The Poverty of Abundance

THE POVERTY
OF ABUNDANCE

Hoover, the Nation, the Depression

ALBERT U. ROMASCO

OXFORD UNIVERSITY PRESS
LONDON OXFORD NEW YORK

OXFORD UNIVERSITY PRESS

London   Oxford   New York
Glasgow   Toronto   Melbourne   Wellington
Cape Town   Ibadan   Nairobi   Dar es Salaam   Lusaka   Addis Ababa
Delhi   Bombay   Calcutta   Madras   Karachi   Lahore   Dacca
Kuala Lumpur   Singapore   Hong Kong   Tokyo

For my Mother and Father
Augusta and Albert Romasco

Preface

The Great Depression was a national experience which permeated nearly all aspects of American society from the time of the stock market crash in 1929 until the nation's entry into World War II in 1941. This study is confined to the Hoover years of the depression. In scope, it does not pretend to touch upon all the ramifications of that experience. No attempt is made here to deal conclusively with the question of the origin or the causes of the depression. This is a problem for the trained economist; and economists, such as John Kenneth Galbraith, in *The Great Crash, 1929,* have offered their evaluations to account for the economic collapse. My study is concerned with the consequences rather than the causes of the Great Depression; it looks at the tree's fruit rather than at its roots.

My purpose is to explore the ways in which American leaders, following the suggestions of President Hoover, used the nation's existing institutions in their efforts to master the economic collapse. Since I have endeavored to see the problem through the eyes of contemporary leadership, both private and public, the selection of the institutions to be examined is more theirs than mine. I have tried, consequently, to re-create the problems facing contemporary leadership, to show the methods they used in their struggle with the forces of economic collapse, and to come to some evaluation of their performance.

In its impact, the Great Depression was both a destructive and an instructive experience. Men and women were blighted, established personal relations were warped, and families destroyed. Familiar ways and institutions, severely challenged to meet new demands, often lacked the vitality to accomplish vital purposes. During the Hoover years, America was littered with debris. Much that was destroyed would never be recovered; much that was salvaged would be transformed and show only slight resemblance to the old. But, after all, this simultaneous demolition and rebuilding is inherent to the process of education. The Great Depression put the American people—especially the leaders of institutions—back to school. What these leaders learned, the old ways and ideas modified or abandoned, the new departures, their successes and failures—in sum, how they attempted to adjust the institutions to combating prolonged economic collapse is what I am concerned with in this book.

New York   A. U. R.
June 1965

Acknowledgments

Writing a book means many things to an author, but for his friends it is a time that tests their good will and tolerance. I am particularly indebted to Professor Walter Johnson of the University of Chicago for his guidance, encouragement, and expert advice. Without him there would have been neither beginning nor end to this project. Professor Daniel J. Boorstin, by his willingness to discuss this and other topics in long, challenging conversations, was a most valuable and generous supporter. In fact, I am deeply obliged to the entire History faculty of the University of Chicago for the unforgettable experience and the cherished years they provided. The entire manuscript was read also by Professor Vincent Carosso of New York University, whose eye for the misplaced word and meandering phrase won my high respect. My grateful appreciation to Professors Richard M. Abrams of the University of California, Berkeley; James S. Chase of the University of Texas; Roger Daniels of the University of California, Los Angeles; and Mr. Thomas P. O'Connor, each of whom read part or all of the manuscript and freely gave me their suggestions. The library staffs at the University of Chicago, Library of Congress, and the National Archives provided indispensable aid, tendered with cheerful courtesy. My thanks to the Arts and Science Research Fund of New York University for their assistance.

Contents

I The Initial Response: Experiment in Voluntaryism and Co-operation

1. Introduction: The Poverty of Abundance, 3
2. Herbert Hoover: Governmental Outlook and Methods, 10
3. The Stock Market Crash: Hoover's Initial Program, 24
4. Business Leadership: The Limits of Co-operation, 39
5. Banking: Cash, Credit, and Confidence, 66
6. Agriculture: The New Individualism, 97
7. Unemployment: Industry and the American Way, 125
8. Social Welfare and the Unemployed: Cities and States, 143

II Hoover's Second Program

9. Herbert Hoover: The Presidency in Peacetime Crisis, 175
10. The President, the Press, and Congress, 202
11. Conclusion: The Dry Well of Conservatism, 230

Notes, 235
Bibliography, 267
Index, 277

The Poverty of Abundance

I

The Initial Response:
Experiment in Voluntaryism and Co-operation

It is a time of testing, not only for our political
and business policies, but for our most fundamental institutions, and even for our whole economic system.*   THOMAS N. CARVER, 1932

I

Introduction: The Poverty of Abundance

> There is no economic failure so terrible in its import as that of a country possessing a surplus of every necessity of life in which numbers, willing and anxious to work, are deprived of these necessities.*   HERBERT HOOVER, 1921

> In all our thoughts and feelings and projects for the betterment of things, we should have it at the back of our heads that this is not a crisis of poverty, but a crisis of abundance.†
>   JOHN M. KEYNES, 1932

Americans in the Hoover years of the Great Depression, 1929–33, were a people perplexed by plenty. They saw the nation's magnificent productive plant intact, its ability to produce unimpaired. And yet, in a land celebrated for its abundance, the people were plagued by scarcity. This paradox confounded the age-old notion of poverty. America's poverty was not cut in the familiar pattern of the past; it represented a new phenomenon. It was the result of rich resources and not of the niggardliness of nature; the outcome of energy and inventiveness, not of indolence and inefficiency; the product of the world's most advanced industrial nation and not of its most backward one. The situation was one peculiar to the modern world of invention and technology. America's poverty was the poverty of abundance.

The world has found it difficult enough to devise new solutions for old problems, but to be obliged to formulate a solution for a new problem is more perplexing still. The Great Depression was in an important particular a new problem, and the poverty which attended it was a new form of poverty. Although the world had experienced many crises of a similar

3

kind in the modern era, the depression which started in 1929 represented a new problem primarily because before this very little positive action had been taken to overcome a national economic crisis. For Americans the Great Depression was an old condition but a new problem.

American leaders' traditional forbearance in the face of economic adversity was due more to design than to conscious negligence. Depressions were regarded as a sort of natural phenomenon: they proceeded according to their own law, they served some useful purposes, and eventually they cured themselves by natural processes. A depression was like a rainstorm; and a sensible man acknowledged his inability to stop the rain, he sought shelter while waiting for the storm to pass, and observed philosophically that at least it was cleaning up the old mess.

Many Americans in 1929 still thought of an economic depression as a periodic and unavoidable rainstorm. The nation's bankers conspicuously held this view. Sensible men, they felt, did well to let the depression run its course; nothing could be done about it anyway, and nothing should be attempted. A depression was the necessary and unavoidable after-effect of a prosperous era with its accompaniment of personal extravagance, reckless business practices, and financial irresponsibility. It was the time for a beneficial readjustment, for re-establishing economic equilibrium, and for washing away the encumbering debris accumulated by unreasonable expectation.

The counsel of the bankers was one of beneficent non-interference. For the federal government, they advised a hands-off policy: let the liquidation proceed so that sound business values and practices might be re-established. They saw this as the quickest, the surest, and the best method for economic recovery. For the people, they urged the time-honored and time-broken virtues of hard work, frugality, self-reliance, and fortitude. Such advice proved singularly inappropriate for conditions of 1929.

If America's poverty had been the traditional one of scarcity and want, the people would have been at least familiar with the adversary they were combating. For, while old problems may often continue to be both difficult and insoluble, they seldom stifle the imagination or paralyze the will to act in the way a novel one does. But instead during the Great Depression America had an over-abundance of food, of commodities, in fact, of everything. The nation was bewildered and thwarted by its own wealth; instead of its mass-production economy having failed, it had seemingly succeeded all too well. The economy was cluttered and stalled by its own unmanageable surplus.

Contemporaries were both aware of and baffled by this economic puzzle. Many saw the riddle well enough, all belabored it, but none seemed able to resolve it. "We still pray," a writer remarked, "to be given each day our daily bread. Yet there is too much bread, too much wheat and corn, meat and oil and almost every commodity required by man for his subsistence and material happiness. We are not able to purchase the abundance that modern methods of agriculture, mining and manufacture make available in such bountiful quantities." And then this question: "Why is mankind being asked to go hungry and cold and poverty-stricken in the midst of plenty?" [1] Or hear the *Nation:* "We are able to produce so much that a good share of us live in perpetual fear of having nothing, and all of us periodically, as at present, stop producing because we can find nobody who is able to buy the things everybody wants. Surely there was never a more insane situation outside of a madhouse." [2] Or more succinctly: "The horn of plenty is too heavy upon our hands." [3] "Why," asked another, "are so many millions in want? Because we have produced too much. Why must they wear shabby clothes? Because we have too much cotton, too much wool, too many mills, and too many mill hands to make cloth. Why must millions live in slums . . . ? Because we have too much . . ." [4] But, why? "Somewhere," another answered, "there has been a breakdown in the application of man's intelligence to economic phenomena." [5]

What needed to be resolved, in short, was not underproduction and over-consumption, but an apparent overproduction and obvious under-consumption. Masters of the techniques of mass production, Americans had yet to learn and apply the techniques of an equivalent mass consumption.

These problems could not be solved by individual resolution. While the breakdown of the economic system affected nearly every individual in the nation, the individual was pathetically ill-equipped either to escape the consequences of the breakdown or even to understand it. In this respect, the Great Depression stood as a great revelation. It revealed the intricate complexity of the modern economic apparatus; it made man's dependence fully evident; and it thoroughly exposed the impotence of the individual in modern society. The individualistic creed, the cherished inheritance of an earlier, simpler society, was shown to be not only inappropriate but an actual hindrance in the struggle against the economic collapse.

Co-operation became the great cry of the day. Some form of unified, co-operative, national effort was needed to cope successfully with the economic crisis. While this much was obvious, the question of what form the collective action should take was more controversial. Some, recalling the great co-operative effort to win World War I, urged a vast expansion of federal authority. Others, convinced that more traditional and less dangerous means were at hand, insisted that organized industry and business leadership should assume the responsibility.

President Hoover's influence was decisive in determining

how the nation would respond to the crisis. Thoroughly convinced of the superior virtues of decentralized authority, and
ideologically opposed to the further extension of federal authority and power, the President committed the nation to an
experiment in voluntary co-operative action. The economic
crisis was to be mastered by the people themselves and not by
the federal government. Through the organized, group action of existing institutions, the resources of the nation
would be combined and concentrated on the task of reviving
the stalled economy. The arts of persuasion would be used in
place of legislative coercion to accomplish a vital national
purpose.

The Great Depression was a time of national adversity, and
periods of adversity proverbially create a reflective mood.
The experience of these years brought the unreflective American people up short, and provided them with the incentive
and leisure — often enforced — to consider the unexamined
assumptions and the slogans by which they had been living.
In the grim atmosphere of economic crisis, when man seemed
the victim of his own creation, and intelligence seemed
balked by the fruits of inventive genius, reflection often led
to despair. To some of the despairing (an attitude most noticeable among writers for the *Nation* and the *New Republic*), it seemed that the capitalistic system was on trial, and
that the outcome of the test was acknowledged failure.

In a sense, they were right: there was a trial, and there was
a judgment. But it was not the capitalistic system itself, or the
laissez-faire conservatism of the bankers, or the individualistic
creed that were being tested and evaluated. It was rather the
men in power, the current custodians of the system — both
private and public — who were on trial. These men represented the viewpoint of enlightened conservatism, and they
followed the leadership of Herbert Hoover. Under his directing hand, the possibilities of enlightened conservatism were
exhausted in the attempt to make the American system work.

In the Hoover years, conservatism had its day in the court of public opinion.

It would be a serious mistake, however, to interpret the Great Depression as a problem which concerned and challenged one institution exclusively — the presidency. To do so is to put too heavy a burden — an unfair and unrealistic emphasis — upon the power of that institution's custodian — Herbert Hoover. The economic collapse was not solely the President's concern, nor did he struggle to overcome it in some sort of splendid isolation. The Great Depression, like all momentous national experiences, engaged many other of the nation's major institutions as well.

A nation's institutions are the traditional agencies, the formalized habits, that have emerged from the experiences of a society in its attempts to cope with the past. History — past experience as it is currently understood — survives as an influence much more pervasively in institutions than in books. A nation's people may not know or little care about the particular episodes of their past, but their lives are decisively influenced by institutions none the less.

Institutions, while shaped by the past, are ever concerned with the present. Their usefulness and validity are not so much determined by past successes as by present opportunities. They exist as functional devices permitting a people to go about its multitudinous affairs with the least possible obstruction. Yet, when paralyzing obstructions do arise, such as the Great Depression, institutions to survive must undergo a process of growth: test, trial, and modification. The quality of a nation's leadership — the men who direct the institutions — largely decides the success or failure of these modifications. Institutions do not function without men, nor can men deal with great obstructions like an economic collapse except through institutions.

Herbert Clark Hoover, as President of the United States, is principally important as the leader of the first of the nation's institutions. In his control of the executive, through his influence upon the conduct of the federal government, and by his prestige among institutional leadership of all sorts, the President set the initial response taken by major institutions. Businessmen, bankers, mayors, governors, and congressmen, social workers, agricultural and labor leaders, all these men — and the institutions they represented — looked to the President for their cues. Hoover was courageous enough to assume this leadership.

It is precisely because Hoover took the reins of national leadership that we must understand his philosophy of government, his attitude regarding federal power, and his concept of the presidency. Hoover's ideas — his governmental outlook and his methods — first determined the manner in which the nation's institutions should respond to the challenge of the depression.

2

Herbert Hoover:
Governmental Outlook and Methods

> The government is more than administration; it is power for leadership and co-operation with the forces of business and cultural life in city, town, and countryside. The Presidency is more than executive responsibility. It is the inspiring symbol of all that is highest in America's purposes and ideals.* HERBERT HOOVER, 1928

> Equality of opportunity is a fundamental principle of our nation. With it we must test all our policies. The success or failure of this principle is the test of our government.† HERBERT HOOVER, 1928

Herbert Hoover has been celebrated and mocked during these long years as the exponent of "rugged individualism." These two words have served as perhaps the most concise and effective caricature in modern American political history. They conjure up a very definite stereotype that obviates any further inquiry, thereby making Hoover's ideas simple, clear, distorted, and misunderstood. But what do the words, as Hoover used and meant them, actually signify? What was the place of the individual in the political and social thought of Hoover? And what was the connection betwen the President's concept of individualism and his concrete governmental programs?

Beginning with the publication of his *American Individualism* in 1922,[1] continuing in his 1928 campaign speeches, and then in a series of press releases, messages to Congress, and speeches during his presidency, Hoover attempted to clarify his position. These pronouncements revealed that at the very heart of the President's philosophy was what he termed the "American system."

The American system, in Hoover's view, was a shorthand expression for what he conceived to be the American philosophy of society and government. A central feature of that philosophy was the economic arrangements, which he saw as distinctive to America. Those who attempted to tag America's essential qualities with neat labels, such as liberalism, individualism, capitalism, or even democracy, missed its unique character. As subtle and complex as the American way of life, America's economic system eluded precise definition.

"Ours is a system," as Hoover expressed it, "unique with America — an expression of the spirit and environment of our people — it is just American." But while difficult to define, the American system could perhaps best be understood, he suggested, by contrasting it with the philosophies (or systems) of other governments. "From experiences in many lands," he said, drawing upon his observations as a world-traveled mining engineer, "I have sometimes compared some of these systems to a race":

> In the American system, through free and universal education, we train the runners, we strive to give to them an equal start, our government is the umpire of its fairness. The winner is he who shows the most conscientious training, the greatest ability, the strongest character. Socialism, or its violent brother, Bolshevism, would compel all the runners to end the race equally; it would hold the swiftest to the speed of the most backward. Anarchy would provide neither training nor umpire. Despotism or class government picks those who run and also those who win.[2]

Because of America's "unique" political, social, and economic systems, it differed fundamentally from Europe. America's political system was unique "because of its decentralization of self-government and its checks and balances which

safeguard ordered liberty and freedom to each individual."
And the ideal "that there shall be equal opportunity among
men," added to the traditional conceptions "that all men are
created equal and are equal before the law" gave force and
justification, Hoover insisted, to the claim of a unique social
system. Now, out of the prior establishment of its political
and social arrangements, America was in the process of
"evolving a unique economic system." [3] Again, it was the
essentially non-European quality of the country's economic
life that marked it as a new departure. America was unique
no matter how one looked at it.

In contemporary Europe, Hoover claimed, the dominant
ideas were the ideas of old: the class struggle between capital
and labor, the practice of viewing and treating labor as a
commodity, and the notion that the mass of laborers was ever
destined to wallow helplessly near a level of bare subsistence.
There the conception of "inevitable poverty" still commanded a general adherence. Europe provided a model of
pitfalls to be avoided.

The American experience was proof against the universal
validity of these European ideas. "By what amounts to a revolution in ideas and methods," Hoover declared, "we have developed a new economic system." Here capital and labor
worked and walked hand-in-hand in a happy harmony to produce more, to distribute more, to raise the standard of living
of all the people. In this amiable concert of interests that prevailed within the American economic system, everyone
profited mutually. Thus had America vanquished the old,
the European specter of inevitable poverty.[4]

Hoover held these developments to be a revolution — a
revolution impelled by three distinctive American ideas in its
political, social, and economic life. And dominating these
ideas — providing the essential cement binding them into a
workable combination — was "the ideal and practice of equal
opportunity."

The genius of the American system, then, was its provision for equality of opportunity. Hoover defined this as "the right of every individual to attain that position in life to which his ability and character entitle him." [5] This characteristic distinguished the American system and accounted for its superiority over all others. Whatever else might be said of these other systems, they all shared one fatal flaw: they had destroyed the "driving force of equal opportunity." Americans should not make the same mistake. "I take it," the President declared,

> that the outstanding problem and the ideal of our economic system is to secure freedom of initiative and to preserve stability in the economic structure in order that the door of opportunity and equality of opportunity may be held open to all our citizens . . .[6]

The reward of a society which guaranteed equality of opportunity and individual initiative was progress. And among the nations of the world, American progress was unmatched for its rapid growth and its wide diffusion. It was essential, if the continuation of progress were to be ensured, that Americans remain steadfastly faithful to their traditional ways.

And here the federal government had an important role. Above all else it could preserve the system that had made America great, and this it could best do by exercising self-restraint. Since each new expansion of federal authority meant a new encroachment upon individual liberty, tendencies to expand that authority must be rigorously checked. The watchword of government should be conservatism; central innovations which would lead to an enlargement of federal authority were to be shunned. "Our great American experiment," the President said,

> has demonstrated that the people will of their own initiative take care of progress if the Government can remove abuse

and help put the signs on the road, stimulation to all of which is part of the job of Presidents. Of Lincoln's great formula the most important one-third is "government by the people," and they will govern themselves outside of the Government when they see the light.[7]

"Permanent advance in the Republic," as he expressed it on another occasion, "will lie in the initiative of the people themselves." [8]

Unfortunately, a number of Americans still failed to "see the light," thereby imperiling right-thinking and progress. Prominent among these were the people who thought of themselves as liberals; this was a misconception on their part, according to Hoover, who marked them as being false to true liberalism. Their central error was to urge more government activity, more government in business, and, inevitably, a bigger and more dangerous bureaucracy. The expansion of bureaucracy measured a people's failure to govern themselves at the local level. Bureaucracy was the antithesis of genuine self-government, a challenge to democracy that never wearied, never rested. "Bureaucracy," Hoover warned — and this from a man who knew it well from his long years as Secretary of Commerce — "is ever desirous of spreading its influence and its power. You cannot extend the mastery of the government over the daily working life of a people without at the same time making it the master of the people's souls and thoughts." [9]

With every new advance of bureaucracy, the sway and effectiveness of true liberalism was by so much diminished. For liberalism, as Hoover understood it, meant a commitment to definite principles which he listed as "political equality, free speech, free assembly, free press, and equality of opportunity." Liberalism, therefore, could not properly pave bureaucracy's road — a road "not to more liberty, but to less liberty." Nor would he have the American people countenance more government even for the sake of greater efficiency. "Even if governmental conduct of business could give us more efficiency instead of less efficiency," he declared, "the fundamental objection to it would remain unaltered and unabated":

> It would destroy political equality. It would increase rather than decrease abuse and corruption. It would stifle initiative and invention. It would undermine the development of leadership. It would cramp and cripple the mental and spiritual energies of our people. It would extinguish equality and opportunity. It would dry up the spirit of liberty and progress.[10]

In this vital matter of government in business, Hoover saw no half-way house along the road; a nation once commencing the trip inexorably went the whole way — and the final destination was national ruin. It was either all or none.

Hoover was much in earnest on this score; he was convinced that his interpretation of liberalism's true meaning was right. It was fortified by observations and reflections from his own experience — lessons learned hard and hard to forget. Flexibility comes easier on theoretical matters than on empirical ones. "I have witnessed not only at home but abroad," the voice of experience said, "the many failures of government in business":

> I have seen its tyrannies, its injustices, its destructions of self-government, its undermining of the very instincts which carry people forward to progress. I have witnessed the lack of advance, the lowered standards of living, the depressed spirits of people working under such a system.[11]

Hoover would save, if he could, liberalism from its misguided friends. For, as he remarked of the American people: "We are a nation of progressives; we differ as to what is the road to progress." [12] Liberalism, as correctly interpreted by Hoover, was one of the proper roads a progressive could take, but only when those traditional values that made progress possible were adequately safeguarded.

Liberalism, in effect, was here smoothly blended with both conservatism and progressivism to meld into one what had seemed three disparate viewpoints. And this was attempted by the simple recourse of asserting that all three were committed to a common end. "Conservative, progressive, and liberal thought," Hoover argued, "have their only real test in whether they contribute to equal opportunity . . . If they do not they are false in their premise no matter what their name may be." Thus Hoover, as the defender *par excellence* of equality of opportunity, became the true inheritor and spokesman of conservatism, progressivism, and liberalism. His philosophy encompassed them all.[13]

Yet, despite Hoover's repeated strictures against expanded federal activity in the nation's economic life, he did not conceive the American system as one of unchecked *laissez faire*. The "free-for-all and devil-take-the-hindmost" attitude was not, he said, his intention or his creed. "Government," he said, "is only in part a negative function. Its purpose is not merely to stand as a watchman over what is forbidden; government must be a constructive force." [14]

Hoover pointed out three different areas where the federal government could properly take constructive action without violating the principles of the American system. Action in these fields was permissible, since it involved matters which individuals or local governments could not accomplish unassisted. Great public works projects, "such as inland waterways, flood control, reclamation, highways, and public buildings," constituted one. Another was to help in "fostering education, public health, scientific research, public parks, conservation of national resources, agriculture, industry, and foreign commerce." And, finally, the government was to assist the flowering of the co-operative spirit.[15]

Government, in short, could be most useful in assisting the

people to deal effectively with modern conditions. Thro
number of devices, such as temporary committees, con.
ences, and commissions, the federal government could utili
the finest talent available in the nation for the study of public problems. The experts would gather, sift, and weigh the
facts. But the findings of these voluntary groups were not to
be used as a springboard for executive action. To use them
for this purpose, the President said, was "anathema." Instead,
the information was to be given to the people. When pos-
sessing all the facts, the people would judge.[16]

Not only were the people to judge for themselves, the President consistently urged that they also act for themselves.
By helping themselves, the people would preserve and
strengthen the traits so vital to progress. In politics they
would serve themselves and the nation best by handling their
problems at the level of local government. The smaller the
unit, the closer it was to the people, the more effectively it
conformed to Hoover's ideal of self-government. "Where
people divest themselves of local government responsibilities," the President cautioned the nation in a radio address, "they at once lay the foundation for the destruction of
their liberties."

> The true growth of the Nation is the growth of character
> in its citizens. The spread of government destroys initiative
> and thus destroys character. Character is made in the com-
> munity as well as in the individual by assuming responsi-
> bilities, not by escape from them.[17]

In Hoover's hierarchy of preferences, local government enjoyed a favored position among the forms of *political* institutions. But this was not his ultimate ideal of self-government.
So deep did the President's dislike and distrust of government action extend, that he felt ideally the nation's business
should be conducted outside of government altogether. As
Hoover himself repeatedly expressed it, "self-government

outside of political government is the truest form of self-government." This should not be mistaken as a plea for anarchy. What he meant was that in the place of government action the nation's business should be carried on by a host of non-governmental, voluntary organizations. The citizens would rule themselves instead of an overweening bureaucracy ruling the people. Only in this manner, he asserted, would the American system be preserved, American traits and ideals fortified, and the march of American progress assured. For the American system was one

> which holds that the major purpose of a state is to protect the people and to give them equality of opportunity, that the basis of all happiness is in development of the individual, that the sum of progress can only be gaged by the progress of the individual, that we should steadily build up cooperation among the people to these ends.[18]

Americans had demonstrated their willingness to co-operate, which made self-government by voluntary organizations possible in a complex society. And Hoover, when Secretary of Commerce, had assisted them significantly. Among such associational activities (voluntaryism) which demonstrated conscious co-operative development, Hoover cited the vigorous growth of civic associations, chambers of commerce, trade associations, labor unions, trade councils, farm organizations, farm co-operatives, and welfare associations. Hoover hoped for even more, but in the meantime he would have government do all in its power to encourage these.

For co-operation offered an alternative superior to political government. Every extension of political government carried a further constriction of individual responsibility which in turn brought disastrous consequences. But the practice of co-operation, as seen by Hoover, was not considered as a diminution or denial of individualism, but an essential adjunct to it. In modern America, the spirit and practice of co-operation would not destroy individualism, it would preserve it. "What the Government can do best," Hoover maintained:

> is to encourage and assist in the creation and development of institutions controlled by our citizens and evolved by themselves from their own needs and their own experience and directed in a sense of trusteeship of public interest. . . .
>
> Without intrusion the Government can sometimes give leadership and serve to bring together divergent elements and secure cooperation in development of ideas, measures, and institutions. This is a reenforcement of our individualism.[19]

Individualism, in a highly interdependent, urban-industrial society, no longer required that one must go it alone. It meant — and it was fostered by — individuals working together in voluntary co-operative organizations. This was the *new* individualism — an individualism tempered and adjusted to the demands of modern conditions.

Since the virtues of individualism, as well as the American system itself, could only be preserved by fostering co-operative voluntary action outside of government, the federal government must encourage its development. This was the proper, the most desirable function that the national government could perform. Its intervention here would not enfeeble the national character; it would strengthen it.

To lead and encourage voluntary action was a function peculiarly suited to the Chief Executive. "Congress," the President held, "cannot determine administrative policies; it cannot inspire or lead voluntary forces." The President's position as head of the government, his prominence as the nation's first citizen and its spokesman, and the prestige of his office all combined to make him eminently qualified to assume this role. The President would lead by stimulating leadership from the bottom. He would see that the business of the nation went forward by encouraging the nation to conduct its own business.

Hoover's utterances on government, economics, and society revealed a strong strain of idealism, but it was an idealism of a peculiar sort. The ideal social and economic system that he spoke of was not something that had to be discovered and perfected; it was not a distant, hopeful prospect of the future. It was rather the tested product of the past. The ideal system was the existing American system — a national heritage that must be defended and preserved. Certainly Hoover looked forward to even greater achievements in the future — the extinction of poverty being his most celebrated goal. But the realization of these new triumphs was to be accomplished by preserving the American system and not by changing or abandoning it. He offered the philosophy of enlightened conservatism; it was a vision of an idealized past, an invocation of the old, and not a search for the new.

The President's idealism was peculiar in another sense as well. He did not attempt to deliver a Sunday sermon, to be expounded, admired, and then forgotten. His creed was one to live by, even in days which were so trying and discouraging that a less strong-willed man would have been sorely tempted to indulge in some discreet backsliding during the weekdays. In Hoover's case, the correlation between word and deed was a close one, and the correlation was evident from the very outset.

Hoover's solution for the agricultural problem is an excellent illustration of his ideology translated into a concrete governmental program. Throughout the presidential campaign of 1928, as well as in his inaugural address, Hoover had designated agriculture as the nation's most pressing problem; as such, it got the benefit of the first treatment of the Hooverian method.

Agriculture was plagued, Hoover held, with a multitude of pests, mostly in the form of an excess of erroneous counsel. Its friends and advisers — the agricultural spokesmen — looked too avidly to direct federal aid. Their hopes were tied to the various versions of the McNary-Haugen bill with its equalization fee, and to its alternative, the export debenture plan. These plans found no favor in the years of the Republican ascendancy — rejected by Coolidge, disapproved of by Hoover. "Certain vital principles," Hoover felt, "must be adhered to in order that we may not undermine the freedom of our farmers and of our people . . . by bureaucratic and governmental domination and interference." Then, specifying his apprehensions:

> There should be no fee or tax imposed upon the farmer. No governmental agency should engage in the buying and selling and price fixing of products, for such courses can lead only to bureaucracy and domination. Government funds should not be loaned or facilities duplicated where other services or credit and facilities are available at reasonable rates. No activities should be set in motion that will result in increasing the surplus production . . .[20]

These explicit reservations effectively excluded both McNary-Haugenism and the export debenture.

Not that Hoover was opposed to the federal government's assisting the farmer; in fact, he was pledged to have it do exactly that. But this aid must be of the proper sort; it must fit the tenets and practices of the American system. "My fundamental concept of agriculture," Hoover told the folks back home in West Branch, Iowa, "is one controlled by its own members, organized to fight its own economic battles and to determine its own destinies."[21] The farmer must have organization; the government would assist him here — then he was twenty-one and on his own.

Hoover proposed that the government establish a federal farm board, composed of men sympathetic to agriculture, and with the power and resources to aid the farmer in achieving economic equality with other groups of Americans. The board would help the farmer principally by establishing nation-wide marketing co-operatives and farmer-owned, farmer-controlled stabilization corporations. The marketing co-operatives would bring order out of chaos: prevent seasonal gluts at terminal markets, by-pass a host of middlemen who nibbled away the producers' profits, and also increase the farmers' economic leverage. The stabilization corporations were to deal with the more vexing problem of agricultural surpluses.

Co-operation, of course, was neither a new concept nor an untried expedient for America's farmers; it was a well-trod salvation path, strewn with the disappointments of past hopes. But Hoover meant to transform past failures into future successes by bringing the full force of government to the aid of co-operation. Had he not, as Secretary of Commerce, personally assisted business groups in highly successful co-operative ventures? Agriculture was also a business, albeit a sadly disorganized one. Hoover as President meant to apply the Secretary of Commerce's methods to agriculture; he hoped for a similar success. The Federal Farm Board would help the farmer bring order to his business, set him upon his feet, and provide him with national organizations. But once these objectives were realized, the government would withdraw, leaving the farmer in control of his own destiny.[22]

This was all to be accomplished without actually bringing the government into business, and without impairing either the farmer's individuality or his initiative. Government would simply furnish the necessary capital to inaugurate and establish the program. "This plan," Hoover explained, "is consonant with our American ideals to avoid the government operation of commercial business; for it places the operation upon the farmer himself, not upon a bureaucracy. It puts the government in its real relation to the citizen — that of co-operation. Its object is to give equality of opportunity to the farmer." [23]

When one speaks of Hoover and rugged individualism, one should remember the Agricultural Marketing Act with its Federal Farm Board; it is an almost perfect illustration of Hoover's governmental ideas and methods translated into practice.

3

The Stock Market Crash:
Hoover's Initial Program

> Many people think that President Hoover's policy for many months was to do nothing about the depression. On the contrary, he had a definite program.* GEORGE SOULE, 1933

On Thursday morning, October 24, 1929, "the great bull market" of the 1920's came to an end. In time, the events of this and subsequent days on the New York Stock Exchange would be identified simply as "the Great Crash." [1] Later, as the panic developed into a definite depression, this period quickly became known as "the Great Depression." For Americans, these October days marked the close of that buoyant interlude, "the New Era." But for Hoover and the American system, these dramatic developments posed a grave and immediate challenge.

Panics and depressions dotted the American past from its earliest days as a nation onward; they were no new affliction. Nor had these periodic disruptions of the nation's economic equilibrium occurred without an accompaniment of loud lamentations — fervent importunities for federal aid. Yet those who clamored for this assistance clamored in vain: they were heard and ignored by a long succession of Presidents. From the presidency of Martin Van Buren to that of Woodrow Wilson, the administrations which confronted depressions refrained from any direct official action.[2] President Warren Harding, faced with the economic collapse of 1920–21, seemed to break with this tradition. He called a national conference on unemployment in 1921, which conducted extensive and valuable inquiries, and made numerous recommendations on appropriate action. But the federal government was not to carry out these proposals; it was the nation's mayors who were urged to act. Little was accomplished.[3] The precedent of presidential inactivity in depression times — waiting unobtrusively for recovery — remained essentially unimpaired.

One theory held that depressions were best met by patient forbearance. Temporary dislocations were to be overcome not by artificial, governmental tinkering, but through a natural process of readjustment. Supported by the authority of Adam Smith, and reinforced by the Spencerian rationalization of biological evolution to economic affairs, the theory was further buttressed by American antipathy to centralized, governmental direction and control. By 1929 this mixture of theory, experience, and tradition had become diffused into a habit of mind.[4] It was as a habit that this outlook achieved its widest influence. "The great advantage of allowing nature to take her course," Stuart Chase pointed out caustically, "is that it obviates thought. . . . There is no need to think, no need to take concrete action. Just sit and wait with folded hands." [5]

Among members of President Herbert Hoover's official family, Secretary of the Treasury Andrew Mellon best exemplified this trait. After the stock market collapse of late October 1929, Mellon emerged as the spokesman and leader of one school of thought within the administration. Mellon counseled non-interference by the government. In his view, the federal government was to stand passively aside while inflated values were liquidated and the economic situation readjusted itself to normal. The Secretary of the Treasury expressed the liquidationist position perfectly with his simple, brutal formula: "Liquidate labor, liquidate stocks, liquidate the farmers, liquidate real estate." [6] It was advice that curiously blended fatalistic and optimistic elements — fatalistic in that it condemned any effort by the government to cushion the reverberations of the crash as futile; optimistic because it believed that an unimpeded liquidation would be brief and beneficial.

President Hoover disagreed with this uncompromising laissez-faire viewpoint. Supported by others within his administration, he maintained that the shock of the market debacle should be cushioned and confined by the use of governmental authority. "To our minds," he later wrote, "the prime needs were to prevent bank panics such as had marked the earlier slumps, to mitigate the privation among the unemployed and the farmers which would certainly ensue." Publicly, the President attempted to allay precisely this same apprehension among the people over the probable consequences of the stock break. In answer to questions as to the possible effect of the crash on the nation's prosperity, at a press conference on October 25, 1929, he made the celebrated declaration that "the fundamental business of the country, that is production and distribution of commodities, is on a sound and prosperous basis." He repeated this reassuring view on November 15 by stating that "any lack of confidence in the economic future or the basic strength of business in the United States is foolish." Many people at the time applauded these remarks and the intent behind them, including the *Nation,* which in a short time was to be a consistent and severe critic of Hoover. "The great task of the next few months." it now wrote, "is the restoration of confidence — confidence in the fundamental strength of the financial structure notwithstanding the strain that has been put upon it, confidence in the essential soundness of legitimate industry and trade." [7]

Yet, in spite of the sweeping nature of his assurances, Hoover did not delude himself about their complete efficacy. His own experience, he said, had taught him "that words are not of any great importance in times of economic disturbance. It is action," he insisted, "that counts." What line of action had he in mind?

The President suggested emergency Federal Reserve policies to establish a sound basis of stable credit and ample capital. He called for the stimulation of business activity by a combined policy of tax reductions, the revival of construction work, and expanded exports. Above all else, he insisted that the success of this program would require "the co-ordination of business and governmental agencies in concerted action. . . ." [8] This last suggestion was the very heart of his program. To aid in achieving this essential co-ordination, Hoover announced his intention of calling a series of conferences with the leaders of the nation's major economic interests.

In late November 1929 there began a steady pilgrimage of national leaders to the White House. It constituted, the *New York Times* observed, "the largest gathering of noted heads of industrial and other corporations in Washington since the resources of the nation were marshalled for participation in the World War." Within nine days — November 19 to 27 — the President met in separate conferences with prominent spokesmen of the railroads, the Federal Reserve System, industry-business-finance, labor, construction, agriculture, and the public utilities. One result of the meetings was a spate of optimistic statements and forecasts. Of far more importance, these leaders promised the President that they would do all in their power to maintain existing wage rates, stabilize employment, and increase construction activity.[9]

Hoover's purpose in calling these conferences was made clearer through a number of presidential press statements issued at the close of each meeting. After conferring a little more than an hour with a group of railroad executives, the President announced that

> The railway presidents were unanimous in their determination to cooperate in the maintenance of employment and business progress. It was stated that the railways which they represented would proceed with full programs of construction

and betterments without any reference to recent stock exchange fluctuations; that they would canvass the situation as to further possibilities of expansion, and that amongst these particular railways it appeared that the total volume of such construction work already indicated an increase during the next six months over the similar period of last year.[10]

This first statement established a model for those that followed. The crucial points included an optimistic evaluation of the business prospects in their particular field, an expressed willingness to co-operate, determination to maintain employment, and the promise to expand construction programs.

The railroad leaders' optimism and their pledge to co-operate with the President in maintaining business prosperity were echoed two days later in the statement which climaxed a presidential conference with twenty-two industrial and business leaders. During his discussion with the business leaders, Hoover said that first the general situation had been carefully surveyed, and "it was the unanimous opinion of the conference that there was no reason why business should not be carried on as usual." Also, in order to absorb any possible unemployment, it was agreed that private and public construction should be expanded in "every prudent direction."

This conference would not, however, deserve to rank as the most significant of the series if it had stopped here. In regard to the vital problem of how these important proposals were to be practically implemented, it was disclosed that:

> The meeting considered it was desirable that some definite organization should be established under a committee representing the different industries and sections of the business community, which would undertake to follow up the President's program in the different industries.

> It was considered that the development of cooperative spirit and responsibility in the American business world was

such that the business of the country itself could and should assume the responsibility for the mobilization of the industrial and commercial agencies to these ends and to cooperate with the governmental agencies.[11]

To co-ordinate and direct the efforts of the nation's businesses in fulfilling its pledges, Hoover, on November 21, asked Julius H. Barnes, chairman of the Board of the United States Chamber of Commerce, to create a central executive committee of outstanding businessmen.

The business leaders' pledges to the President also included, according to another release of the same day, an assurance not to "initiate any movement for wage reduction," along with a strong recommendation that the entire country follow this example. This startling assurance by business was matched by the labor representatives, who agreed to refrain from demanding any new wage increases. If pledges were an accurate prelude to performance, then this conference represented a remarkable achievement.

Hoover's program was advanced a step further when he enlisted the active co-operation of the state governors. His purpose here was to make doubly certain that adequate construction work would be undertaken to absorb the unemployed. State and local activity would add impressive weight to that promised by the federal government and private business. "I should like to feel," Hoover wrote to each of the governors, "that I have the cooperation of yourself" and the local officials. "It would be helpful," he added, "if road, street, public building and other construction of this type could be speeded up and adjusted in such fashion as to further employment."

Three more conferences followed — with representatives of the construction industry, the three major agricultural organizations,[12] and the public utilities. While nothing substantive was added to the program in these meetings, they did serve to dramatize the national backing that the President had gained for his program.

Meanwhile, Julius H. Barnes, charged with the important role of implementing the pledges of business, was busy planning the organization of his agency. Barnes, in full agreement with what he termed Hoover's "very encouraging picture of industry," announced that he would shortly call together a "fairly large group of trade association representatives," to assess accurately the business situation, and "through mutual confidence and exchange of information of purposes, to disprove inaccurate and disturbing rumors."

"This conference," he continued, "will furnish certain information, from which we will endeavor to determine where the key logs are located and take them out by co-operation with all the industries and with agencies of the Government. If we can loosen the key logs, the flow of ordinary business will float down the river." The key logs in Barnes's estimation appeared to be the severe decline in construction which had begun the year before. "It seems to be true," he generalized, "that every recession in the building construction industry is followed by a recession in general business." [13]

The National Business Survey Conference, the outcome of Barnes's efforts, convened for the first time in Washington on December 5, 1929. The "more than 400 'key men,' representing every branch of industry, finance, trade and commerce," had gathered to devise effective "means of carrying out President Hoover's efforts to stimulate and stabilize business." [14] Hoover was on hand to explain his program personally.

"You have been invited," he informed his distinguished audience, "to create a temporary organization for the purpose of systematically spreading into industry as a whole the measures which have been taken by some of our leading industries to counteract the effect of the recent panic in the stock market." While it had been accompanied by some unemployment, the major effect of the stock break was "to create undue pessimism, fear, uncertainty and hesitation in business." If unchecked, these emotions "would, by feeding upon themselves, create difficulties." Nor could these difficulties be dispelled by mere words. "If we could do so, the merest description of the fundamental stability of our vast organism of production and distribution, touched with the light of the future of the United States, would cure it instantly." The situation called for action.

Hoover briefly reviewed the three lines of action already initiated since the market collapse. The Federal Reserve System, supported, as he claimed, by the current "strong position of the banks," had moved to reduce the discount rate to ensure that investment capital, previously monopolized by the stock market, would now be available for normal business needs. This policy would help shore up faltering public confidence.

Next, he referred to the recent Washington conferences. The promise of employers and labor leaders to retain existing wage levels would protect consuming power; and, he emphasized, it would dispel "fear from millions of homes."

The third line of action — to promote by voluntary action the "expansion of the construction and maintenance work of the country" — had also been discussed at the Washington meetings. The major purpose of the present gathering, Hoover stressed, was "the extension and organization of this work."

Past experience taught that construction work was "the greatest tool which our economic system affords for the establishment of stability." On this point, according to Hoover, the experts agreed. Their immediate task, then, was to make the movement for expanded construction "systematic in all branches of the industrial world." And for the business leaders to undertake it voluntarily, he pointed out, inaugurated something new in the relationship between industry and government. Co-operation would replace the "dog-eat-dog attitude of the business world" in the past.

Hoover stressed the immense challenge that the nation's

deranged economy presented the business community. "A great responsibility and a great opportunity," he declared gravely, "rest upon the business and economic organization of the country." [15]

We might, at this point, re-examine briefly the major features and the underlying assumptions involved in Hoover's evaluation of the stock market crash and his program for dealing with it. According to popular opinion, past experience taught that a stock market crash signaled an impending depression. But, also, a severe decline in new construction invariably preceded a market collapse. While new construction was partly dependent on the need for new facilities, it was even more dependent upon the availability of low-interest, long-term credit. Yet, whenever a booming stock market existed, this credit became increasingly more difficult to come by. The more prolonged the bull market the more effectively it monopolized the sources of available surplus credit.[16]

This absorption of credit was one consequence of the spectacular earnings in common stocks, which in turn forced credit rates gradually up to a level where only the expectation of spectacular returns would justify borrowing. In time, the high-interest rate — particularly on loans on the call-money market [17] — came to represent a curiously mixed symbol of expectation and apprehension. The high-interest rate registered the sanguine expectations for the future; simultaneously it worked to deny funds for basic economic activities essential to sustain those future expectations. The inevitable crash was merely a matter of time.

The heritage of this way of thinking has been reflected in the ambivalent American attitude toward prosperity ever since. Periods of prosperity are anticipated with pleasure and, once achieved, enjoyed with apprehension. The immediate post-World War II years are a nice illustration of this complex interplay of expectations — recorded especially well in the pages of *Fortune*. Prosperity invariably fosters unreasonable expectation, thereby inducing inflationary pressure; and this outcome is largely responsible for the eventual undoing of prosperity. Prosperity, then, undergoes the transition from vigor to decay by the excessive growth of its original components. Prosperity, it appears, is much like happiness: elusive of control and when pursued too vigorously ending in disappointment.

Although past experience taught the sobering lesson that the ultimate outcome of prosperity was depression, it suggested also a more hopeful corollary: that is, the eventual outcome of depression was in turn a new period of prosperity. Moreover, experience, such as the most recent panic-depression cycle of 1920–21, indicated that the process of recovery followed roughly the reverse course of the crash-depression process. After the painful but necessary liquidation of inflated values, money and credit were released from the deflated market. Investors with surplus or idle capital, once convinced that the bottom of the deflationary spiral had been reached, cautiously sought new investment opportunities.[18] This renewed willingness to invest might be described as the outward sign of an inward state of mind — "confidence." And confidence, like investment, is always based upon optimistic future expectations.

Such moderate expectation and revived confidence in future prospects, this reasoning held, completely altered the long-term credit market. Now, with ample funds at reasonable rates available once again, construction revived. And for observers sensitive to the operation of the business cycle, the construction revival was the first sign of the upward swing.[19]

Hoover was thoroughly familiar with this frame of thought. But, while Hoover agreed with much of the accepted wisdom on business cycles, he disagreed completely with the major premise of the deflationists; that is, he rejected their assumption that business cycles were "natural" and thus unavoidable. The intelligence of man might miti-

gate even this scourge.[20] The proof of his disagreement was
the initial program he worked out immediately after the collapse of the great bull market. In effect, the President's program was an attempt to arrest the downward plunge of the
business cycle at its very inception. He meant to short-circuit
the familiar pattern of the past before it could develop in all
its paralyzing ramifications. This ambitious undertaking
might be achieved, it was thought, if two major objectives
could be realized.

Hoover had to convince businessmen that the familiar pattern of response, based upon the lessons of the past, could
now be safely abandoned. In fact, some of the old maxims
had to be disregarded so that they would not come about.
Businessmen, whenever convinced that deflation was immi-
nent, acted in a manner which accelerated the downward
swing of the economy. They retrenched. Inventories and
orders were cut. Prices were reduced. The work force was
pared. And those fortunate enough to hold their jobs worked
at a lower wage scale. Businessmen, in a word, liquidated.
They liquidated in anticipation of a severe deflation, thereby
making a reality the very state of affairs they feared and from
which they sought security. Economically they scurried to
their storm cellars.

This behavior, and the climate of opinion it confessed,
proved highly contagious. Everyone — wholesalers, retailers,
manufacturers — retrenched. The result was another twist of
the screw downward: inventories were cut, orders were cut,
production was cut, wages and employment were cut, purchasing power and consumption were cut. And on and on it
went in a vicious downward spiral where every cautious
measure grasped to achieve personal security only acted to
sap the security of everyone. This spiral — especially in such
a highly complex and intricately interdependent economic
structure as ours — could continue until only the very strongest business, banking, and industrial units survived.[21] It

would end only when confidence was restored. And confidence would not revive until businessmen somehow decided that the downward spiral had reached bottom. "No one cares," as one editor tersely explained the dilemma, "to make commitments as long as there is a chance that the price paid today may be less tomorrow." [22]

It was this nightmare that Hoover foresaw and wanted to avoid. If businessmen could be persuaded to retain confidence in the basic soundness of the economy, the impulse toward caution and retrenchment would be minimized. The presidential business conferences were designed to promote these ends. In addition, the conferences were meant to ensure that businessmen acted in a fashion which would maintain stability. Instead of retrenching, they were to proceed with business as usual. Instead of anticipating trouble, they were to behave as if conditions were normal. And by pledging to maintain wages, prices, and employment they would minimize rather than augment the potential deflationary impact of the market collapse. "It was," as Walter Lippmann remarked, "an open conspiracy not to deflate." [23]

Hoover's second major objective was to stimulate construction — that harbinger of a new period of prosperity. The National Business Survey Conference was created primarily for this purpose. The cure would not be left to exert itself only after a disastrous delay and through chance; it was to be applied at once by artificial means. The combination of these factors — confidence, business as usual, expanded construction — would shorten the downward phase of the business cycle from a prolonged period to a matter of months. "The conception behind this policy," economist George Soule noted, "was that the stock-market crash was an isolated affair, and business could be quarantined against its effects." [24]

Little can be said, or indeed was said, in criticism of the President's aims. Instead, it was highly praised. *Business Week* called Hoover's program "a momentous experiment

— the greatest since the war — in the possibilities of constructive cooperation between business and the Government for the public protection and welfare." "For the first time in our history," the economists Foster and Catchings wrote, "a President of the United States is taking aggressive leadership in guiding private business through a crisis." And his course was a correct one, they added. "President Hoover's plan is sound. The expansion of private capital facilities and public works *at the right rate* is all that is needed to keep men employed and business active during this winter." "I can recall," another recounted, "no such regimentation of public sentiment since the days of the World War. Mr. Hoover may have his little difficulties in controlling the Senate, but as a crystallizer of public opinion, in the present instance at least, he has been just about 99 per cent successful." And the *New York Times,* more restrained but approving, added: "The President's course in this troublous time has been all that could be desired. No one in his place could have done more; very few of his predecessors could have done as much." [25]

Hoover wanted to prevent the stock market crash — for which he was not responsible — from triggering a depression. But good intentions cannot of themselves solve such problems. The crucial test was whether his program would work.

Yet, curiously, the success or failure of Hoover's program was almost wholly outside his direct control. For despite the fact that Hoover had been far more active than previous Presidents faced with a depression crisis, his initial program hardly committed the federal government to a major role in meeting the nation's danger. The President's role was actually confined to that of an influential adviser and well-placed cheerleader. The President's function was pointing the way to others, who, prodded on by encouragment from the White House, would provide the necessary leadership and energy to implement his ideas. The brunt of his program rested on the nation's traditional institutions. Combined by mutual pledges and a common aim, they were to act in a concert of good will and co-operation to surmount a major economic crisis.

Among these institutions, the chief burden was undoubtedly put upon business leadership. Business leaders, aided by the positive help of the banks and the negative help of the labor unions, were to ensure that business proceeded as usual. Assisted by the cities, the states, and the federal government, they were to spearhead the movement to expand construction. Meanwhile, the existing private and public social welfare agencies were to care for whatever unemployment these measures failed to prevent.[26] Hoover believed that the nation's traditional institutions, inspired with new vigor and the will to co-operate, were sufficient and capable to meet the challenge.

In considering Hoover's response to the crash during these first months, one is struck by the total absence of reform proposals. Hoover's program did not require change but a new spirit within existing institutions. While the collapse itself and its potential repercussions were not minimized, the need for structural changes in the nation's traditional economic arrangements — which had permitted such a devastating collapse — was completely neglected. The operations of the securities exchange, for example, with its esoteric practices — short-selling, margin accounts, investment trusts, inside and outside pools, bear raids, and call loans — were not to be probed for weakness and strengthened by reforms. Instead of reform, the stock market was to be immunized from the healthy body economic. There was, in other words, no assurance or indication that Hoover's program would protect the nation against a similar recurrence in the future.

Hoover's optimistic assumption may well explain why one of the nation's most important institutions was excluded from participation in his program. Since investigation and reform were not called for, there was no need for legislation.

Congress had no apparent place in the ambitious plans of a Republican President. During these early months of domestic crisis, Congress was in session, but Hoover showed no inclination to enlist its aid. With Congress excluded, and the role of the presidency confined to inspiration and exhortation, the authority and power of the federal government could not be said to be committed in any direct sense.

This was precisely what Hoover wanted. It was not desirable, in the President's scale of values, that the crisis should be met by federal intervention. It was much more desirable that it should be met and overcome by the institutions which he had called upon, and this task was to be accomplished voluntarily by co-operative effort. In these first months, Hoover made the issue clear. The nation's institutions were challenged. All that remained was the test: were these institutions capable of overcoming a major, domestic economic crisis by voluntary co-operative action?

4

Business Leadership: The Limits of Co-operation

The historical role of Mr. Hoover is apparently to try the experiment of seeing what business can do when given the steering wheel.*

NEW REPUBLIC, 1929

Leadership in America is more easily identified than defined. In politics, for example, leadership is customarily associated with specific Presidents rather than with the presidency. We persistently deal with the subject by contrasting strong Presidents, such as Wilson and the two Roosevelts, with weak Presidents, such as Buchanan and Harding, rather than by constructing categories of strong and weak presidencies. The qualities of leadership, therefore, do not appear abstracted and classified; they are personified and illustrated. Men, not attributes, constitute leadership. In our thinking, the nature of leadership is one of variety and not of patterned uniformity. Leadership in America, to put the matter somewhat differently, is considered an individual and not an institutional phenomenon.

But only in relatively recent times has leadership become associated with politics and politicians. Before the Great Depression, it was far more usual for Americans to equate leadership with business and businessmen. Americans thought and spoke not of captains of politics, but of captains of industry.

American leadership became closely identified with businessmen in the period from the Civil War to the 1890's. For this was a time when individual enterprise displayed a surging energy and achieved its most impressive results. A swarm of individualistic businessmen, possessed of genius, ruthlessness, imagination, and power, translated their visions and obsessions into a reality of transcontinental railroads, of factories and cities. And, incidental to their unco-ordinated, personal strivings and motives, they unwittingly transformed America into a modern industrialized nation. It was an achievement which owed little either to a sense of togetherness or to a spirit of co-operation.

The quarter-century following the Civil War was economically a creative, a building age. A new America was made, and it was made without benefit of plan. Since it had happened that way, it was easy to see how the accident of planlessness should subsequently be elevated to a positive virtue. As a result, there developed an aversion to planning and to the governmental interference that planning implied. This reaction found one expression in the creation of a simplified litany of success. The major phrases of this democratic chant are familiar to us all: unfettered freedom, personal initiative, individual opportunity. These words became the slogans that were used to explain our greatness. Individualism and progress became cause and effect.

This experience and the rationalizations it induced were to distort seriously the American perspective. Individualism was projected backwards and forwards. We had achieved greatness because of individualism, and individualism would make us greater still. To understand individualism was to comprehend all that was peculiarly American. Our history was merely the chronicle of the successive triumphs of the individualistic spirit.

This attitude, of course, greatly oversimplified our heritage. People forgot that much in our past exemplified the co-operative spirit, and co-operation now seemed alien to the American temper. For the definition of leadership, however, this rationalization fostered its own potent heritage, one grounded in habits of mind that hardly encouraged a co-operative spirit within the business community. "The American tradition," as one business leader confided, "does not favor cooperation. Business men and bankers will join in cooperative efforts only when driven by necessity." [1]

If life, like words, were subject to precise definition, applied with consistency, and governed by logic, then such contradictory ways of life as individualism and co-operation could not conceivably exist simultaneously within the same person. One quality would necessarily preclude the other. But in life, as we well know, contradictions often exist comfortably side by side. We speak, for example, of a virtuous sort of a rogue, or call a friend a sociable individualist. Today, in political discussions, we hear a good deal of talk about progressive-conservatives and conservative-liberals. Many dismiss this terminology as either jargon or an absurd confusion of thought. Actually, these designations capture current complexities of life by doing violence to words and to the neat, logical categories they tend to impose. In life, in spite of the old adage, we do always try to have our cake and eat it too.

It was this type of feat which the Hoover program in effect called business leadership to perform. It demanded that they break through the formidable obstacle of words. What was wanted badly for the national welfare were co-operative-individualists. This was to require a great deal of businessmen.

Some contemporaries were optimistic; they thought that what was wanted could be supplied. For these, a favorite argument was that the long experience of businessmen in conducting their own concerns without government interference had incidentally conditioned business leaders for the much broader task of collectively correcting a floundering national economy. "If it is practicable," a business leader argued, "for a single industry to regulate and balance production by planning ahead, by diversifying and other means, it would seem to be quite as practicable by the same means to keep prosperity on an even keel." [2] Despite its plausibility, it was faulty reasoning. It was much like saying that a horse permitted to run free and unbridled was actually in training to pull harnessed in a team.

Considering the daily experience of business leaders in conducting their enterprises, and adding to this the rhetoric of individualism, the obstacles to a successful co-operation among businessmen appeared overwhelming. Businessmen, the Dean of the Harvard School of Business Administration wrote, "have a fine understanding of their own business, too little grasp of their industries as a whole, almost none of the relation between their particular interests and our general social and economic structure, and far too little grip on the social consequences of their activities." [3] Nevertheless, it would be a mistake to view the situation as one of unrelieved gloom. There was one ray of light. This was the trade association.

Trade associations were co-operative organizations of businessmen engaged in the same industry. The purposes of the associations were to study production and distribution problems of the industry, promote the common interest of its members, and increase their profits.[4] This movement, in short, deviated in practice from the rhetoric of individualism. For through these associations, the business community attempted to encourage co-operation within a particular trade or industry. Co-operation — in purchasing, selling, and price fixing — was to replace the old, unrestrained, cutthroat competition. Order and efficiency were to displace chaos and waste.

Despite the smoke screen raised by the rhetoric of individualism, business co-operation had existed for a long time. Trade associations antedated the Civil War. But their development through the 1890's was slow. The chief obstacle for this movement, which aimed at circumventing competition, was the intense individualism characteristic of most businessmen of that time. "The association movement," as one student has observed, "was considered revolutionary doctrine, and did not seem to fit into a business world where every man was a law unto himself." [5]

In the 1890's a new factor checked those promoting trade associations. Congress enacted the Sherman Anti-Trust Law. Yet, despite the legal obstruction of this new legislation and subsequent court decisions, "neither the growth of associations nor their price activities" was checked. Ways were found to circumvent the law. In the following years — right up to the American entrance into World War I — the trade groups proceeded to the organization of associations national in scope. Whether accepted outwardly as respectable or not, the trade associations flourished.[6]

Respectability would eventually come to the association movement. This acceptance, both by the government and by the entire business community, was hurried by national necessity. World War I created it; and, at the time, winning the war seemed to override all other needs. Trade associations were found useful in fulfilling the war effort; they oiled industrial co-operation. And many of the businessmen who had personally participated in this wartime, co-operative experiment were impressed with its achievements. "The war," as one historian has remarked, "confirmed the triumph of large-scale industrial organization." [7] Co-operation worked; it was efficient and paid good returns — so businessmen learned the practical value of associations. They also gained valuable experience in the methods of co-operation.

After the war, adverse Supreme Court decisions in American Column and Lumber Company *et al. v.* United States, and United States *v.* American Linseed Oil Company *et al.,* of 1921 and 1923, momentarily checked the advance of the trade association movement. These decisions were modified later, in 1925, by the Supreme Court in Maple Flooring Manufacturers' Association *et al. v.* United States.[8] This decision created a new atmosphere, one in which the trade associations could proceed apace. Thereafter, the friendly eye of Republican administrations watched their development approvingly. The Federal Trade Commission and the Justice Department now abandoned their brief hostility of 1921–25, and resumed the friendly attitude of the war years. The Secretary of Commerce in the Harding and Coolidge administrations, Herbert Hoover, shared this approval. Under his direction the Commerce Department actively participated in promoting the growth of associational activities.

These activities, Hoover felt, seemed necessary; to encourage their development promised the best hope of forestalling the distasteful alternative of governmental control.[9] To Hoover, the powers of the federal government were always the force held in reserve. Before utilizing them, he would exhaust the possibilities of voluntary action.[10] It would be difficult to point to a more devoted adherent of this principle. Hoover's persistent adherence to this article of faith created much bitter criticism of his presidency.

This experience with trade associations supported the hope for business co-operation at the time of the stock market collapse. Upon this slender foundation, the effort to utilize voluntary action would have to be built. It offered the best available alternative to governmental interference. Hoover was quick to exploit its full potentialities. It was not caprice that brought him to choose the chairman of the United States Chamber of Commerce for the job of mobilizing the business community.

In 1929 the United States Chamber of Commerce served as the leading spokesman of the business community. It was through this organization, whose membership included 1700 business organizations, that the President made effective contact with the nation's trade associations. The December 1929 meeting of the National Business Survey Conference was in actuality a small gathering of the Chamber — indeed, the same club by another name. "Although many were representatives of large concerns," *Business Week* reported, "it is significant that most were spokesmen for national business organizations." Julius Barnes, when planning this conference, rightly referred to it as a "meeting of trade association representatives." [11]

The strength of the business community's co-operative spirit was, therefore, concentrated in the National Business Survey Conference. The initial test of its effectiveness would be determined by the success with which it met the President's challenge. The test, in brief, would be whether it succeeded in stabilizing employment, maintaining wages, and expanding construction. Here, in the words of the President, was indeed "a great responsibility and a great opportunity." [12]

Hoover's choice of Julius Barnes was singularly fortunate. The viewpoints of the two men were remarkably harmonious. Hooverian phrases and ideas threaded their way easily in the fabric of Barnes's speeches and writings. Here was expressed the same conviction that the stock market crash was an unfortunate but peripheral event, that the essential structure of business remained sound and unimpaired. He had the same optimistic view that the business community possessed sufficient cohesiveness, leadership, and co-operative spirit to surmount the difficulties of maintaining stability. A more congenial partner for Hoover could hardly have been found.[13]

Besides, Barnes was strategically located. As chairman of the Chamber of Commerce of the United States, he was in close touch with its one million members as well as with the nation's trade associations. He was the vital link with those business organizations which, impressed by their successes in organizing stability within their own industries, refused any longer to accept the business cycle as an inevitable economic law. Barnes enthusiastically shared this optimism. "Why should there be," he asked, "tacit acceptance of a former theory of cycles which involved extravagant inflation, to be followed by discouraging depression?" [14]

Not long ago, he admitted, business had "bowed unquestioningly before the fetishes set up by some of the older economists who invested certain sequences of cause and effect with the sanctity of inexorable economic law — not because they could not be controlled but because they were not understood." It was only within the last ten years, he noted, that the tranquillity of this economic fatalism had been seriously disturbed. More detailed studies by younger economists first shook this belief in business cycles and raised questions about their inevitability. Now, he said, "we have begun to doubt that variations in demand and supply are of mysterious origin, accepting them, rather, as the results of our own lack of foresight."

Business was now prepared to act. The willingness displayed to undertake to stabilize industry, Barnes declared, "marks an end of the fatalism with which industry and commerce have been in the habit of contemplating the periodic fluctuations embraced in the business cycle."

Barnes not only approved, he applauded business's ambitious new undertaking. It was justified, he thought, because this was not merely a change in opinion; it was accompanied and strengthened by an important change within the business structure. No longer was business a mere conglomeration of unco-ordinated parts. The day of the small, autonomous business unit was passing. "This is the day," he proclaimed, "of the trade association and of concerted effort in local chambers of commerce." [15]

Associations — those business units of a larger mold — were attempting to utilize the best aspects of two traditions. In them, the "individual initiative" of the older day was combined with the advantages of "large-scale effort" of the new day. "It would be an inspiration to all who believe in self-government of the people," he said in a radio address, "if there could be constructed now such an example of team-play as would show that voluntary service is superior to government compulsion." And, later, in a similar vein: "It is time for collective common sense and for the most intelligent voluntary team play." [16]

This broadened outlook of co-operative individualism, together with the structural changes in organization, made people hope that the downward spiral could be arrested. The National Business Survey Conference constituted for the business community a "novel social experiment." It was, Barnes pointed out, "the first attempt to marshal national economic resources to the accomplishment of a national purpose." Business, by its willingness to accept this responsibility, "undertook to shape its own destiny rather than leave it . . . to the varying winds of fortune." [17]

As the leader and spokesman of this national, co-operative effort, Barnes was eager that the public understand fully the function, methods, and the organization of the National Business Survey Conference. He accomplished this largely by making speeches and writing a number of articles throughout 1930. In these he made clear that the function of the National Business Survey Conference, now an organized body with headquarters at the United States Chamber building in Washington, D.C., was a multiple one.

The National Business Survey Conference, besides being a temporary organization, was a purely voluntary one. Consequently, it could not command obedience to its program. It had to persuade. Large industry, small business, and even householders were among those who had to be persuaded in one fashion or another. Large industry, Barnes maintained, could not be expected to hold to production levels that exceeded current demand. Such a policy would result in overproduction and only worsen conditions. Instead, what was needed was an industrial program which would preserve con-

suming power while "production marked time." Big industry
should increase construction and invest in the modernization
of plants and equipment. Small business, meanwhile, could
help ensure the success of the President's policy by immediately commencing all necessary repairs, improvements, and
expansions. Even the nation's householders had a part in this
scheme. They could contribute by making home improvements, including "the extra sunporch, new fixtures for the
bathroom, new floor in the cellar." [18] Each new expenditure
— from improvements in the largest of industrial plants to
the household bathroom — was urged in the interest of the
common welfare.

This policy was an attempt to reverse well-established
habits. In times of economic uncertainty, people usually
saved. They saved to provide some measure of personal security for themselves. But the National Business Survey Conference was now attempting to persuade a people who had
been taught to regard frugality and foresight as virtues that
the time had come when these virtues were vices. What was
appropriate for a past day was obstructive today. The habit
must be abandoned. People were urged to spend on home
repairs, business improvements, modernization of equipment, and new construction. By spending, they would sustain
economic stability, and thus provide for everyone's personal
security. The task of persuasion obviously was not to be an
easy one.

The National Business Survey Conference had also to reassure. After the market crash, rumors of disaster were ramp-
ant. These had to be dispelled. If left unchallenged, "they
might eventually have brought about the panic of which they
were only the imaginative forebodings." While this was primarily a psychological problem, it was no less real for that.
"It is obvious," Barnes declared, anticipating a famous
Rooseveltian phrase, "that the thing to be feared most was
fear, which would result in hesitation and timidity and the

clogging of undermined confidence." Rumors and fears fed upon ignorance. If the people were given the facts, if they could be made to understand the true state of affairs, then ignorance would be dispelled, fear checked, and confidence restored.

A major function of the National Business Survey Conference, consequently, was to provide the people with accurate facts about the state of the economy. "It was felt," Barnes explained, "that American judgment, supplied with knowledge of accurate conditions, could be trusted to reach dependable conclusions." [19] Barnes, it is apparent, was fully convinced of the correctness of his own optimistic diagnosis of the economy. He was equally convinced that all right-thinking folk, when given the facts, would arrive at the same conclusion. Statistics were to give only one message — a reassuring one.

These functions of the Survey Conference — persuasion, reassurance, and education — were to be performed by its two committees. The small Executive Committee of twenty-one men, chosen for their broad business outlook, was headed by Julius Barnes.[20] This committee was to be assisted by the larger Advisory Committee composed of 170 men. Each member of the Advisory Committee represented an organized industry,[21] and they were responsible for making detailed studies of the nation's industries with the aid of the trade associations. The Executive Committee, after evaluating the information gathered by the Advisory Committee, was "to shape and direct major policies."

The Survey Conference, drawing upon the chambers and the trade associations for its information, promptly began to issue periodic reports on the condition of major industries.[22] In one of its first gatherings, at the United States Chamber of Commerce building in Washington on January 23, 1930, the Executive Committee ventured to evaluate business conditions for 1930. After the meeting, a delegation, led by Lewis E. Pierson, chairman of the Irving Trust Company of New

York, called upon Hoover to present its conclusions. Looking back upon the events of the last quarter of 1929, the Committee acknowledged that the economy had suffered a recession. But it had been short-lived. "This recession, due to causes other than those involved in the business structure," they declared, "has left no major problems to be solved."

As for future prospects, the Committee announced that its survey of major industries indicated that production and consumption figures all were "encouraging." The consensus of the members was "that the situation had become so far normal that no unusual methods need be considered for the stimulation of business beyond the policies of progress which ordinarily mark American industry." This statement, made by those who reputedly knew the facts, was indeed optimistic. The danger, so much feared, that the stock market crash would precipitate a depression had resulted instead in a mild, short recession. And that recession had now been mastered. The job undertaken by business leadership, it now appeared in January 1930, was terminating successfully. The Survey Conference was to be blessed with a short-lived tenure.

The facts, unfortunately, like the recently expired bull market, failed to sustain this comfortable expectation. Succeeding reports acknowledged this only obliquely: a note of caution was heard; an engaging humility replaced the complacent self-confidence. The figures, as Chairman Barnes quaintly expressed it, were now to be given "without presuming to draw conclusions." The ostensible reason for this restraint was that it would permit the people to form their own opinion. Perhaps so, but this procedure incidentally permitted the people the opportunity of having no one to blame for error but themselves.

The facts, especially as time went on, were not at all encouraging. By the end of 1930, Chairman Barnes was not only scrupulously refraining from drawing conclusions, but he was careful not to make any forecasts of general trends as well. The facts were telling a single story, but not the one that had been anticipated — and definitely not a reassuring one. Eventually the Survey Conference was heard from no more; its expiration lacked the ceremony and fanfare that marked its inception. A brief public notice, buried in the back pages of the *New York Times,* stated that the National Business Survey Conference had been dissolved on May 6, 1931. The White House explained that there was no significance in its dissolution; its "pioneer work" was finished, and other agencies had taken over its function. Its work (if one ventures to call it such) consisted of meetings and conferences, answering correspondence, and issuing optimistic statements. When optimism was clearly untenable, the Survey Conference quietly faded away.[23]

To maintain a claim to leadership, it is not sufficient merely to propose. One must also dispose. One major objective of business leadership was expanded construction. How well did business leadership do in translating its pledge into reality?

At the time of the President's conferences, the business leaders went beyond optimistic statements and pledges of co-operation to estimate anticipated expenditures on new construction and modernization. These figures were conspicuously reported by the press, and the emphasis they received was undoubtedly due in part to the conviction that a prime need of the moment was psychological reassurance. Here was optimistic opinion backed by optimistic action. Business was fundamentally sound; it would act that way. Conditions were normal; business would spend that way. Beyond reassurance, the figures represented in dollars and cents a stated objective of business leadership.

The figures were impressive. At the time, government building construction was the most important sector of the construction field because of its effect on general business. According to estimates by the President's Committee on Economic Changes, public construction accounted for 35 to 40 per cent of the nation's total construction, employing approximately 900,000 workers. The representatives of the building construction industries who attended the November 22, 1929, conference "estimated that projected state highway construction and improvement contemplated an outlay of $1,100,000,000 in 1930." A similar amount was anticipated as a result of county and city roadwork. In all, construction in this field was expected to amount to $2.2 billion. These figures were revised upward subsequently by Secretary of Commerce Robert P. Lamont. On January 19, 1930, he stated, using statistics compiled by the new Construction Division in his department, that the total expenditures by the states for public works was estimated at $3 billion. When federal construction work was added to this, the total, he announced, was $3.3 billion.[24]

The railroads, with a work force of 1,750,000 employees, ranked next to public building. Railroads paid out annually to their employees nearly $3 billion in wages. For the materials and supplies necessary to their operation, they spent on an average more than $1.25 billion a year. In addition to these outlays, new capital investment averaged annually more than $750,000,000. The railroad leaders in their conference with the President spoke only generally of their industry's construction plans. But, according to the New York *Herald Tribune,* "it was learned unofficially, that the nation's railroads have projects in mind that would require an aggregate budget of more than $1,000,000,000 in the next year." [25]

Public utilities, ranking third in importance, averaged annually between $700,000,000 and $900,000,000 for construction and development. At the conclusion of the utility leaders' conference with the President, on November 27, a statement was issued by Matthew Sloan, president of the National Electric Light Association, for the thirty-five executives present. "The electric light and power, manufactured and natural gas, and electric railway utilities," he said, "contemplate the expenditure of $1.4 billion during 1930 for new construction and expansion of facilities, an increase over the corresponding expenditures for 1929 of $110,000,000." In addition to this sum, $410,000,000 was to be spent to maintain existing facilities. This meant a total expenditure for the utilities of $1.8 billion.

On January 19, 1930, Secretary of Commerce Lamont announced that the figures of anticipated expenditure in 1930 for both public works and public utilities amounted to a grand total of $7 billion. Lamont pointed out that this total did not include residential construction, commercial and industrial building, or other private activities, which, in 1929, had amounted to more than $3 billion.[26] If construction work in this sector held up during 1930, total investment would amount to an impressive $10 billion.

The importance that business leadership attached to construction was further emphasized by the creation of a special committee to deal exclusively with construction problems. Under the auspices of the National Business Survey Conference, more than a hundred representatives of construction and building industries met in Washington in late January 1930 to devise ways of encouraging building activities through concerted effort.

The first step was to organize. The National Building Survey Conference, a committee composed of representatives of the major building industries, was created. Fenton B. Turck, Jr., vice-president of the American Radiator Company of New York, was named chairman.

Next, the committee defined its objectives. They planned to convince the public, by publicizing information through the mass media, that current conditions were "especially favorable" for new building; to conduct a national survey of all construction work presently underway; and to discover ways which would more easily promote the financing of building projects. *Business Week* summed up this program nicely when it reported that the National Building Survey Conference was "to make propaganda." [27]

The federal government, meanwhile, was taking steps to make more propaganda. A Division of Construction was established within the Department of Commerce. It proposed to keep a close check on developments in construction and to provide a continuous follow-up on local construction projects. From this source, as well as from the other interested organizations, a constant stream of new projects, bigger figures, and exhortations inundated the country throughout 1930.

Hoover himself set the example for much of this optimistic outpouring. Government studies, he announced in early March, indicated that business leaders had responded heartily to the call to expand construction. Figures of announced contracts for January and February were, he said, 40 per cent higher than the usual seasonal totals. For the entire year, Hoover anticipated a higher total than the 1929 figure. In April, Hoover signed a bill authorizing $125,000,000 annually, for three years, for a road-building program.[28]

In late June, Hoover summed up the record of the first six months in a radio message to the Governors' Conference at Salt Lake City, Utah. He thanked the governors for their co-operation in promoting construction throughout the states. Government figures, he informed them, showed "that the totals expended or contracted for in new public works and betterments by National, State and local governments in these last six months have not been less than $1.7 billion, and that this exceeds even the boom year of 1929 by over $200,-000,000 . . ." [29] In the private sector the record was even more impressive. Business leaders, he said, "have shown courageous faith in the future and their expansion of employment which they have provided in construction and betterment works exceeds even the $200,000,000 of increase over 1929 accomplished by the public authorities."

Chairman Barnes, in the meantime, moved his oar to the President's pace. In the National Business Survey Conference's summary report of business conditions, issued on April 27, he declared "that large American industry is fully carrying out the construction program forecast by them last December. . . ." In June, he reported that big industry was continuing to carry out its pledges. In both cases, statistics were cited in support of his contention.

Assistance came from other quarters. The Treasury Department, for example, announced that it would assist the President's stabilization program by suggesting to Congress that it increase current appropriations for public building construction by $15,000,000 annually. The Navy Department publicized contracts for $23,000,000. Similar releases came from the War Department and the Department of Interior. Mayors who had building figures to cite were listened to with attention. Even Harvard and the Universities of Chicago and Minnesota, where $25,000,000 of new construction was under way, were gratefully noticed.[30]

In October, Hoover announced the formation of still another voluntary committee. On October 22, Colonel Arthur Woods was chosen to head the President's Emergency Committee for Employment. Colonel Woods, formerly Police Commissioner of New York City and member of the President's Unemployment Conference of 1921, was primarily concerned with the unemployment situation, and he considered that boosting construction was not unrelated to this problem. And several days prior to the Colonel's appointment (perhaps in an effort to show that, while ingenuity was taxed, invention was far from exhausted), Hoover designated Secretary of Commerce Robert Lamont as chairman of a freshly conceived Cabinet Committee on Unemployment.[31] Boosting took on new vigor.

"The Committee's object," Woods explained, "is to encourage and urge the immediate construction of public buildings which normally would be spread over a period of years, concentrating as much as possible of the normal building program of public works for the next few years into the next few months." To encourage others, Woods announced that Irénée du Pont had informed him that the E. I. du Pont de Nemours Company was carrying out a program along the lines suggested by the Committee. The company and its subsidiaries, with seventy plants throughout the country, would accelerate its plant repair, renewal, and replacement work. This program, it was estimated, would expend several million dollars.[32]

The Colonel also had some advice for the people. "Everybody knows," he said, that "prices are low." For those with fixed incomes, "it might be well to buy ahead." By supporting the "buy now" campaigns, purchasers would aid in providing increased employment. They would also save by buying at the low prices.[33] Here certainly was an alluring formula: spend to save!

In more sedate language, Woods used a similar appeal upon educational leaders. In a letter sent to more than 250 colleges and universities, he urged administrators to speed up their construction programs. "I am informed," he wrote, "that the falling costs of building construction are in themselves an important reason for accelerating plans and operations, thus securing greater efficiency in the use of endowed funds." [34]

Additional examples of this sort could be listed indefinitely. But even then the essential question would remain to be answered. What did it all signify? Much of what this activity meant is now fairly obvious. Beyond demonstrating that business leadership and government were prolific in their ability to create committees, this organizational preoccupation was evidence of the significance that business leadership attached to applying psychology to public problems. While it was considered economically important that construction be expanded, it was equally important that the public should be persuaded that it was being expanded. The primary concern was clearly with public confidence, and it was evident that business and government leaders thought that this factor could be manipulated.

Whether consciously intended or not, there was a certain coherence to these attitudes. If confidence were primarily a state of mind, and states of mind were subject to psychological manipulation, then business leaders were clearly the element best suited to undertake the manipulation. Since in public estimation, business leaders were the acknowledged authority in economic matters, they enjoyed the prestige that comes of association with past achievements. What better device than for the committee to gather together the most prominent members of the group, to co-ordinate their pronouncements, and to maximize the impact of their prestige value? The National Business Survey Conference and its counterparts were much like the conductor who reduces many voices to the sound of one.

Business leadership had put its prestige on the line when it made its pledges and optimistic estimates. As it turned out, however, the actual performance of business leadership in the construction field was not impressive. The simple fact was that construction did not expand; it contracted.

According to statistics compiled by the F. W. Dodge Corporation, the most accurate source on construction activity,[35] total construction contracts awarded in 1929 amounted to $5.75 billion. This represented a 13 per cent drop from the 1928 high of $6.6 billion. In 1930, total construction contracts awarded amounted to $4.5 billion. In 1931, they dropped to $3 billion and the following year to $1.3 billion.

Private construction showed the greatest decline. In 1929, all forms of private construction had accounted for 75 per cent of construction work. By 1932 it was down to 42 per cent of the total. Public construction was held to near record figures in the first two years after the stock market collapse. The totals were approximately the same in 1928, 1929, and 1930 — about $1.75 billion annually. There was a moderate decline to $1.5 billion in this sector during 1931. The first large reduction in public construction appeared in 1932, when total volume dropped to half that of 1931. In 1932, as *Business Week* vividly described it, "the construction industry . . . hit bottom with a depressing bump." [36]

A glaring disparity existed between promise and performance. Nor was this the end of the performance; for business leadership had made other commitments as well. It had pledged to maintain the wage level. What sort of performance did it make here?

If the price level had remained stable, the task of maintaining the wage level would have been relatively simple. But a declining price level completely altered the situation. To adhere successfully to its pledge of maintaining wages under these circumstances was a far more exacting test than business leadership had anticipated. They were obliged to pay the same wage level in dollars appreciating in value at the same time that the prices they received for their products — when they could be sold — was steadily declining. As one editor expressed the problem, "Prices on the decline subdue the spirit of enterprise." This difficulty was not foreseen at the beginning, and business leaders undertook the task with a high resolve. At the time of the Washington conferences, Henry Ford, always one step ahead of his business brethren, declared that it was not sufficient just to hold the existing wage scale. "Wages must not come down," he insisted, "they must not even stay on their present level; they must go up." The Ford Motor Company, he said, "will announce a wage increase shortly." [37]

This was an encouraging example, but it would be a mistake to equate individual action, however meritorious, with the responsibility that business leadership had assumed. In

1929 and the years following, the issue was not whether a particular group of business leaders — those who attended the conference — held steadfastly to their promises in their own enterprises. This was incidental to the major purpose, which was to activate and lead the entire business community to a common determination to maintain wages. The reputations of the captains, the crew, the trade associations, the chambers of commerce, the National Business Survey Conference, the very concept of business leadership itself, were at stake in this undertaking.

Almost from the beginning, the undertaking was marred by failures. *Business Week,* in January 1930, urged a "comparatively small" group of waverers to "call off that wage cut!" While "American industry," it reported, "made practically no use of that 'liquidation of labor' which heretofore has been its first response to threatened depression," there were some exceptions. "Not all concerns — not even all the large corporations, presumably most progressive — met the situation with calmness and good-will. Some automotive companies . . . laid off and discharged employees with what seemed precipitous haste." [38]

There were scattered reports of other evasions of the wage agreement. The New York *Journal of Commerce* in February reported that weavers at the Delgado Cotton Mills of Wilmington, North Carolina, walked out when their wages were cut. The *New York Times,* at the same time, told of workers at the Riverside and Dan River Cotton Mills of Danville, Virginia, who had their wages cut 10 per cent.[39]

On March 7, President Hoover declared that "the undertakings to maintain wages have been held." On May 1, in an address at the annual dinner of the United States Chamber of Commerce, he said that "for the first time in the history of great slumps we have had no substantial reductions in wages. . . ." Henry Ford, later in the month, warned that "issuing optimistic statements on the one hand and lowering

wages on the other is a sure way to prevent betterment."
Those who lowered wages, Ford insisted, were hitting the
country when she was down.[40]

Contradictory claims of success and failure were to distin-
guish the wage effort from beginning to end. In an attempt
to penetrate beyond opinion to fact, *Business Week* undertook a general investigation. Despite conflicting reports of
wage cuts and wage increases, it found that the majority of
large employers were attempting to retain their rates of pay.
"They may," it was conceded, "be reducing employment by
lay-offs and part time, but piecework rates and pay per hour
remain as before." [41]

Not all employers were even this conscientious. "In smaller
cities," *Business Week* explained, "some employers are taking
advantage of the present situation to save money. They are
doing this with an untroubled conscience since they made no
pledges and do not feel bound by the wage truce." Textile
companies were conspicuous in this connection. In addition,
there were reports from Chicago, Cleveland, and Los Angeles
of lay-offs, cutting hours of work, and wage reduction.[42]

In some industrial lines, such as the building trades, where
wage rates were unchanged, unemployment mounted alarm-
ingly. According to the Building Trades Council, 90,000 of
the 120,000 building trades workers in Chicago were unemployed; in St. Louis, 75 per cent; in Milwaukee, 40 per
cent.[43]

In August 1930 the *Commercial & Financial Chronicle* (an
ultra-conservative weekly financial newspaper in New York)
gave its personal estimate of the experiment.

> The brilliant conferences held in Washington last fall did
> a little good, no doubt, but only a little. They did not pre-
> vent unemployment, which increased almost steadily there-
> after. They did not stabilize the prices of commodities, which
> have fallen since. They did not increase building operations
> beyond the appropriations for public buildings and roads,

as the past statistics of building will show. They did not keep up the price of wheat, which is now ruling at exceedingly low levels. They did not prevent a recurrence of stock smashes, for at least one other of large dimensions has occurred since. Nor, in truth, can it be said they kept up the scales of wages for the pressure of unionization is largely responsible for this.[44]

This adverse judgment was at sharp variance with administration statements. The panorama of 1930 when seen from the White House appeared quite different. Hoover found the prospect not unpleasing. A White House release of April 2, 1931, described the President "as being highly pleased with the manner in which the principal industries of the country have supported him in his determination that wage scales shall be maintained during the depression." [45]

How are these disparate evaluations to be explained? What actually was happening to wages during 1930? Had statistics any help to offer in clarifying this babble of voices? The most extensive compilation, that of the United States Bureau of Labor Statistics, was based upon information involving some 3,000,000 wage earners. According to the Bureau, there were wage cuts averaging 9 per cent in 23 establishments, and wage increases averaging 9.2 per cent in 35 establishments, during the period from November 15 to December 15, 1929. From December 15 to January 15, 1930, there were 26 reported wage cuts averaging 9 per cent and 54 increases averaging only 2.9 per cent. These figures, *Business Week* pointed out, indicated that initially the wage truce had held fairly well. But, it noted, the proportion of cuts to raises was increasing with time. In the period from January 15 to February 15, for example, there were 25 cuts averaging 10 per cent to 16 increases averaging 5.3 per cent.[46]

By May 1930, Bureau figures showed that since November 1929 there had been a total of 231 concerns which had reported wage cuts involving 30,000 employees. "These cuts," *Business Week* reported, "were spread over many industries, from agriculture to woolen and worsted goods. In only a few industries," it concluded, "are there indications of concerted action toward lower wages; most cuts seem to have been made independently." [47]

In October 1930 the National Industrial Conference Board took issue with those contending that wage reductions were general. It based its opinion upon the selfsame monthly reports of the United States Bureau of Labor Statistics. These figures showed, it asserted, that in a period of a year (July 1929 to July 1930), 56,941 persons took wage cuts while 31,565 received wage increases. The difference — 25,376 persons — amounted to "slightly more than eight-tenths of 1%" of the 3,000,000 persons studied. Available evidence, it concluded, showed that the number of workers suffering wage cuts was practically negligible. [48]

The wage statistics were clearly inconclusive, largely because they were inadequate. The compilation of the Bureau of Labor Statistics was based upon information voluntarily reported by some 12,000 establishments representing 54 manufacturing industries. It was, consequently, only a sample, and one confined to wages in manufacturing. It is not surprising, therefore, that the available statistics left unresolved the issue of whether business was or was not maintaining its pledge fully. The controversy continued for another year largely because commentators were confused over the precise responsibility business leaders had undertaken on the wage problem.

Different commentators, in discussing wages, simply were not talking about the same thing. Some construed the presidential business conferences to mean that the attending individuals had only undertaken to maintain existing hourly rates of pay within their own enterprises. Laying off workers and reducing their hours of work were not, by this construction, considered violations of the intent of the conferences.

Others based their evaluation upon a slightly broader interpretation of the conferences. These held that both lay-offs and part-time employment, when resorted to by those industries represented at the conferences, marked a retreat from the original pledge. Finally, the broadest interpretation was one based upon the intended purpose of the conference as orginally defined by Hoover and Barnes.

Business leadership, according to this view, had voluntarily undertaken to mobilize the entire business community in a collective effort to protect the workers' purchasing power. This was to be achieved by increasing construction, by retaining the existing wage level, and by stabilizing employment.[49] Considered in this context, business's effort to honor its wage undertaking clearly had begun to collapse at the very outset. Only by using the narrowest construction of the commitment (which almost everyone quickly did) was it possible to pretend that it had been kept.

This is not to say that some business leaders did not make a genuine effort. For example, the railroad leaders, despite a sharp drop in traffic, attempted to live up to their promise. Leaders in the steel industry also made a decided effort, although with less success. Nevertheless, there is no disguising the fact that these efforts were limited — especially as time went on — to the narrowest construction of the undertaking. And even viewed thus narrowly, success was partial. James A. Farrell, president of the United States Steel Corporation, in a speech before the American Iron and Steel Institute, openly acknowledged this. "We are living in a fool's paradise," he declared, "if we think every steel manufacturer in the United States has maintained what is generally known as the current rates of wages." [50]

So that even by the narrowest construction, the wage experiment eventually had to be acknowledged as a failure. This conclusion became inescapable on September 23, 1931. The United States Steel Corporation announced a general wage cut of 10 per cent, effective October 1, that involved

220,000 employees. Similar announcements followed immediately from the Bethlehem Steel Corporation, Youngstown
Sheet and Tube, and Jones and Laughlin Steel Corporation.
In the next few days the remaining independents took similar action. "We held to the old wage rate," Charles M.
Schwab of Bethlehem Steel declared, "as long as our balance
sheets would permit. But with the liquidation of prices and
values in all directions it was necessary to yield to economic
law." [51]

The decision to cut wages was not confined to steel. General Motors announced a 10 to 20 per cent cut in all salaries.
The United States Rubber Company reported that it
planned to go on a five-day week. Wage cuts were announced
by the coal, copper, and textile industries. Within days of
United States Steel's action, it was estimated that 1,700,000
workers had already been affected.[52]

"The policy was experimental," the *Commercial & Financial Chronicle* concluded, "and it proved a flat failure, not
only in the steel trade, but in trade in general." [53] The failure, it might have added, was not one involving the wage experiment alone; it was a failure of the very idea of business
leadership.

André Maurois, returning to visit an America deep in depression, found its people greatly changed. "People have discovered," he remarked, "that in order to conduct big business
properly one must be something more than 'a good fellow.'
They are beginning to examine rigorously reputations and
assertions which used to be taken for granted." [54] American
writers by their own comments fully substantiated the im-
pressions of the French observer.

Elmer Davis saw a great deflation of "the smart man."
Leaders of industry and finance, he declared, "are about as
thoroughly discredited as any set of false prophets in history,
and most of them," he added, "know it." "It is easier to believe," another writer commented bitterly, "that the earth is

flat than to believe that private initiative alone will save us." The editor of the *Nation* fully agreed. "As for leading us out of the crisis," he wrote, "the captains of industry have plainly no vision, no plan, no economic program." The Dean of the Harvard School of Business Administration summed up the widespread disillusionment. "The inability of business and political leadership to rise to the new heights required by an unprecedented situation," he observed in 1933, "is the most disturbing fact of the three and a half years ending March 4." [55]

These bitter evaluations can only be understood when we recollect the high place that business leadership occupied in public esteem. Great claims to prestige, especially when based upon a reputation for leadership, such as business enjoyed prior to the Great Depression, cannot survive failures in overcoming pressing problems. In times of drought the venerable rainmaker must bring rain. Failure forfeits veneration, and anger takes its place — an anger intensified by disillusionment. In the years of the Great Depression, public disillusionment was great. The prestige of American business leadership never has suffered a more shattering fall.[56]

Hidden behind the disillusionment of contemporaries, however, was a more fundamental lesson. This was that the organization of the business community, and its schooling in great co-operative efforts, were insufficiently developed to permit it to meet successfully a major economic crisis. American business was far too diverse and complex to be treated as an entity and committed to a common program. Yet, to misjudge the capacity and unity of business leadership in the days immediately following the stock market crash was but human. But to continue making the same mistake when the depression deepened, and after voluntary action and co-operation had demonstrably failed, was tragic. Something beyond traditional ways was required.

5

Banking: Cash, Credit, and Confidence

Surely America has small claim to genius in banking; rather must she bow her head in shame.*
RAY B. WESTERFIELD, 1931

"To business men," the editor of the *Business Week* remarked, "banking is an esoteric mystery; central banking, its quintessence — the thirty-third degree. They don't want, or feel they can't hope to know anything about it; are thankful if they can keep out of its range." If difficult to businessmen, banking was incomprehensible to others. "Only a handful of people," one writer concluded, "even think they understand much about the fundamental principles of finance."[1] So that in banking matters, the community at large relied upon the experts — the bankers.

Banking, of course, is not unique in this regard. The modern world is cluttered with esoteric matters with which people must none the less deal. Unable to understand these matters, but compelled to deal with them daily, the ordinary person must perforce depend upon the specialists.[2] Self-sufficiency in such a world is a recognized impossibility. Not only do we lack self-sufficiency, we even lack sufficient knowledge to enable us to evaluate the competency of the specialists. As a result, in our dealings with specialists of all kinds — from the automobile mechanic to the doctor and banker — we cannot rely upon explanations in forming our judgment of their competency. We must resort to a more simplified standard of evaluation. We must rely upon what we do know and can judge — results.

We compensate for our ignorance of the mysterious terminologies and procedures of the specialist by simply asking whether his expertise works. If his ministrations do work, we trust the man. Trust, in the modern world, becomes a necessity, since the unspecialized are unavoidably dependent upon the specialized. "We are to-day, in America," as one writer declared bluntly, "approaching a new age of faith, in which the individual, in an era of corporations, super-corporations, giant banks, and investment trusts, is driven to rely mainly on his faith in the character of those with whom he deals, to whom he entrusts his savings, and who control the destinies of the corporations in which he invests." [3]

In the 1920's, intelligent Americans felt particularly incompetent in matters dealing with money, banking, and investment. The initiates in security investments, for example, spoke of all the others as "investment illiterates." "To-day the situation confronting the small investor," a contemporary admitted, "is utterly bewildering." And yet, since the bull market offered such attractive prospects of gain, the bewildered were anxious to share its advantages. "The American saver of today," an observer remarked, "sees that there is a persistent increment in industry which accrues to the wise investor. He wishes to be one of these wise investors." [4] The problem for the non-specialist was how to go about it.

One way that the anxious investor resolved his difficulties was by engaging a broker. A broker, however, was not completely satisfactory. Since he was but one man, he was limited in his knowledge and contacts by that fact. What was wanted was something similar to the modern medical clinic — an institution with specialists in all branches of the field, one that would properly inspire trust, one that the small investor could use. And that is precisely what was offered to the bewildered investor.

The investment trust, while originally developed in Great Britain, was imported to the United States, and, as so often happens to imported institutions, was quickly modified to exploit peculiarly American potentialities. As in name, so in function did it become an instrument perfectly fitted to satisfy the needs of the anxious but uninformed investor. Its phenomenal success in the years leading to the stock market collapse fully attested to its utility. According to one writer, investment trusts were sometimes organized "as fast as two or three a day" during 1929. In 1930, some five hundred investment trusts were estimated to have approximately $3 billion at their disposal.[5]

The justification for the investment trust, and the reason for its success, was that it provided a simple solution to a vastly complicated matter. The well-advertised experts associated with the investment trust — prominent bankers, brokers, and economists — provided the investor with a satisfying sense of security. The investor's sense of inadequacy was lulled by the assurance that his money was safely in the hands of men thoroughly versed in the operations of the securities market. A contemporary writer nicely plumbed the psychology of the uninformed in relation to the investment trust:

> the idea was that if you put your money with this or that investment trust you had nothing more to think about. The trust would play the market for you, knowing always when to buy and what to buy. The trustees were on the inside. Moreover, the operations of the trust, besides being informed, were to be scientific in the very latest sense. The bankers who put their names to it provided the information; professors of economics, who studied charts and geometric curves, provided the science.[6]

The investment trust is merely an exaggerated illustration of essential factors involved in modern life in general and banking in particular. For banking is an institution built upon trust. Without the trust of depositors, there could be neither banks nor banking. In terms of dependence, the relationship of an individual to a banker is much like that of a

patient to a physician. To the physician, an individual entrusts his health; to the banker, his money. Both are prized
possessions. Neither can be neglected with impunity. Perhaps
because it handles a more quantitative element than does
medicine, banking undoubtedly is the more pervasive institution. "Scarcely any of us," as the historian James Truslow
Adams remarked, "can escape a banker." He "enters into the
life of all of us, rich or poor, at every nook and cranny." [7]

The factor of trust was a basic, although often unacknowl-
edged, element involved whenever contemporaries discussed
confidence. No discussion of any aspect of the depression was
complete without some reference to confidence. Everyone
talked of it, and the variety of its uses fairly matched its use.
Individuals were chided for lacking it, leaders were exhorted
to restore it, groups were accused of undermining it, and the
public was urged not to lose it. Due to the lack of confidence,
it was said, the depression had deepened. Without it, investors woudn't invest, bankers wouldn't lend, and businessmen
wouldn't borrow. It was asserted also that when confidence
was restored the depression would end. "Every day," one
writer stormed, "we are told that all this country needs for
economic recovery is confidence. That is not only a fact: it is
the most patent fact in the whole situation." [8] By common
consent, confidence was important; but there was an uncom-
mon amount of confusion over what it meant.

Confidence may be viewed as an idea without definite content, or as an idea of so many diverse associations so as to
represent virtually something without content. In such cases,
it is more profitable to deal with the concept by illustration
than by definition. The best illustrations of confidence, the
ways through which it may be understood, are in its relationships to banking and credit.

"So long as we have our present individualistic private
banking structure," one editor pointed out, "public confidence in it is absolutely essential. Without such confidence, it

cannot function." The validity of this statement can be quickly established by citing a few facts about the American banking structure. In 1929, there were 25,110 banks in the United States. Of this total, 7530 were national banks — chartered and supervised by the federal government through the Federal Reserve System. The national banks, with some twelve million depositors, had total deposits of $19.5 billion.[9]

There were, in addition to the national banks, 17,580 state banks. These banks, chartered under the laws of the forty-eight state governments, were governed by rules as diverse as the number of state governments. The state banks had "perhaps twenty-eight million depositors and 34½ billion dollars in deposits." The American banking system, as a whole, then, was composed of 25,110 banks operating under forty-nine different sets of laws. These banks possessed $54 billion in deposits, and $9.5 billion in capital funds. This was invested by the banks mainly in the $17 billion of securities they held, "and in the 42 billions of loans which they had extended to business men, farmers, and going industrial and commercial enterprises."[10]

To these facts add the important point that 90 per cent of American currency was in the form of bank checks. In other words, 90 per cent of all transactions were conducted on credit. This meant, as one writer expressed it, that "the dollar in any given instance . . . is no better than the bank on which the check for it is drawn." And the bank, he might have added, was no better than the collateral of its loans. Obviously, in such a situation, if the depositors lost confidence in their banks, credit and the banks could no longer function. The problem was stated simply by one writer: "All of us have on deposit in the banks of the land fifty billions of dollars. If we should all go to the banks tomorrow morning and demand our deposits the banks, from all sources, could give us only a scant five billions."[11] This danger, which faces banks at all times, makes the bankers' preoccupation with the problem of confidence quite understandable.

The prevailing opinion held by contemporaries in the wake of the stock market crash was that the banks were in a particularly strong position. Julius H. Barnes, for example, stated immediately after the market break that "there is now no fundamental weakness and no commodity price inflation, and we have a strong banking situation, with adequate credit in sight." Hoover, in his annual message to Congress on December 3, 1929, declared that Federal Reserve measures, undertaken after the crash, "together with the strong position of the banks has carried the whole credit system through the crisis without impairment." He repeated this assurance two days later in addressing the first gathering of the National Business Survey Conference.[12]

Business Week reported that "the position of the banks, which emerged from the stock market disturbance as the strongest element of the financial structure, considerably brightens the 1930 outlook for business and industry. The stability of the banks, so greatly emphasized in recent weeks, remains unquestioned." Later in the year, the American Bankers' Association announced at its annual convention that "the country is to be congratulated that the banking and credit situation continues fundamentally sound." [13]

Many commentators went even further than this and viewed the Wall Street crash "as something of a blessing in disguise." The relief with which those of this opinion greeted the crash was based upon the conviction that the speculative boom had monopolized a vast amount of the world's capital. The collapse had released much of these funds previously tied up in speculation. Cash and credit were now more readily available for normal business development. "Confidence," according to this viewpoint, "did not, therefore, have a fatal fall in the United States in 1929; the aftermath of the Wall Street panic was not fear; it was an admixture of relief, quandary, and resolution." [14]

While it was recognized that the Wall Street crash had created problems which banking had to solve, these problems were not considered at all formidable.[15] Readjustments were certainly required, but the strong position of the banks would facilitate these. While it was necessary to ease credit, the Federal Reserve System's traditional devices — the discount rate, bill rates, open market operations, and direct action — were thought fully adequate to provide for this need. There was, in other words, initial agreement with Hoover's contention that the traditional banking institutions, operating in established ways, were sufficiently strong to meet the needs of business.

The Federal Reserve System began to apply its stock of techniques for easing credit immediately after the first serious rumblings on Wall Street. During the last three months of 1929, it purchased $350,000,000 of United States securities and $100,000,000 of banker acceptances. The Federal Reserve System continued the policy of moderate open market buying of United States government securities throughout 1930. At the same time, it continued decreasing the discount rate of negotiable paper (banker acceptances or bills and commercial paper) eligible for rediscount at the Federal Reserve banks. By the end of 1930, banker acceptance rates were down to $1\frac{7}{8}$ per cent from the autumn 1929 rate of $5\frac{1}{8}$; rediscount rates on commercial paper had dropped from $6\frac{1}{4}$ to $2\frac{7}{8}$ per cent. Call money (brokers' loans for those dealing on the Stock Market) was at 2 per cent. The year, in brief, was "one of low rates for money." [16]

The Federal Reserve System continued this easy credit policy throughout the greater part of 1931. In fact, "during the summer reserve bank rates were at the lowest levels that had ever prevailed, the official buying rate of acceptances being at 1 per cent for the principal maturities and the discount rate of the Federal Reserve Bank of New York at $1\frac{1}{2}$ per cent . . ." After checking the record back to 1760, one newspaper reported that "no instance can be found of a central bank rate lower than 2%." The New York rate of $1\frac{1}{2}$ per cent, it concluded, "has no parallel in the world among central banks." [17]

The theory underlying this program was that the Federal Reserve, by these methods, would expand the reserve holdings of member banks,[18] and, as a consequence, put these banks in a position to increase their loans. By lowering the discount rate — the rate of interest charged by the Federal Reserve banks for accepting eligible paper from its member banks — the member banks would be encouraged to bring their paper in for rediscount to their Reserve bank. In this way, the member banks could increase their reserves. For every dollar added to the member banks' reserves, the basis was established for a tenfold increase in credit. That is, $1000 of additional reserves in excess of legal minimum requirements would provide the basis for $10,000 in credit.[19] One drawback in achieving this result by a lower discount policy, however, was that the initiative was not with the Federal Reserve; it was with the member banks. All that the Federal Reserve could do was to lower the rate, but it was up to the member banks to bring in its paper for rediscount.

In open-market operations, on the other hand, the initiative was with the Federal Reserve. The decision of when to buy United States government securities, as well as how much it would purchase, was wholly in its hands. By purchasing, for example, $1,000,000 of federal government securities, the Federal Reserve would increase member bank deposits and reserves by the same amount; and this would provide the basis for $10,000,000 in credit. While it was theoretically possible for bank loans to increase by $10,000,000, it was neither necessary nor inevitable that it would actually happen. In credit policy, unfortunately, much more is involved than simple arithmetic. "Credit," as Roy A. Young, Governor of the Federal Reserve Board remarked, "is one of those peculiar instruments which seems to work in opposite directions simultaneously, so that the benefits secured in one operation frequently are counteracted by forces that work in just the opposite direction." [20] In this instance, despite Federal Reserve discount and open-market policies, the anticipated result did not occur.

The reason it did not occur was due primarily to the fact that the bankers did not proceed according to theory. Instead of the member banks using the additional funds to expand their loans, they used them to decrease their indebtedness to the Federal Reserve banks. As a result, instead of a tenfold increase in loans, there was little or none at all. All that happened was that the member banks used the funds to improve their liquidity by decreasing the amount of their borrowing from the Federal Reserve. Bankers were obviously more concerned with improving their liquid position than they were in expanding their loans. This action demonstrated, to borrow contemporary terminology, a definite lack of confidence. If confidence had not taken "a fatal fall" in the autumn of 1929, it appeared to be primarily due to delayed action. In 1930 there was little doubt that a significant fall had taken place. The reasons for the bankers' timidity and caution are easily explained.

The economy in 1930 had turned sharply downward. Business failures during the year amounted to 26,355 — a new record. The rate of general manufacturing operations at the end of the year was 14.9 per cent below the December 1929 rate. Automobile production was two million cars less than the 1929 total. Steel-ingot production was down 27 per cent, and steel mills were operating at only 38 per cent of capacity. Distribution of goods, measured by freight-car loadings, showed a material decline. Factory payrolls were down 35 per cent. Retail trade was in much smaller volume. Business demand for bank credit was reduced. Commodity prices were down.[21] Only unemployment was up. This was depression, and it had a direct effect upon banking.

Banking, in an economic disturbance of this magnitude, did not escape unscathed. Disquieting weaknesses were soon exposed in the reputedly strong position of the banks. The first signs of serious weakness in the banking structure came from the rural areas. Small rural banks had been in trouble for a number of years. Suddenly, in November 1930, a new crop of suspensions occurred in the South and West. The trouble began with the failure in Louisville of the National Bank of Kentucky. An affiliate, the Louisville Trust Company, closed at the same time. The failure of the parent banks was followed by that of other affiliated banks in the group. The collapse quickly spread beyond this group, and at least two other distinct groups went down in the chain reaction that ensued. Banks in seven states were affected: Arkansas, Kentucky, Missouri, Illinois, Iowa, Indiana, and North Carolina. Before the dust settled, one hundred banks in these states had suspended. For the entire country, six hundred banks went down in the last sixty days of the year.[22]

It was a bad time for banks. For the entire year, 1345 banks failed — another new record. Total deposit liabilities of the suspended banks amounted to $865,000,000 — another record. This compared with 642 bank failures in 1929, and the previous record of deposit liabilities, in 1926, of $272,000,000.[23] In Canada, merely by way of contrast, there were no bank failures.

Among the nation's commercial banks, the country banks and the small city banks experienced difficulties long before the large metropolitan banks were involved. Their difficulties, in fact, antedated the stock market collapse. Country banks, with loans heavily secured by farm lands, "had shown, in the main, only precariously small earnings or actual losses throughout the years following the post-war collapse of prices for farm lands and farm products." The small city banks were similarly hurt by the decline in land values. In their case, the

trouble stemmed from the collapse of the nation-wide real estate and building boom, which left the banks with loans secured by overpriced real estate.[24]

The stock market crash found these difficulties already
present and caused new ones. The collapse of security values
not only diminished the value of bank assets held in securities, it also endangered a large number of the banks' loans to
customers which were secured by stocks. The situation confronting country and small city banks was summed up co-
gently by one writer: "With few important exceptions," he
observed,

> the security loans and investments of the banks, like the real
> estate loans and investments, were in practical effect frozen,
> and had been frozen even during the period of prosperity;
> for no large part of them could be liquidated under any cir-
> cumstances without smashing the market and reacting on
> business generally.[25]

While it clearly was not a time to sell, banks were often
obliged to sell, for the situation was one that alarmed depositors, undermined their confidence in their banks, and
drove them to withdraw their deposits. In order to meet
depositors' demands, banks were forced to sell their best securities, and this further weakened the banks. Since many
other banks were being forced to the same expedient, the
securities market became overloaded. There were simply too
many sellers and not enough buyers. Stock prices, seriously
weakened since the crash, were depressed even further. The
bond market, an island of strength in the securities market
after the Wall Street crash, now in December 1930, began a
"downward plunge." [26] In this demoralized market, the high-
est grade securities — stocks and bonds — were sold at prices
far below their intrinsic value, leaving the portfolios of the
smaller banks cluttered with the poorer and even less marketable securities. At a time when depositors' trust was being

undermined by the increasing number of reported bank failures, bank assets were virtually frozen. The larger banks were not long immune to these same forces.

On December 11, 1930, the Bank of the United States, a large New York City institution, closed. Net deposit liabilities at the time of its suspension amounted to $161,000,000. Two other large banks had closed during the year — with deposit liabilities of $38,000,000 and $35,000,000.[27] These failures were a prelude to the larger difficulties which characterized banking in 1931, and which now engulfed many of the large metropolitan banks.

Bankers acted promptly to protect themselves. Charles F. Speare, financial editor of the Consolidated Press Association, observed clear signs that self-protective measures were being emphasized in banking policy — especially noticeable among the larger banks. "The remarkable liquid position of the banks and trust companies in New York and in other metropolitan centers of the United States," he noted in January 1931, "as well as that of many so-called 'country banks,' is the outstanding feature of the statements now being published . . ." Liquid assets — cash on hand, cash due from other banks, call loans, and United States government securities — were held at a higher percentage of total assets than at any time since the period following the 1907 panic. In many cases banks had built up their cash reserves to figures from two to three times above normal.[28]

Bankers, whose behavior was central to any policy for restoring confidence, lacked confidence themselves. The scramble of the bankers to attain a strong liquid position helped to undercut the effort to reassure the public. For as the banks increased their liquidity, the volume of loans and credit outstanding was curtailed. The total amount of loans and investments held by all banks at the end of 1931 was "about $9,100,000,000 less than in the autumn of 1929. . . ." At the very time that they were being urged not to retrench, businessmen found that it was increasingly difficult and more expensive to obtain credit. "Despite the energetic efforts of banks to bring down other important items in the cost of living," an observer declared, ". . . the rates charged by banks to the rank and file of borrowers have in most cases remained unchanged, or have actually increased." [29]

Even though the bankers resorted to the policy of excessive liquidity in order to protect their banks against frightened depositors, there were limits as to how far the policy could safely be carried. "No bank," as Charles Speare warned, "can ever be entirely liquid. If it were forced to maintain cash reserves, call loans, government obligations and short-term securities in the amount equal to its deposits it would be an unprofitable enterprise and would have to go out of business." [30] Not only would the policy of liquidity, if carried to extremes, eventually put all banks out of business; even to attempt it would defeat the very function that banks were designed to perform. Bank credit would be destroyed.

The upshot of events in 1931 was that the large metropolitan banks found themselves facing the same dilemma that earlier had confronted the nation's smaller banks. This dilemma, as *Business Week* reported it, was twofold:

> Assets are weakened by general price and earnings declines . . . Widespread commercial failures have left in bank portfolios notes of questionable value. Heavy declines in security and commodity prices and earnings have left notes with insufficient collateral. The drop in the price of foreign securities, deposits frozen in other banks by failures, and signs of weakening of municipal bond prices due to tax defaults are other troubles among the assets of the banks.
>
> Simultaneously, banks are being drained of their funds. Depositors are frightened by hearing of banking difficulties, by bank failures, and by multitudinous rumors. Deposits have been withdrawn and hoarded in almost unparalleled

amounts in some sections of the country, $600 millions in the last year [1930]. Foreign depositors have needed their own funds, have withdrawn hundreds of millions of dollars. All this has occurred just at the time when assets are most difficult to convert to cash to meet this demand.

The best banks have rapidly done the obvious thing of seeking liquidity, many in advance of the need. They have pressed for repayment of loans, have sold weaker bonds as rapidly as possible in a thin market, and have declined to make any but the most liquid loans.[31]

The bankers, quite understandably, were striving merely to protect themselves. Nevertheless, the attempt was inadvertently intensifying the price decline, which was a central factor in the banks' difficulties. Instead of expanding credit, loans were curtailed; instead of improving their liquidity, bank assets were undermined; and bank depositors, frightened rather than reassured, increasingly lost confidence in the banks. Here was a dilemma with the elements of a poignant human comedy. For as one editor declared: "Business can recover only when stability of prices is restored, for such stability is the basis of confidence." If this were so, then bankers had done little to foster their own salvation. They had, in fact, been consistent critics of whatever co-operative efforts had been undertaken to maintain the price level.[32]

The bankers' attitude toward schemes for artificially holding the price level was unmistakenly shown by their hostility to the experiment in maintaining existing wage rates. The bankers' misgivings began to emerge publicly early in 1931. In April, for example, the *New York Times* disclosed that "reports attributed to the White House were that the chief pressure for a wage reduction was coming from a source described as 'the bankers.' " Commissioner Ethelbert Stewart of the Bureau of Labor Statistics, according to the *United States Daily*, stated bluntly that "he regarded the attitude of the banks as the real menace. . . ." The banks, he elaborated, are "thinking in terms of the political economics of Adam Smith and are not progressing away from it, while manufacturers are." "Some banks and bankers," he added, "are hell-bent to get wages back to the 1913 level. I have said this often and I repeat it." This contention was supported by the Secretary of Labor, William N. Doak, who insisted, according to the New York *Journal of Commerce,* "that the only serious proposals for reduced wages are emanating from banking circles." [33]

Other spokesmen outside the administration came to the same conclusion about bankers. *Business Week,* in a report on the wage question, wrote that the "vocal proponents of wage cutting — chiefly of the banking fraternity — maintain that a depression is not time to increase real wages by maintaining wages while living costs fall; that lower prices are essential to develop new markets; that lower costs are necessary to achieve lower prices." Labor leaders were even more emphatic and specific — they cited names — in singling out bankers as the leaders of a movement to reduce wages. William Green, president of the American Federation of Labor, in an address at Houston, Texas, informed his audience that "many representatives of labor believe that a group of powerful banking and financial interests are attempting to enforce a general reduction of wages." In support of this contention, Green identified a number of prominent bankers who recently had made statements in favor of wage reductions.[34]

The bankers' opposition to the policy of maintaining wages, and the satisfaction they expressed when the attempt was definitely abandoned, was merely one expression of their conservative economic orientation. Bankers held views which most closely approximated orthodox, classical, economic thought anywhere in American life outside of academic circles. Bankers rejected the assumption — basic to Hoover's initial program and to the purpose of the National Business

Survey Conference — that the business cycle could be controlled. "The nineteenth century had its cycles and recovered," Stuart Chase remarked sarcastically of the economic conservatives, "and the nineteenth-century minded lean up against this historical analogy as though it were the Rock of Ages." "As a guide to social policy," economist Leo Wolman wrote, "recourse to the procedure of deflation is nothing more than an appeal to mystic forces whose potency we have long since come to suspect." [35]

Yet the counsel of the bankers remained one of unabashed old-time economics: thrift, hard work, and fortitude.[36] It was counsel that became more and more irritating to others. Businessmen attending the national meeting of the United States Chamber of Commerce in May 1931 were openly antagonized by the bankers' strictures. "Again and again," as one editor reported his impression of the meeting,

> one encountered uncomfortable evidences of the widespread feeling that the creative purposes of modern business management had been and were being somehow frustrated by the conservatism and hostility of financial forces. Irritation was especially evident toward some bankers' condemnations of business and labor for overproducing, over-expanding, and over-spending, and the platitudes about thrift and hard work which so often constitute the financial diagnosis of depression and its decalogue of recovery.[37]

The bankers' response to the economic emergency was not to draw together and attempt to surmount the crisis by cooperative undertakings. Far from it. Their response was that of the unreconstructed individualist. Bankers, William T. Foster declared in exasperation, seemed "committed beyond hope of recall to the view that whatever is, should continue to be, and nothing much can be done about it." [38]

On a Friday morning, October 20, 1931, a revealing exchange took place between Senator Robert M. La Follette, Jr., and Albert H. Wiggin, chairman of the governing board of the Chase National Bank of New York.

THE CHAIRMAN. Then, I take it, you believe that there is nothing which can be done that will be effective in saving us from these great fluctuations in business activity which we have experienced in our past history?

MR. WIGGIN. I do not think so. A man only lives so many years and his experience only lasts with him so many years. New generations succeed and they will make the same blunders in the next generation and succeeding generations as were made in the first. I do not think an economic council would do any harm, do not misunderstand me.

THE CHAIRMAN. You would not be opposed to an effort being made in that direction?

MR. WIGGIN. Any more than I think the Federal Reserve advisory council does any harm, but I can not see that it does any good, and it is an expense.

THE CHAIRMAN. Your counsel is one really of despair, then. We are going to suffer these terrific dislocations and the suffering that goes with them on the part of the people generally?

MR. WIGGIN. I think you are looking for a superman, and there is no such thing. Human nature is human nature. Lives go on. So long as business activity goes on we are bound to have conditions of crisis once in so often. We may learn from each one how to avoid that particular difficulty the next time, but you are always going to have, once in so many years, difficulties in business, times that are prosperous and times that are not prosperous. There is no commission or any brain in the world that can prevent it.

THE CHAIRMAN. You think, then, that the capacity for human suffering is unlimited?

MR. WIGGIN. I think so.[39]

After concluding his testimony, Wiggin requested permission to read into the record what he termed an authoritative opinion by Benjamin M. Anderson, Jr., economist of the Chase National Bank. It was an opinion, he added, with which he entirely agreed. The statement was a thoroughgoing defense of laissez-faire economics. It repeated in technical terms what Wiggin had just finished saying with such refreshing bluntness. "Under this system of free, private enterprise," he read,

> with free movement of labor and capital from industry to industry the tendency is for an automatic balance to be maintained and for goods and services to be supplied in right proportions. A social order is created, a social cooperation is worked out, largely unconscious and largely automatic, under the play of the impersonal forces of market prices and wages.

Then, after this reaffirmation of the primacy of the law of supply and demand in American economic life, the alternative way — central government control — was examined. But this was quickly dismissed as an impossibility.

> The ability to understand the highly intricate economic life of to day, the ability to see through it and to see the different parts in relation to one another, to coordinate wants and efforts, to distribute resources properly among conflicting claimants — this ability does not exist.

In addition to Wiggin, there were others of a conservative bent who regarded Anderson's opinions with high regard and appreciation. The editor of the *Commercial & Financial Chronicle,* for instance, quoted a speech by Anderson approvingly and at length.[40] Speaking at the Ohio Bankers' Convention in Toledo on June 10, 1931, Anderson characterized current thinking about the depression in terms of two opposing schools of thought. These were, he said, the purchasing-power school and the economic equilibrium school.

The adherents of the purchasing-power school, according to Anderson, saw "the causes of depression in deficiency of purchasing power, and would seek to find the remedies by artificial increase of purchasing power in one way or another." He included, as members of this school, the advocates of credit expansion through cheap money policies; "those who urge increased expenditures and condemn savings in times of depression; the faction which favors heavy borrowing by government for public works and oppose wage cuts . . ."

The other school of thought — the one to which Anderson adhered — saw the major problem of depression as "a disturbance in the economic equilibrium, and would expect things to right themselves again and business to go on actively and satisfactorily when balance is once more restored." Purchasing power and production, in this view, were not considered as separate things. In orthodox fashion, he insisted "that purchasing power grows out of production and that ability to consume depends upon ability to produce." Equilibrium would be achieved by natural processes and not as a result of outside manipulation and control. "The equilibrium view relies upon the automatic forces of the market place to restore equilibrium when it once has been broken rather than looking to governments and to central banks to guide and control the process of re-equilibration."

This view "is very skeptical," Anderson added, perhaps unnecessarily, "of government interferences." The fact was that depressions were considered as serving a necessary function. "The equilibrium doctrine looks upon periods of reaction and depressions as, properly, periods of liquidation of credit and improvement of the quality of credit, as times for the paying of debts and the restoration of sound credit conditions." [41]

Whether or not all bankers subscribed to these ideas in precisely this fashion must remain a matter of conjecture. It is clear, however, that as a group bankers acted in a manner not noticeably at variance with them. Unfortunately, as time and the depression went on, an ever-increasing number of banks were included in the liquidation process. How far would the bankers be willing to see the liquidation proceed?

Raising this question reveals a characteristic of the American response to the Great Depression that seems now to have been largely forgotten. This was the tendency to consider impersonal, economic forces in a personalized, moralistic fashion. There lingered, for example, a distinct aura of old-time morality about the devotees of classical economics. This trait was particularly evident in the thinking and behavior of bankers. Bankers viewed economic behavior, like salvation, as an individual affair. Attention was focused on the individual and, more specifically, upon individual wrong-doing. Economic righteousness consisted of conducting business according to the dictates of economic law. Those who violated the law, like those who transgressed the commandments, were regarded as extravagant and profligate.

Depression was thought of as a time of chastisement. Wrong-doers now received their just deserts: they were liquidated. And liquidation was viewed as a selective process — a winnowing out of heretical practitioners. But for the righteous, there was justification: they remained solvent. The end result was the restoration of a healthy economic structure and a return to good, sound, business practices.

Unfortunately for the bankers, things did not work out this way — the events of 1931 made this abundantly apparent. During that year, liquidation continued at an increasing and truly alarming rate. Not only did the liquidation process go beyond expectation, it showed a disconcerting lack of discrimination. Unaccountably, it engulfed the unrighteous, the righteous, and the self-righteous without discrimination. Economic forces proceeded with scant regard for moral distinctions — deflation affected the assets of all banks. Alarmed depositors, incapable of distinguishing between conservative and careless bankers, became distrustful of all of them. This wholesale distrust seemed to be confirmed by the mounting yearly number of bank failures. In 1931, a new record of bank failures was established. For the entire year, 2298 banks failed with deposit liabilities of $1.6 billion. A disquieting, additional factor was that failures among the larger banks were no longer an exception to the rule. "The average size of banks that suspended in 1931," the Federal Reserve Board pointed out, "was larger than in any of the previous 10 years. . . . The increase in the average size . . . was due chiefly to the fact that a relatively larger number of suspensions was in the larger towns and cities." [42] Judged pragmatically, no bank could be regarded as safe any longer. Trust — that vital ingredient to stable banking — had been seriously shaken.

Bankers were in good part responsible for the public's loss of confidence in the entire banking structure. The large number of bank failures during the preceding years, even though confined primarily to small banks, weakened confidence in all banks. By ignoring the problem that these failures exposed, by failing to devise some collective means of protecting the weaker banks, the stronger banks unwittingly allowed the very foundations of banking to be undermined.

Bankers were unable to see the utter inappropriateness of attempting to isolate themselves from the effects of impersonal, economic forces. They seemed incapable of escaping the delusion that safe, conservative banking practices would protect their own particular institutions and bring them safely through the debacle. Living in an interdependent, specialized world, where trust was vital, bankers doggedly continued to operate upon the basis of individual effort and responsibility.

How long the bankers would have persisted in this course of action if left to their own devices is an interesting but unanswerable question. Individual effort was indeed finally supplemented by an attempt at co-operative action late in 1931. But the banking community did not provide the initiative for this important departure. The initiative, the conception, and the guiding spirit of this co-operative banking venture was solely that of Herbert Hoover.

The President, alarmed at the rapid deterioration of banking conditions, decided that the emergency warranted definite executive leadership. The first public indication of this resolve came in September 1931, when he conferred with government banking and financial experts in an attempt to devise some effective measures of bank relief. Fear, he recognized, was a major factor in the banking crisis — a fear now as widespread and evident among bankers as it had been for some time among depositors. "The center of weakness . . ." Hoover recalled, "was obviously in our banking and financial system — the element most sensitive to fear." [43]

As bad as the situation already appeared, it was made worse on September 21, when England went off the gold standard.[44] The English decision aggravated all the misgivings which were seriously clogging the proper functioning of the banking system — hesitation, fear, and, above all, distrust. The President's response was to bring direct pressure on the bankers.

On Sunday evening, October 4, President Hoover slipped out of the White House and went to the home of Andrew Mellon on Massachusetts Avenue to meet secretly with a group of forty private banking and insurance leaders. Gathered at the Secretary of the Treasury's home were prominent Wall Street bankers — representatives of the country's largest banks: the Chase National, the National City, the Guaranty Trust Company, and J. P. Morgan and Company.[45] Hoover's purpose was to convince the bankers that the emergency made imperative some form of co-operative action by them on a national scale. The program which Hoover submitted was designed to reassure depositors and bankers alike, halt the policy of excessive liquidity, encourage the resumption of normal loan policies, and loosen up credit.

Hoover insisted that the responsibility should properly be assumed by private enterprise — that for it to do so would "demonstrate its ability to protect both the country and itself." Only a few of those present showed enthusiasm for the President's contention; others argued that the task was one that the government should undertake.[46] But Hoover wanted the government to step in only as a last resort.[47] Near midnight, when the meeting ended, the bankers had not yet reached a decision. They did agree, however, to appoint a committee, headed by Governor George Harrison of the Federal Reserve Bank of New York, to take up the President's proposal with all the New York banks at a meeting the next day.[48] They asked the President for a written statement of his program for this purpose.

"As I said last night," Hoover wrote Governor Harrison the next day, "we are in a degenerating vicious cycle." "The only way to break this cycle," he concluded, "is to restore confidence in the people at large." This objective might be achieved, he submitted, if the New York bankers took the lead in a co-operative effort to mobilize the nation's banking resources. Specifically, he proposed that the New York bankers take the initiative in persuading the banking community to create a credit association with a $500,000,000 capital fund. This fund would be used to assist threatened banks and prevent bank failures by rediscounting paper ineligible at the Federal Reserve.[49] In addition, he suggested that the association aid the depositors of suspended banks by making loans against the assets of closed banks.

Within the next two days, the committee of New York bankers met twice at the New York Clearing House to consider Hoover's suggestions. On October 6, the twenty-four bankers present agreed to organize the National Credit Corporation.[50] This outcome — far overdue — was unquestionably the direct result of the President's urgent prodding.

Later in the same evening, Hoover summoned to the White House administration officials, and, although Congress was not then in session, thirty-two senators and representatives of both parties. He explained the seriousness of the situation, and reported on the co-operative association which the bankers had agreed to organize to combat the emergency. In the event that the bankers' effort should fail, he proposed additional relief measures that would require congressional action. At the close of the three-hour conference, Hoover had received assurances of support from all but two of the congressmen — John Nance Garner and William Borah withheld their approval.

In his public announcement the next day of the formation of the bankers' association, Hoover asked that all the country's banks support the movement. "It is," he insisted, "a movement of national assurance and of unity of action in an American way to assist business, employment, and agriculture." The movement was quickly under way. The New York bankers, Governor Harrison announced, were busy organizing to carry out the President's plan.[51]

The directors of the National Credit Corporation held their first formal meeting on October 17. Mortimer N. Buckner, president of the New York Clearing House and chairman of the New York Trust Company, was elected president. The Corporation formally opened for business on November 7 at its headquarters in the Federal Reserve Bank building in New York.[52]

The National Credit Corporation was the bankers' counterpart of the businessmen's National Business Survey Conference. Like the earlier, now defunct organization, the National Credit Corporation was a non-governmental, voluntary organization. It represented for bankers a similar excursion — although more strange to them than to businessmen

— into the unfamiliar realm of co-operative action. "It substituted," as one commentator remarked, "a practical, co-operative means of operation for an impractical, individual effort of banks working alone." It was, again like its business counterpart, a grass roots organization. The difference between them was minor: instead of working through trade associations as the business group had, the National Credit Corporation operated through local associations of bankers. Where these did not exist, they were created.

For the American public, the National Credit Corporation put banker prestige on trial. "The plan," the editor of *Business Week* noted astutely, "puts private leadership and the philosophy that sponsors it to its supreme test. The public is bound to judge the soundness of this philosophy by the results achieved." Here, at long last, was an issue in the mysterious world of banking and finance that the American public could judge pragmatically.

For Hoover, there was the satisfaction of knowing that the crisis would continue to be met in the "American way." Voluntary co-operation by private enterprise would be tried anew. Government control — at least for the moment — had again been averted.

The National Credit Corporation was incorporated in Delaware but carried on its loaning operations through a subsidiary organized under the laws of New York State. Any operational bank (suspended banks, as Hoover had recommended, were not included) could become a member — and all banks were urged to join — by subscribing 2 per cent of its total time and demand deposits. These subscriptions provided the Corporation with its working fund. If the full $500,000,000 were subscribed, then the Corporation would have that amount available for loans. In other words, the Corporation did not create new credit. The amount available for loans would equal the amount subscribed by the member banks.[53]

Loans from the Corporation were permitted only to the member banks. To secure a loan, a member bank applied directly to its local association, which, after examining the collateral it offered, decided whether the loan should be granted. If approved by the local association, the funds were immediately provided by the National Credit Corporation. The decision of the local association, since it was liable for all loans that it approved, was considered final by the parent body.

Proponents maintained that the National Credit Corporation would benefit the banks individually, banking in general, and the country as a whole. For the individual bank, the immediate advantage of membership in the Corporation was that it would offer a means to utilize its sound but slow assets — assets not eligible for rediscount at the Federal Reserve System.[54] If a bank, for example, were embarrassed by heavy deposit withdrawals at a time when its available cash and liquid assets were depleted, it could borrow the necessary funds from the Corporation on its slow, not readily marketable assets. This would permit the embarrassed bank to escape the resort to otherwise unavoidable alternatives: selling its slow assets for whatever they would bring on a depressed market and hastily calling in its loans.[55]

Banking as a whole would also be benefited. When assets are dumped on a depressed market, it not only depresses the market even further, it also diminishes the value of similar assets held by all the other banks. Banks, frightened by the decline in value of their assets, are all the more reluctant to make additional loans.

This disastrous process, in fact, was actually what had been taking place, and it was precisely this process that the National Credit Corporation was meant to stop. While providing help to the bankers who needed it, the Corporation was intended to reassure all bankers. And, since frightened bankers do not lend readily, reassuring them was no easy matter.

This is what was intended; it was not what was accomplished.

The National Credit Corporation was launched amid cheers and sanguine expectations for its success. "The essential significance of the move," *Business Week* commented, ". . . is that, so far as it works, it means a definite end of the deflation process and an aggressive beginning of reinflation. It has been obvious that this is the only way out of the depression." The American Bankers' Association, at their annual convention, adopted a resolution which declared that "the operation of this pool . . . should immediately remove the restrictions upon credit throughout the United States that has been the cause of so much anxiety to bankers and the public and should serve to re-establish confidence throughout the length and breadth of this country." [56]

General editorial comment was favorable. "The President's plan," the *New York Times* wrote, will "mobilize the banking resources of the country in a common defense against the unjustified loss of public confidence that has lately produced runs on sound banks, hoarding of currency, and reckless liquidation of securities." One writer, referring to the "dramatic fashion" in which the Corporation began, noticed correctly that "front-page publicity was one of the most important factors in the entire situation." [57]

The National Credit Corporation, conceived in September, launched so auspiciously and with such fanfare in October, was by December an acknowledged failure. "After a few weeks of enterprising courage," Hoover recalled in his *Memoirs,* "the bankers' National Credit Association became ultra-conservative, then fearful, and finally died. It had not exerted anything like its full possible strength. Its members — and the business world — threw up their hands and asked for government action." [58]

Contemporary evaluations were not quite so harsh. "It has always been our belief," one editor remarked, "that this Credit Corp[oration] was in the nature of a magnificent gesture, of some value psychologically, but not likely to be of great utility otherwise." [59] There was ample evidence to support this evaluation in the testimony given by public and private officials at the Senate hearings considering the proposed Reconstruction Finance Corporation.

Governor Harrison of the New York Federal Reserve Bank, for example, frankly acknowledged in his testimony the importance that had been attached to the psychological factor:

> The difficulty . . . with the situation throughout the country at the time the credit corporation was formed, was an unholy fear on the part of many bankers that this unreasoning withdrawal of deposits which was going on at that time, might continue and might put them in a position where they would be embarrassed.
>
> The mere creation of the corporation, which provided a pool to which they could go if they had to, relieved the minds not only of the depositors but of many of the bankers as well. . . . The whole psychology of the bankers' mind — especially the smaller country banker, who did not have a very good city contact — was immediately changed.

Eugene Meyer and Ogden L. Mills used a similar argument. The creation of the National Credit Corporation, Mills informed the senators, "had an immense psychological effect on the restoration of confidence when it was badly needed." "After all," he asked, "what is credit but confidence?" [60]

If credit and confidence were so closely linked, how much credit had the National Credit Corporation actually made available? That is, how much of the $500,000,000 pool had been used for loans? No one at first seemed to know. Finally, when the question was put to Governor Harrison, it was answered. "Frankly," he replied, "there have not been very many loans made." When pressed by the senators for a definite figure, Governor Harrison answered that the Corpora-

tion had "advanced around $10,000,000." [61] Considering the
nature of the crisis and the importance that had been
attached to the Corporation, how was the small amount of
loans granted to be explained? And since the bankers' pool
was virtually untouched, why were they urging the government to form the Reconstruction Finance Corporation?

Melvin A. Traylor, president of the First National Bank of
Chicago, not only had the answers to these questions, he also
explained the failure of the bankers' co-operative venture:

> The National Credit Corporation was formed as a volun-
> tary act by the banks of the country to meet an emergency
> which they felt clearly existed at the time. That emergency
> arose because of the inability . . . for perfectly solvent banks
> to borrow against their collateral. There are two avenues
> open to solvent banks. Those that were members of the Fed-
> eral reserve bank had that avenue open for rediscount or
> borrowing, and all banks had their correspondent relation-
> ships with the larger city banks from whom they might bor-
> row.
>
> The public feeling was that a number of banks throughout
> the country had assets that were perfectly good, but, because
> of their character, too slow to meet the requirements either
> of the Federal reserve bank or the other correspondent banks.
> This emergency corporation . . . was formed, therefore, for
> the purpose of making loans to solvent banks against these
> slow assets — and admittedly slow . . .
>
> What it really meant . . . was that the pooled assets of
> the larger banks or those subscribing to the pool . . . would
> be loaned to the borrowing banks against a character of assets
> which . . . was slow . . .
>
> The result is that to the extent this pool loans against these
> slow or frozen assets, they are taking into their portfolio, or
> participating in, through their guaranty, which is joint by
> the members of each association, assets which . . . are sub-
> ject to criticism as slow and nonliquid.

To pursue to the end the operation of the National Credit Corporation, would mean taking $500,000,000 out of the larger liquid banks, and tying it up in the character of loan that . . . can not be quickly or readily liquidated.[62]

The nation's strong banks were clearly unwilling to jeopardize their own position by taking over the slow assets of the weaker banks. Bankers, in creating the National Credit Corporation, accepted the forms of co-operation but refused the substance. Money was available for loans, but bankers were extremely reluctant to lend it. "To be safe," Rexford Tugwell commented, "a credit pool must be conservative; to be effective it must be generous." It was the refusal to be generous that made the entire venture a mere gesture.[63] The ingrained, individualistic temperament of the banking community was not to be so easily altered.

But the viewpoint of the bankers was only one element of the problem. Even if all the nation's bankers had acted in perfect concert, the issue of credit would not have been solved. For credit involves more than the ability and willingness of bankers to make loans; there must be investors willing to take the loans. And the decision to invest cannot be divorced from market conditions. When the normal pattern of buying and selling of one hundred and twenty million people is deranged, it is futile to insist that the cure of the malady is to ignore it.

When the economic system is functioning properly, few people concern themselves by asking why. It is only when the mechanism breaks down that the importance of understanding it becomes apparent and pressing. Only then do we appreciate the complexity of this intricate, delicately balanced system. In times of prosperity, we say that confidence is abroad in the land. In times of depression, when the economic system fails to work, we say that confidence has absconded — it has skulked away.

Confidence reflects the mood of the people. It is the outward manifestation of deeper causes; it is the symbol we use when the economic system is working right. The attempt to expand credit was to go beneath the surface and to deal with one of the underlying causes. Besides the problem of credit, there was the problem of a declining price level. These were problems which, during a period of serious economic crisis, were clearly not to be solved by the timid and confused efforts of voluntary co-operative action.

6

Agriculture: The New Individualism

> My fundamental concept of agriculture is one
> controlled by its own members, organized to fight
> its own economic battles and to determne its own
> destinies. . . . We propose with governmental
> assistance and an initial advance of capital to
> enable the agricultural industry to reach a stature
> of modern business operations by which the
> farmer will attain his independence and maintain
> his individuality.*   HERBERT HOOVER, 1928
>
> You fellows, better organized, got yours while
> the farmer, unorganized, failed to get anything.†
>   ALEXANDER LEGGE, 1930

Like a tenacious perennial plant, the agricultural problem
blossomed with each harvesting season. But its yearly recurrence brought no joy to the hearts of farmers, nor did it cheer
the government officials who sought its solution. Each new
blossoming merely deepened the gloom of the onlookers. If
the farmer and his allies were often discouraged, it was not
because they regarded their plight as a mystery beyond com-
prehension; despair started when they turned to talk about
solutions. The farm question may have been one, but the solutions were many.

One can easily detect — among farmers, agricultural experts, and government officials — a general agreement about
what constituted the farm problem. Hoover, who shared in
this consensus, briefly summarized the "multiple causes" of
agricultural distress in his message to Congress on April 16,
1929. The farmers suffered from heavy indebtedness, a condition inherited from the 1920 deflation and compounded subsequently by increased railroad rates, higher local taxes, and
lower prices for agricultural products. Low prices were

clearly the crux of the matter, the cumulative effect of several factors: selling on the world market, which involved the American farmer in an intense, unregulated competition with foreign products which were produced by cheaper labor and, often, on better, virgin soils; disorderly and wasteful marketing methods; and chronic overproduction — the result of specialization, mechanization, and the continued utilization of marginal lands brought into cultivation to meet wartime exigencies.[1]

Farm surpluses thus became a tangible and daily reminder of agriculture's problems: a simultaneous measure of the American farmer's astounding productive success and his dismal business failure. "The general result," as Hoover stated it, "has been that our agricultural industry has not kept pace in prosperity or standards of living with other lines of industry." [2] The poverty of abundance — a paradox soon to encompass the entire American scene — was first evident in agriculture.

The common criticism made against the farmer was that he was not businesslike; he persistently ignored the canons of economics both in his thinking and in his methods. Despite the repeated admonitions of friends and critics alike, he continued to produce in excess of demand. After years of monotonous repetition, the outcome of this unbusinesslike behavior was predictable: glutted markets and low prices. It was regarded as axiomatic, for example, that in the marketing of staple crops the surplus — that portion of the total crop in excess of domestic demand — governed the price. And even if it represented merely a small part of the crop, it was the fraction (the 5 or 10 per cent sold on the world market) that determined the price of the whole.[3] It was a case of the man-of-war following in the wake of a dinghy.

The farmer, in explaining his dilemma to himself and his fellows, summarized the economic situation by simply declaring that he received the low world price for his crops instead of the higher American price. Yet it is a curious fact that, although the farmer centered his discussion of agriculture's ills on prices, it was not really prices that were at the bottom of his grievances. It was his standard of living and the discrepancy he observed between his standard of living and that of most other Americans.[4] The farmer's true discontent was that he wanted a fair share of the good things of life, and he was not getting it.

The farmer, in short, was less the aspiring businessman than the disgruntled consumer. The businesslike way to combat low, world prices was to curtail production to the domestic demand, thereby eliminating the troublesome export surplus altogether. Although this solution was tediously urged time and again, it made little impression upon the nation's farmers, or, for that matter, upon the principal farm organizations. Instead, the National Grange consistently advocated the export debenture plan; the American Farm Bureau Federation was equally consistent in its support for the equalization fee.[5]

The common element in these favored solutions was that neither made any provision for curtailing production. Both plans permitted the farmer to produce as much as he would; both ignored the business solution of controlled production. Instead, the depressing effect of the surplus upon the domestic price was to be broken by dumping the excess abroad at prevailing world prices. By these schemes, the farmer sought to establish a two-price system: a high domestic price for the bulk of the crop and the world price for the surplus. But since the surplus would sell at a price lower than had been paid for it to the American farmer, a loss was necessarily involved — one that varied in proportion to the size of the surplus.

The equalization fee plan provided for making up this loss by a levy upon all participating farmers. It was expected that the enhanced income from domestic sales at protected prices would amply compensate the farmer for the slight loss involved in disposing of the troublesome surplus. The export debenture plan proposed to accomplish the same object; the only difference was in the mechanism. Export debentures equal in value to the loss of disposing the surplus were to be issued to the farmers who sold on the world market. The farmer, in turn, would sell the debentures — at a small discount — to foreign traders who would use the debentures for payment of import duties. This devious and confused procedure cloaked a straightforward purpose: the loss here would be paid by the United States Treasury in reduced import-tax receipts. Or to be more accurate, the ultimate effect was that the farmer would receive an indirect subsidy from the nation's taxpayers.[6]

Agricultural spokesmen justified these demands by contending that they were merely designed to make the tariff benefit the products of the nation's farms. They insisted that the farmer was just as much entitled to the protection and benefits afforded by an effective tariff as other types of producers — groups who had long waxed prosperous beneath the tariff umbrella. The American market should be preserved for American producers; their slogan was "made for Americans in America by Americans." "If we are going to have a protective system," Senator Norris of Nebraska wrote, "then there can be no logical reason why the farmer who produces the food which we eat should not get the same protection which the manufacturer gets from our tariff laws. Any other system is not just." [7] Nor did the farm leaders feel that they were asking for special privileges by having their proposals enacted in legislation; when critics made this charge, the farmers were indignant and offended. After all, they demanded nothing more than others received; the precedents for such a course were numerous, clear, and sanctioned by long usage. And the one they cited most often and most loudly was the established protective policy for manufactured products. In this respect, the farmer wanted nothing more than to be a businessman.

In addition to this "me-too" argument, farm leaders (facile masters of the timely statistic) effectively buttressed their case by simply pointing to the acknowledged difficulties suffered by the farming third of the population. The standard of living of the agricultural community was indeed not that of other Americans. The disabilities which plagued farmers were certainly genuine; and the aspiration basic to nearly all farm proposals — the attainment of a higher standard of living — was of a sort to elicit a sympathetic response from similarly oriented Americans.

To farm spokesmen, this combination of economics, arguments, and appeals seemed irresistible; and fully convinced themselves, they found it difficult — as the convinced often do — to imagine that others, once informed of the essential facts, would not find their solution completely persuasive. Yet, President Coolidge had not been persuaded; and, as it turned out, neither was President Hoover.

Hoover's attitude toward the agricultural problem was a complex mixture of sympathy and criticism, a view that compounded economics with morality, and resulted in a program that aimed to achieve hard-headed business results and idealistic objectives simultaneously. The genuineness of Hoover's sympathetic understanding of the farmer's plight was well attested by his reiterated pledge, made during the campaign as well as after his election, that the agricultural problem would be the incoming administration's first order of business. "The most urgent economic problem in our nation today," Hoover declared to fellow Republicans in his acceptance address, "is in agriculture. It must be solved if we are to bring prosperity and contentment to one-third of our people directly." "The object of our policies," he continued, "is to establish for our farmers an income equal to those of other occupations; for the farmer's wife the same comforts in her home as women in other groups; for the farm boys and girls the same opportunities in life as other boys and girls." [8] In these sentiments, Hoover was at one in heart and mind with the nation's farmers and their spokesmen.

This harmony of sentiments, however, did not extend to solutions. Hoover thoroughly disagreed with the basic assumption which he believed underlay the thinking of farm leaders: the idea that agriculture constituted one industry, beset by one common problem, and thereby susceptible to one solution. This preoccupation with a single answer seriously hindered agriculture's friends, for it augmented "the difficulty of finding a complete solution," while it also had the divisive effect of provoking the opposition "of those branches of agriculture to which that formula would not apply." "The industry is not a single industry but is a dozen specialized industries absolutely different in their whole economic relationships."

Hoover's thinking on agricultural matters was more sophisticated and complex than that advanced by the principal agricultural organizations, and explains, in part, his persistent opposition to single-formula solutions, such as the equalization fee and the export debenture. Instead, his analysis led him to formulate a more comprehensive approach; a program involving tariffs, transportation rates, marketing organizations, surplus control, and prices. "The first and most complete necessity," Hoover stated, "is that the American farmer have the American market. That can be assured to him solely through the protective tariff." Effective agricultural tariffs would protect farmers "from the competition of imports of farm products from countries of lower standards of living." The modernization of the nation's inland waterway system — joining the Great Lakes to both the Gulf and the Atlantic — would provide farmers with cheaper transportation, and, along with that, ensure producers a larger share of the price paid by consumers for agricultural commodities.

The dribbling away of profits would be further checked by a thorough reorganization of the marketing system via the creation of nationwide, farmer-owned and farmer-controlled, commodity co-operatives. Finally, the marketing co-operatives were to be supplemented by the formation of stabilization corporations which were specifically designed to prevent seasonal gluts and surpluses.

In defense of these comprehensive proposals, Hoover invoked the prestige and success connotations that clung to any mention of "business" or "business methods." "This is not," he assured the farmers, "a theoretic formula. It is a business proposition designed to make farming more profitable." Methods that had been tried, tested, and proved successful in business were now to be applied to the industry of agriculture; and Hoover was confident that the experiment would produce handsome results. Had he not already fully demonstrated the soundness of this approach? His evidence was experience. "During my term as Secretary of Commerce," he recalled,

> I . . . steadily endeavored to build up a system of co-operation between the government and business. Under these co-operative actions all elements interested in the problems of a particular industry such as manufacturer, distributor, worker, and consumer have been called into council together, not for a single occasion but for continuous work. These efforts have been successful beyond any expectation. They have been accomplished without interference or regulation by the government. They have secured progress in the industries, remedy for abuses, elimination of waste, reduction of cost in production and distribution, lower prices to the consumer, and more stable employment and profit.

"I should wish," he concluded, "to apply the same method to agriculture."

Had Hoover stopped here, the problems confronting him

would have been formidable enough; to fashion the inchoate agricultural industry into a disciplined, co-operative business undertaking was a bold and ambitious task in itself. Yet Hoover unavoidably added serious complications for himself and the success of his program by insisting upon the attainment of results which were extraneous to a purely business-like treatment of the agricultural problem. These were unavoidable complications because Hoover never actually regarded farming as merely a business. He revealed his true sentiments when he remarked: "The farm is more than a business; it is a state of living."

For Hoover, then, an acceptable resolution of agriculture's ills must not only assure farmers a greater profit; it must also be so designed as to preserve a way of life — a way of life that stirred memories of Hoover's own youth on the farm, an experience that had helped to fashion his ideals and philosophy — fostering values which he cherished and would now protect. Speaking at his birthplace, West Branch, Iowa, Hoover looked to the past as a guide for the present:

> Our fathers and grandfathers who poured over the Midwest were self-reliant, rugged, God-fearing people of indomitable courage. They combined to build the roads, bridges, and towns; they co-operated together to erect their schools, their churches, and to raise their barns and harvest their fields. They asked only for freedom of opportunity and an equal chance. In these conceptions lies the real basis of American democracy. They and their fathers gave a genius to American institutions that distinguished our people from any other in the world. Their demand for an equal chance is the basis of American progress . . . Here there are no limits to hope, no limits to accomplishment; our obligation today is to maintain that equal opportunity for [the] agricultural as well as for every other calling.[9]

Hoover would link the values shaped by a heroic, pioneering past to the industrial present; traits, qualities, and methods that had achieved progress then would, if preserved, assure continued progress hereafter. He would give no encouragement to any solution which tended to undermine the farmers' way of life. Increased profits the farmer must certainly have, but not at the expense of fundamental values; otherwise the price paid for profits might well be too dear.

Considerations of this nature — vital to the understanding of all of Hoover's policies — were decisive in his rejection of the favored formulas of farm leaders. "Certain vital principles," he cautioned, "must be adhered to in order that we may not undermine the freedom of our farmers . . . by bureaucratic and governmental domination and interference." The first of these principles was that "there should be no fee or tax imposed upon the farmer." The second: "No governmental agency should engage in the buying and selling and price fixing of products." And closely tied to these, a third: "No activities should be set in motion that will result in increasing the surplus production." [10] Without specifically mentioning by name either the equalization fee or the export debenture plan, Hoover pronounced them both as dangerous and unacceptable.

It was from similar considerations that Hoover rejected another — and much more businesslike — suggestion for improving agriculture's economic status. In assessing the environment created by modern industrialism, he remarked: "The whole tendency of our civilization during the last fifty years has been toward an increase in the size of the units of production in order to secure lower costs and a more orderly adjustment of the flow of commodities to demand." Yet, despite this awareness, Hoover rejected the proposal that agriculture follow this trend by consolidating small farms into huge farm factories. "Farming," he stated emphatically, "is and must continue to be an individualistic business of small units and independent ownership." The necessary efficiencies of combination must be achieved by co-operative marketing — in the field of distribution, and not by enlarging the unit of production. Agriculture must not be "converted into a mass-production machine." [11]

Hoover rejected this business idea from the same grounds that caused him to reject the farm formulas: these were innovations that would introduce an inevitable train of consequences disruptive of precious attributes of the American heritage — personal initiative, individuality, and independence. Hoover's plan, on the other hand, would both profit the farmer and preserve his way of life. "This plan," he explained, "is consonant with our American ideals to avoid the Government operation of commercial business; for it places the operation upon the farmer himself, not upon a bureaucracy. It puts the Government in its real relation to the citizen — that of cooperation. Its object is to give equality of opportunity to the farmers." [12]

The fruit of Hoover's pledges and his philosophy was the Agricultural Marketing Act of June 15, 1929: "An act to establish a Federal Farm Board to promote the effective merchandising of agricultural commodities in interstate and foreign commerce, and to place agriculture on a basis of economic equality with other industries." The Federal Farm Board, a seven-member body with the Secretary of Agriculture, Arthur M. Hyde, as an *ex officio* eighth, authorized a $500,000,000 revolving fund for making loans to co-operative associations. This money was to be used to accomplish the stated objective of the act — economic equality — by assisting farmers to establish efficient merchandising organizations. It was designed also to permit them to construct or purchase necessary marketing and processing facilities; encourage "the formation of clearing house associations"; undertake educational (or promotional) work among farmers — persuading them of the advantages of co-operating with the venture; allow the co-operatives to make more liberal commodity advances to their members; and, lastly, create stabilization corporations for handling surpluses. Advisory committees (for cotton, wheat, and other major commodities) were also to be established; and these groups, composed of experienced representatives of the trade, were to support the vital interests of the producers before the Federal Farm Board.[13]

In its spirit and its details, the Agricultural Marketing Act was drawn to Hoover's specifications. Members of both the House and Senate Committees on Agriculture and Forestry, where the bill was debated and written, were fully appraised of the President's farm ideas, and they were governed by his wishes. Efforts to expand the measure — in particular, the attempt to graft the export debenture plan to the bill in the Senate — were decisively defeated.[14] This was clearly Hoover's bill, accurately reflecting his commitment and his reservations: an attempt to achieve the double ends of progress and preservation of the way of life and business that was agriculture.

Opponents of the bill argued that the Federal Farm Board lacked the necessary powers to deal effectively with the basic problem of agricultural surpluses, and that any proposed solution that denied the vital powers required was no solution at all. Clarence Cannon, congressman from Missouri, summed up the opposition's case: "It fails by every major test. It does not make the tariff effective. It does not control the surplus. And it contains no provision against overproduction." Others, while agreeing with Cannon's judgment, saw the futility of opposing Hoover and his supporters; the alternatives were clear: either Hoover's bill or none at all.[15]

Senator George W. Norris, an advocate of the equalization fee, urged his friends not to attempt to block the administration. "I believe," he wrote, that "those of us who favor farm relief ought to put no stone in the way of Mr. Hoover's friends to get this law passed at the short session." Yet, Norris was neither enthusiastic over the Hoover program nor persuaded that it would succeed. Explaining his pessimism to another correspondent, he stated: "Congress is now confronted with the proposition of passing a bill to take care of the surplus without the equalization fee in some guise or other. To my mind, this is a practical impossibility." At best, the Hoover bill might do some good, but it would not solve the farm problem. The situation, as Norris described it to George N. Peek, one of the originators of McNary-Haugenism, was that "Congress is going to pass a law to satisfy President Hoover and anything that does not satisfy him cannot get into the law." "If it were not for President Hoover's objections," he added, "there is no doubt but that this debenture amendment would prevail by a good majority." [16]

This grudging support of the Hoover program was characteristic of the outstanding farm spokesmen in Congress. Senator Thomas J. Walsh of Montana, a supporter of the export debenture plan, was decidedly lukewarm in his comments on the measure. "After nearly ten years of agitation and effort," he wrote, "the only form of farm relief that Congress has been willing to accord is the cooperative marketing act, which experience has shown amounts to nothing practically." But Walsh, as well as other farm spokesmen, was in a difficult position: the act was inadequate; it would not achieve its professed objective; and, yet, it was a beginning. "The marketing act," he wrote in evaluation, "does not amount to much as a measure of farm relief, but we have been advocating for years cooperative marketing as the remedy for some of the obstacles to successful farm management, and the act should be . . . distinctly helpful toward the establishment and maintenance of a general cooperative farm marketing organization." [17]

South Dakota's Senator Peter Norbeck, describing to Norris the position that he would take, remarked that since "Mr. Hoover is evidently willing to assume the responsibility, I want him to have it." Norbeck also suggested to Senator Charles L. McNary of Oregon that he refrain from pushing his own bill; instead, he recommended that the farm leaders first should give Hoover a chance to make good on his pledge to agriculture. "I am going to cooperate with him if he has anything substantial," he concluded, " — but why deprive him of the opportunity." McNary, chairman of the Senate Committee on Agriculture and Forestry, after his initial enthusiasm for Hoover ("Wonderful," he congratulated Hoover on his election. "We will now solve that vexing farm problem"), was somewhat less optimistic at the time the agricultural bill was enacted. "The present Act," he stated publicly, "will probably require amendment by supplemental legislation from time to time." This idea that the Agricultural Marketing Act merely represented the beginnings of a solution expressed a common judgment among farm leaders. "Those having the interests of agriculture at heart," Senator Walsh wrote, "are satisfied that it is good as far as it goes. The only complaint is that it does not go far enough." "Our fight," Senator Norris explained, "was not against farm relief, but it was to get as much farm relief in the bill as possible. Failing to get all that we fought for, we accepted it as a compromise, believing that it is better to have half a loaf than no bread." [18]

The Federal Farm Board, the focus of all these high hopes and serious reservations, held its first meeting at the White House on July 15, 1929, where the President gave the members a short pep talk — emphasizing again the importance of businesslike methods. Hoover had chosen as chairman a successful businessman from the farm machinery field. It was a choice that underscored his intention of resolving agriculture's difficulties by introducing the organizational efficiencies of modern business to the folks back on the farm.

Alexander Legge, president of International Harvester, knew these methods from the inside; but, in addition, he was a man who spoke the Hoover idiom. "The Agricultural Marketing Act," he explained to the members of the national Chamber of Commerce, "supplies the means necessary to help the farmer help himself. His success will depend largely on his own willingness to do his part." Answering business criticism of the Act — charges that it was socialistic or anarchistic — he reminded his fellow businessmen that they made no complaint when government aided business, industry, transportation, and banking. "All the farmers are trying to do, with Farm Board assistance, is, by acting together, to apply the same methods and business principles to their industry that were adopted in other lines long since." [19]

The trouble with agriculture, Legge told the farmers, is that it "has operated as an individual enterprise competing with organized effort in other industries — individual action and planning as compared with collective thinking and acting." What the farmer most needed was organization; he had to combine, drastically reduce the number of sellers, and market his product through one organization alone. The Federal Farm Board was prepared and willing to assist the farmer in attaining these ends. "The major policy of the Board will be the expansion and strengthening of the co-operative movement."

Yet, like Hoover, Legge was also swayed by principles and values that lurked just beneath the hard-headed, realistic talk. "The Federal Farm Board, as now organized," he cautioned, "is not going to buy or sell any commodity, agricultural or otherwise. It is our duty to assist you in doing a better job of this yourselves." Then, more bluntly, in the very words and tone of the Hooverian language: "The improvement of agricultural conditions must be based on self-help. . . . In the long run . . . the Board will render the greatest service to agriculture and to the nation by helping the farmer to help himself." [20]

Legge fully agreed with farmer opinion that the basic cause of agriculture's difficulties centered in the problem of low prices; but, as a businessman, he insisted that prices were — and should be — determined by the market and not by government tampering. "The Board," he warned farmers, "can not raise prices arbitrarily." "Prices," he explained,

> are determined by basic economic conditions — by the demand for a commodity, the supply available to meet that demand and the manner in which that supply is fed to the market. What the Board hopes to do is to assist farmers to become better able to compete with other groups in the markets of the nation and the world. It expects by aiding in the development of cooperative associations to make possible economies in marketing and stabilized marketing conditions, and to assist farmers to obtain their just share of the national income.[21]

Thus the Federal Farm Board's aim was to assist the farmer to stabilize his operations and thereby bring about the long-sought goal of higher prices; and it was authorized to pursue this aim through two principal agencies: the national cooperatives and the stabilization corporations. The question of which of these two agencies would receive primary emphasis by the Board in its stabilization efforts was a crucial one — recognized by both Board members and farm spokesmen. And a split in opinion occurred immediately.

"The principal work to be done by the Board," Senator McNary announced publicly at the time of enactment, "must be through the instrumentality of the stabilization corporations." [22] That McNary, a long-time leader of the farm interests in the Senate, should emphasize this part of the act is understandable: the stabilization corporations could operate directly upon the price problem through government purchase of surpluses. Yet, what McNary regarded as the Board's principal work was considered to be merely a minor and secondary expedient by the Board's chairman.

Legge attempted to dispel the confusion over the Board's position on stabilization by writing directly to McNary. Stabilization involved two distinct processes he explained.

There was, first, the "normal" operations; and behind this, a second form, which Legge termed "extraordinary or emergency" operations. Normal operations included practically everything the Board was currently attempting. "Every measure taken to increase the effectiveness of cooperative organizations in any commodity, or improve their financial position, to centralize or correlate their activities so as to make their operations more effective, is in itself a process of stabilization." And, then, he added significantly: "It is our hope that as time goes on this activity will in most cases prove to be all that is needed, the result, of course, depending on how successful we are in working out large, well-managed organizations, which will control a sufficiently large percentage of the product to make their influence felt on the market." [23]

The principal work, in short, was to be done through the national co-operative associations; the work of the stabilization corporations was to be intermittent — coinciding with extraordinary or emergency conditions. In such cases, "the operation would consist of buying and taking off the market some considerable part of the tonnage so as to relieve the pressure, and carrying the product until some future date in the hope that there would be a more favorable opportunity of disposing of it." Clearly there was a wide divergence of viewpoint here: Legge regarded as extraordinary precisely those measures which the farm leaders wished to make the principal or normal operations of the Board. Hoover, in appointing Legge, had found another mirror for his own form of individualism.

The Federal Farm Board accordingly devoted its initial efforts to the creation of national co-operative associations for each of the major farm commodities. In realizing this aim, the Board was aided by the prior existence of an extensive network of co-operative associations, largely local and regional in scope. In 1929, there were some two million farmers (one-third the total number) who were members of approximately 12,500 co-operative associations.[24] By consolidating these numerous competing associations into several large organizations, the Board hoped to increase significantly the farmers' marketing leverage. The first effort, illustrating the nature of the Board's problem and its accomplishment, was in grain.

American farmers marketed annually approximately 1.4 billion bushels of grain of all kinds; 40 per cent of this total was handled by more than 4000 grain co-operatives, and the remainder by private dealers. In a series of meetings (beginning in July 1929), representatives of the co-operatives conferred with Board members and agreed to the formation of the Farmers National Grain Corporation. Incorporated in October, with headquarters in Chicago, the new national organization represented a combination of three different types of co-operatives: farmers' elevator associations, terminal sales agencies, and pools for common marketing. In those parts of the country where large-scale co-operative associations did not yet exist, they were to be formed.[25]

To ensure that the National Grain Corporation ultimately would be farmer-owned and farmer-controlled, the local associations were to purchase stock in the regionals, while they in turn were to subscribe to the stock of the national organization. It, in turn, would make all loans through the participating co-operatives (and not directly to the individual farmer), using government money from the revolving fund initially, until such time as the farm organizations should be sufficiently established and strong to assume the entire financial burden. Fortified with this readily available loan money, the co-operatives would be able to assist the individual farm member by providing him with three options of sale. He could "sell his grain for cash on the day of delivery at the local market at the prevailing competitive price"; he could "store his grain in a licensed, bonded warehouse, receive an advance on it and 'call' the day any time during the market-year when he want[ed] it sold"; or he could "enter it in a pool, receive an advance on it and take the average price with all other growers for grain entered in the pool." [26]

By these inducements, the Federal Farm Board was able to entice the individualistic farmer into greater participation in the co-operative movement. By June 30, 1930, the Farmers National Grain Corporation included twenty-five stockholding associations with a total membership of more than a quarter of a million producers. During its first year of operation, the national organization "handled at terminal markets about 196 million bushels of grain, or three times as much as was handled on terminal markets by grain cooperatives prior to the organization of the Farmers National." [27]

The Federal Farm Board quickly expanded its activities to include other major crops in this national co-operative pattern. During its first year of existence, 1929, the Federal Farm Board established national co-operative marketing agencies in wool, cotton, beans, livestock, and pecans. In August 1930 it added another by creating the National Beet Growers Association; and in the following May, it established the National Fruit and Vegetable Exchange.[28] If the Board had been favored with normal times during its period of inception, it might have approached its objective, or at least have had a chance to accomplish its goals; but it was not to be so blessed by circumstances. Instead, the Hoover program and the Board were not even at midstream in their efforts to ford the agricultural problem when they were suddenly overcome by a devastating flash flood in the guise of the stock market crash.

The stock market crash precipitated what was termed a "sympathetic" decline in agricultural prices. When farm prices continued to drop sharply in the following months, however, the Federal Farm Board shifted from normal to emergency operations; emphasis was now placed where farm

leaders originally wanted it — on stabilization or price support with government funds. So in spite of the producer's intent, the stabilization corporations, authorized by law but
held in the wings, suddenly came forward to stage center.

The first sign of the Board's emergency policy was given
with a brave flourish in a press release of October 21, 1929:
"The Federal Farm Board believes that the present prevailing prices for cotton are too low." Cotton farmers were urged
to hold back their crop; and, to assist farmers in adhering to
this policy, the Board announced that it would supplement
current farmer borrowing from government and commercial
banks with additional loans sufficient to equal a total of 16
cents per pound of cotton. The farmer would thereby be in a
position to pay off his obligations without the necessity of
selling his crop at a declining price. The Board had $100,-
000,000 available to back its bold bid, and it stated that it was
ready to go to Congress for more if it were needed. Five days
later, an identical announcement was released concerning
wheat; and, again, another $100,000,000 was pledged,
coupled with a readiness to ask Congress for more.[29]

The story of wheat is illustrative of the Board's efforts and
the ultimate outcome of its stabilization venture. In response
to the Wall Street crash, the Board in October established a
flat scale of wheat prices ($1.18 per bushel in Chicago),
which it pledged to support by loans through the National
Grain Corporation. These loans supplemented existing ones
from commercial and Federal Intermediate Credit Banks,
thereby permitting growers to borrow between 85 and 90 per
cent of the money value on their stored crop, which served as
collateral. The Board's immediate object was to prevent
grain held as collateral for loans from being dumped on the
market; in some cases, in its anxiety to avoid this, "the Board
even guaranteed banks margins pending refinancing." [30]

For the moment, the Board's policy seemed successful, but
by the turn of the year wheat prices again weakened. To re-

sist this, the Board took a second, bolder step: it authorized the Farmers National Grain Corporation to buy wheat at the loan value. When this measure also proved inadequate, the Board went the full length of the Agricultural Marketing Act by creating, in February 1930, the Grain Stabilization Corporation with an initial credit of $10,000,000. The stabilization corporation immediately started to buy cash wheat at market prices (the "pegged price" had already been abandoned) as well as to purchase May futures. On March 6, the Board publicly stated the aim of its new program. "The Grain Stabilization Corporation," it announced, "will continue buying wheat at the market and remove from the market whatever additional quantity that may be necessary to relieve the pressure and prevent any considerable decline in wheat prices." "The Farm Board," it concluded determinedly, "is prepared to advance to this farmer's organization, whatever funds are necessary for that purpose." [31]

In the first phase of this extensive price-holding operation — between February and June 1930 — the Board "held control of a quantity of wheat equal to approximately one-half of the visible supply of wheat." Some of this was disposed through export; still, on June 30, the Board owned 65,000,-000 bushels of wheat and futures. At a cost of $90,000,000 in government funds, the Grain Stabilization Corporation could point to only disappointed hopes: wheat had fallen in price by 33 cents a bushel. In the face of this large holdover, together with the big 1930–31 crop that already was beginning to move to market, and its failure to stabilize wheat prices, the Board decided to abandon the policy of price-support through government buying. In the Board's judgment, "the situation faced in the early summer of 1930 did not . . . warrant further action of the same sort at the outset of the crop year of 1930–31." Instead, the only assurance given to farmers and grain dealers was that the Board would not suddenly dump its accumulated holdings on the market. "The grain trade need have no apprehension of competition from the wheat held by the Grain Stabilization Corporation during the coming months," the general manager of the corporation stated. "In no event," he assured, "will this 1929 stabilization wheat be thrown on the market in a way to depress prices." [32]

Despite the Board's public announcement, within a month it commenced a second and larger price-support effort to protect the 1931 wheat crop. The Stabilization Corporation began by buying some futures in August; during September and October, as prices continued to decline, purchases were stepped up. By November, with wheat down to 73 cents a bushel at Chicago, the Stabilization Corporation was authorized to purchase as much wheat as was necessary to check any further price decline for the 1931 crop. Large purchases were now made in an effort to firm the market; and, by June 1931, the Board had added 192,000,000 bushels of wheat to its previous holdings. At a cost of $169,000,000, the Board succeeded in temporarily raising the price of wheat to 81 cents a bushel, or, approximately 20 cents a bushel above the world market price. [33]

The Federal Farm Board had aimed to achieve one objective, but to its chagrin it failed in that and only succeeded in producing an unwanted result. Instead of lifting wheat prices, it accumulated a total stock of 257,000,000 bushels of wheat. Faced with the prospect of making the temporary and emergency stabilization program a permanent one, the Board decided to abandon the policy altogether. Or, as the Board phrased it: "It was decided . . . that wheat farmers had been given as much assistance through stabilization purchases as was possible with the Board's limited resources; and that the future policy should be one of gradual liquidation to work down the supplies on hand." [34]

Senator McNary, in assessing the record of the Federal Farm Board from 1929 to May 1933, marked it down as a failure; he also provided figures which fully sustained his evaluation. During this period, the Board made approximately $1.15 billion in loans to agriculture. Nearly $746,-000,000 (or 65 per cent of the total) was loaned to the grain and cotton stabilization corporations for the purpose of maintaining prices. In addition, $200,000,000 was loaned to the agricultural co-operative associations for price-support activities. The major concern of the Board consequently — as well as the vast bulk of its resources — was centered upon a direct price-support program. In conducting this extended emergency operation, the Federal Farm Board suffered a $344,900,000 loss from its $500,000,000 revolving fund.[35] It was a high price to pay for meager returns: agricultural prices were more depressed and the farmers more discontented than ever before.

In justifying its policy, the Farm Board argued that it was not equipped to cope with the prolonged emergency conditions of a general depression. Its limited financial resources were inadequate to stabilize prices of crops which were consistently over-abundant. From the very outset of its existence, the Farm Board had insisted that farmers curtail production. "The obvious and economic remedy for the overproduction of wheat," the Board declared in its first report, ". . . is curtailment of production, with a view of reducing and, if possible, eventually eliminating our export surplus so that the tariff might become effective on American prices." Yet, to accomplish this essential objective, the Board could rely only upon voluntary co-operation. Working together with the federal and state extension services, the Board attempted to persuade wheat growers to reduce their 1930–31 crop by 10 per cent. Cotton planters received similar advice.[36] Despite these efforts, the campaign to limit production voluntarily was a complete failure. "Many farmers," the Board ruefully observed, "hold a theory that their neighbors are likely to increase their acreage whenever general advice is given to reduce, with a view to cashing in on the higher prices that may be in prospect." "The experience of the past two years," it stated in 1931, "shows it is futile to engage in stabilizing purchases for any product over a period of years in the face of a constantly accumulating surplus of that product." [37]

The experience and the feeling of discouragement felt by the Farm Board were succinctly summarized by its chairman, Alexander Legge, in a letter to Senator Thomas Walsh early in 1931:

> A long time ago we pointed out the facts regarding the wheat situation to the American wheat growers and stated that in our judgment there was no hope for a reasonable return as long as they continue raising wheat for export. Correcting the trouble does not mean they should quit raising wheat, but simply that they should raise about twenty per cent less of it. Notwithstanding the fact that it seems to be clear that they would get more money for the eighty per cent than they are receiving for what they produce, they continue to come back with some other proposition.
>
> This problem cannot be solved by building warehouses and storing wheat, as the wheat must find an outlet eventually. What these farmers apparently expect the Government to do is to continue buying up the present surplus and storing it while they go on producing an additional surplus. . . .
>
> We have tried earnestly to persuade the American wheat growers to put their production on a domestic consumption basis which would insure their getting a fair return, but the present indications are they are going to continue producing the biggest surplus they can possibly raise until such time as enough of them starve to bring about the adjustment in that way.[38]

Finally, in desperation, the Farm Board urged farmers to destroy a portion of their crops. Cotton producers were asked to plow under every third row of cotton. But these suggestions, like so many others made by the Farm Board, were ignored. The farmers lacked the discipline and unity to carry out an effective program of production control by voluntary co-operation. No one knew this better than the farm leaders themselves. As John Simpson, president of the Farmers' Educational and Co-operative Union, remarked to members of the Senate Committee on Agriculture and Forestry, "One of the first fundamentals is that the farmers will not organize. There is no use deceiving ourselves any longer and saying that we will solve our problems ourselves through organization." [39] Despite the Farm Board's exertions to harrow and sow among farmers the seeds of the new individualism, it succeeded in reaping only thistles and thorns.

Farm senators were critical even of the Farm Board's motives and aims during its price-stabilization phase. James C. Stone, who had replaced Alexander Legge as chairman of the Farm Board, declared in a speech at Hutchinson, Kansas, on March 25, 1931, that if the Board had not undertaken its second stabilization effort (from November 1930 to June 1931), there would have been incalculable consequences for the nation's business. If prices had been allowed to drop a few cents more below their November 1930 level of seventy cents, banks, which had loaned to farmers, who put up wheat as their collateral, would have dumped between forty and fifty million bushels on the market in order to protect their margin. This development, Stone maintained, might easily have plunged wheat below fifty cents a bushel, and "would have meant financial disaster not only to the farmers who still had their wheat on hand, but would probably have meant the closing of hundreds of banks in the Middle West." [40]

Farm senators quickly inferred that the Farm Board, after it had publicly announced that it would no longer attempt to hold up the price of wheat, had reversed itself and undertaken a further and more extensive price-support program primarily to relieve bankers and not the farmers. As Senator Norbeck pointed out, the resumption of the stabilization program occurred when two-thirds of the wheat crop was out of the hands of farmers and in the possession of bankers — and farmers could hardly be helped by supporting the price of wheat they no longer owned. While Senator McNary differed on the amount of wheat no longer in the farmers' possession, he agreed in the opinion that the principal objective was bank relief.[41]

When the Farm Board definitely abandoned emergency commodity-buying in June 1931, farm leaders in and out of Congress immediately resumed their long-standing demands for a more forceful government program of agricultural support. They knew that the emergency operations had failed; but, unlike the Board, they felt that the failure was due to timidity and lack of resolution. From the beginning, farm senators and representatives had prodded, urged, and demanded a more extensive and forceful government program. In a steady stream of letters and telegrams, they applied pressure on Board members to take the next step — and then another. Early in the game, they demanded that the Board commence a government price-support program through the creation of stabilization corporations; later they insisted that the program should be continued until prices were actually raised. They urged that additional loans be made to farmers by the government on the security of farm commodities; they suggested that the Board withhold its accumulated stocks of farm produce for two years or more; they protested against the proposed plow-up; and, instead, they proposed that Congress authorize the Board to establish minimum prices on cotton and wheat. What all these congressmen urged in common was more direct and more forceful government action.[42]

Like the congressional wing of the farm bloc, the leaders of the principal farm organizations picked up their old plans and ideas where they had temporarily been left while they waited to see what was wrought by Hoover's Agricultural Marketing Act. They did not want to repeal that Act, but amend it to incorporate the old discarded farm formulas. Louis J. Taber, master of the National Grange, wanted the export debenture substituted for the now discredited stabilization corporations. Edward A. O'Neal, president of the American Farm Bureau Federation, maintained that while the marketing act was fundamentally sound, it was insufficient to take care of the exportable surplus. What it needed, he insisted, was a strong, new arm: the equalization fee. Advanced ground was taken by John Simpson, president of the Farmers' Educational and Co-operative Union. "The one thing that is necessary to be done to save agriculture," he argued, "the one big thing, is to get for farmers the cost of production for that part of their product that is used in this country." And that meant that government should fix minimum prices.[43]

They wanted an end to Hoover's half measures and the enactment of their own favored farm programs. Their reaction to the voluntary domestic allotment plan illustrates their impatience with moderate proposals. M. L. Wilson, professor of agricultural economics at the College of Agriculture of Montana, explained that the plan was designed to increase the purchasing power of agriculture while avoiding objectionable secondary effects, such as increased acreage, government control, and government appropriations, as well as the difficulties involved in a two-price system — thereby avoiding any necessity for European dumping of surpluses. Wilson estimated that this plan, the work of Dr. W. J. Spillman of the Agricultural Department, Dr. John Black of Harvard, and himself, would increase the purchasing power of producers of five commodities by about $700,000,000. Vital for the success of the plan, however, were two essentials: an excise tax on processing to finance the program, and the voluntary co-operation of 60 per cent of the farmers of each commodity who would agree to decrease their acreage.

Farm leaders were decidedly cool to this proposal; it simply did not go far enough to improve significantly the farm problem in a time of emergency. While its carefully worked out safeguards might favorably impress men who shared Hoover's moral scruples, the farm leaders were largely indifferent to methods but vitally concerned with results. As Senator Smith Brookhart of Iowa remarked, an increase in the farmers' purchasing power was absolutely essential, but the increase needed was more in the vicinity of $6 billion than a meager $700,000,000.

Consequently, instead of abandoning old formulas for a new, inadequate plan, the major farm organizations proposed a combined plan that included the equalization fee, the export debenture, and a proposal for government licensing of all producers prohibiting them from selling any commodity below the cost of production. This was offered as an amendment to the Agricultural Marketing Act, leaving to the Farm Board the option of which plan or combination of plans to use.[44]

By early 1932, the depression and the failure of Hoover's agricultural program had led the administration and farm spokesmen to widely divergent conclusions. Hoover, after allowing the Farm Board to experiment briefly with emergency measures, drew back in alarm from continuing a program which involved far too much government action. Farm leaders, on the other hand, saw the lesson of three years of depression as one necessitating a more extensive commitment of federal assistance and control. The common ground between the two viewpoints, at best a narrow strand at the outset, was progressively eroded until it had disappeared completely. The Agricultural Marketing Act, with its twin aims of progress and preservation, had ended in failure. "There

will be but few mourners at the grave of 1932," Senator Mc-
Nary concluded gloomily. "Without regret and without grief
that year passes into history." [45] Senator Norris was of the
same mind, only more emphatic and specific. "As long as Mr.
Hoover stays in the White House," he concluded, "I have no
hope whatever of any relief for stricken agriculture." [46]

7

Unemployment:
Industry and the American Way

> After mechanized warfare the bitterest thing in modern life is unemployment. Wars come and go. Unemployment goes on in season and out.*
>
> STUART CHASE, 1929

The Great Depression, like the Great Plague, was a catastrophe that touched the life of an entire society. The causes of the depression may have eluded most Americans, the cure for it may have been unknown, but the impact of the economic collapse was unmistakably evident to all. "Not since the Civil War," the editor of the *Survey* concluded gloomily, "have we known a conflict which devastated American homes like this depression." [1]

The victims of this devastation naturally turned for assistance to the economic experts; yet from them they received scant comfort — and even less enlightenment. Indeed, to listen to the experts was to hear a vocabulary of abstractions. In order to comprehend this complex economic phenomenon one had to make a baffling plunge into the most difficult aspects of economic theory. The dialogue of the experts was a Babel to the non-specialist; he was excluded by the technical meaning and precise interrelationship of such terms as money, investment, savings, foreign trade, international exchange, and the gold standard. More dismaying still was the failure of the experts to reach some concensus. How were the non-specialized to judge between the conflicting theories of the experts?

The fact was that popular judgment, as well as popular understanding, was unequal to the task. The non-specialist lacked the competence, if not the interest as well, to deal with the abstraction. Yet, no matter how vague the depression might be as an abstract economic concept, it was vivid as an experience. And it was the experience of the depression that counted with the mass of Americans.

The depression impinged upon the lives and thoughts of Americans most forcefully, most concretely, and hence most intelligibly, in the form of unemployment. It was unemployment that brought the depression home to Americans: literally brought it in through the door, into the pantry, and onto the kitchen table. While this direct personal experience with unemployment touched only the lives of the unemployed and their families, the fear of becoming unemployed gradually seeped through the entire society. "It is no longer possible to believe," a writer observed, "that jobs are part of the natural order of things; nor is it reasonable to assume that if the one you have is lost you can readily get another. The result is that fear has become the dominant emotion of contemporary America — fear of losing one's job, fear of reduced salary or wages, fear of eventual destitution and want." [2]

The problem of unemployment in all its forms — seasonal, technological, and cyclical — was not new to the American scene. In one aspect or another it was a perennial concern. Now, however, it was present in all three of its forms combined so that its impact was more extensive, severe, and pressing than ever before. "Unemployment," as one contemporary expressed the prevailing view, "has become a permanent feature of American life." [3]

Unemployment was an experience shared by many individuals, but solution of the problem was clearly beyond the individual's capacity. This was the great tragedy of unemployment in a highly interdependent society. The individual's helplessness in modern society was starkly exposed when the economic system failed to function properly and unemployment became national in scope. "These are men and women," one writer described the unemployed, "who have no control over discount rates, or credit, or the manipulation of bull markets and bear markets, yet they are the first victims of the battles fought in those high and mysterious regions." "The worker today," the *Nation* realistically observed, "does not and cannot control the conditions of employment; he is likely at any time to find himself out of a job by reason of causes entirely unrelated to his acts and choices." [4] Both escape and solution eluded the unemployed.

An individual might, of course, trudge the streets in search of some job, but if no jobs of any sort were to be had, he could not create one of his own initiative. All that he could do was to wait for the industrial system to revive again. "To hold, as some do," Stuart Chase wrote, "that any worthy man can secure a job if he only applies himself diligently enough is to be guilty of a total, and almost criminal misconception of the course of the industrial revolution." The editor of the *Survey*, a close student of unemployment, agreed: "Such chance as the city worker has for swift reemployment when he is laid off under normal conditions pindles out in times like these. All the skill, moral worth and back muscles in the world won't bring him anything in a factory town when its works are running short or are closed down and when a hundred other men are lined up waiting at the mill-gate." The individual workman, as Frances Perkins told a congressional subcommittee, "is utterly helpless, because he is in a situation in which there is no work. The result is we can not look to individual initiative to help these people through the unemployment crisis." The president of the American Federation of Labor, William Green, testifying before the same subcommittee, emphasized the same conclusion. "Unemployment is a problem which has plagued workers and communities for decades and is beyond the power of individuals or groups to cope with. It is a social as well as an industrial problem and requires the joint efforts of every organization . . . concerned with it." [5] If, previously, unemployment could be viewed as an individual concern, now many were coming to recognize it for what it really was: a problem that concerned the entire society.

Actually, society had developed a number of defenses against unemployment and for the relief of the unemployed, and Americans had learned to expect assistance from a number of different institutions. The responsibility of providing relief was soon fixed upon those very institutions on which the people customarily leaned for help. Private industry, labor unions, and private charity were the first line of defense; in reserve, were the cities and the states. How unemployment was handled provided the mass of Americans with a pragmatic standard of judging their institutions. They could easily determine by their own experience (or by taking the latest estimate of the unemployed) whether old ways and institutions were successfully meeting the unemployment problem or not.

Moreover, the pragmatic-unemployment yardstick could be used for other measurements. For while the public may have been unable to grasp the intricacies of a national policy designed to overcome the depression, there was little doubt of its ability to understand that the failure to decrease unemployment meant the failure of that particular policy. And for anyone to insist that a policy was adequate while the number of unemployed continued to increase, was to tempt not only the public's credibility but its wrath as well.

Hoover actively encouraged the people's natural tendency to look to the old ways for adequate assistance in coping with unemployment. At the time of the Washington business conferences, when he presented his initial program to ward off depression, the President had taken the position that the old, established ways would care for whatever unemployment might arise. He held tenaciously to this conviction as the depression deepened.

Late in 1930, when an insistent demand for some form of federal aid began to develop, the President "flatly denied a rumor that an extra session of Congress might be called to cope with the situation . . ." "No Special Session," he announced firmly on October 24, "is necessary to deal with employment. The sense of voluntary organization and community service in the American people has not vanished. The spirit of voluntary service," he insisted, "has been strong enough to cope with the problem for the past year and it will, I am confident, continue in full measure of the need." [6]

Reporting to Congress on December 2, 1930, on the state of the union, Hoover spoke reassuringly about unemployment. "The local communities through their voluntary agencies," he declared, "have assumed the duty of relieving individual distress and are being generously supported by the public." In a press statement, issued on February 3, 1931, he said:

> The basis of successful relief in national distress is to mobilize and organize the infinite number of agencies of self help in the community. That has been the American way of relieving distress among our own people and the country is successfully meeting its problem in the American way today.

Later in the month, the President spoke to the nation in a radio address and reiterated his conviction that "the American Way" was sufficient to handle unemployment:

> Victory over this depression and over our other difficulties will be won by the resolution of our people to fight their own battles in their own communities, by stimulating their ingenuity to solve their own problems, by taking new courage to be masters of their own destiny in the struggle of life. This is not the easy way, but it is the American way.[7]

This insistence that the nation's voluntary institutions, operating in the old, established ways, were fully able to deal with unemployment was just another way of saying that federal intervention and control were unnecessary. Not only was federal aid unnecessary, it was undesirable. In that direction lurked grave dangers to the national character. "I am confident," Hoover averred, "that our people have the resources, the initiative, the courage, the stamina and kindliness of spirit to meet this situation in the way they have met their problems over generations."

If the voluntary relief provided by private charity should prove insufficient in handling distress, then, according to Hoover's viewpoint, "our American system requires that municipal, county and state governments shall use their own resources and credit before seeking such assistance from the Federal Treasury." And, finally, as the very last resort, Hoover declared:

> I am willing to pledge myself that if the time should ever come that the voluntary agencies of the country together with the local and state governments are unable to find resources with which to prevent hunger and suffering in my country, I will ask the aid of every resource of the Federal Government because I would no more see starvation amongst our countrymen than would any senator or congressman. I have the faith in the American people that such a day will not come.[8]

But it would be a serious mistake to portray Hoover as the solitary defender of what he conceived to be the American way of coping with unemployment. There were numerous others who shared his conviction that unemployment had to be handled by "voluntary organization," "community spirit," and "voluntary service" if cherished aspects of the national character were to be protected and preserved. For example, charity was a method proclaimed as the bulwark of the old way while the dole was identified with the new way of direct federal aid.[9]

The volume of contemporary strictures against the dole was impressive, and the critics of the dole were invariably warm supporters of the American way. The opponents of federal aid made the dole a symbol of all that was undesirable and un-American. It represented a repudiation of self-reliance, self-help, and voluntary giving. Hoover's Secretary of War, Patrick J. Hurley, argued (in June 1932) against a congressional proposal to establish a $100,000,000 fund for direct relief:

> My own opinion is that we have not yet come to the time when we should abandon the principles and the system that sustained your forefathers and my father and mother when they went into a new country and had to find means to sustain themselves without this dole that we are talking about now. . . .
>
> The thing that you are proposing to do, to give a gratuity to an individual, is divesting men and women of their spirit, their self-reliance. It is striking at the very foundation of the system on which this Nation is builded. . . . You can not get my consent to the inauguration of a system that deprives American men or women of their spirit of self-reliance, or creates a condition whereby they will be led to believe that they can live by the sweat of some one else's brow. What we need to-day is an effort to put everyone back to work, to create in them the courage, the stamina, the will to take care of themselves.

"I disagree," the Secretary concluded, "with all who think that there is not still opportunity for the man with the nerve and the capacity and the desire. Oh, there is not a fortune, we know, in hard times, but there is a living and I do not want to deprive any citizen of his or her spirit of self-reliance." [10]

To adopt the dole in America meant a surrender to European debasement. To quote the contemporary refrain: Look what the dole has done to England! The English dole, an exasperated writer declared, has become "a term of pity and derision, looked upon as a sort of cancerous sore by a vast majority of Americans who have not the least idea what it really is, what it has accomplished, or even how it came into existence." [11] None the less, those who saw the dole in this light argued vehemently that America could do without it. And to do without the dole, in their opinion, meant dealing with the problem of unemployment by traditional methods.

Federal aid, in any case, was to be scrupulously shunned. The proper approach to unemployment was a preventive one, and preventive measures were the responsibility of business and industry.[12] "The ailment," a business spokesman insisted, "is a business ailment, and the remedy, if one is to be found, must be a business remedy." [13]

The effect of Hoover's predilections, his program, and the pronouncements of his supporters was to fix the primary responsibility for dealing with unemployment clearly upon traditional institutions. A convincing performance by these institutions was essental if unacceptable alternatives were to be avoided.

Industry was the foremost institution for dealing with unemployment by voluntary methods. Industry's most important responsibility, in this respect, was a preventive one: keeping its labor force intact and at work. This policy assumed that industry possessed the means of minimizing the number of unemployed even at a time of grave economic uncertainty. This was what Hoover asked of industrial-business leadership, and this was what the representatives of industry pledged themselves to attempt.

At the time, however, stabilization meant more then a temporary willingness by industrialists and businessmen to refrain from laying off workers, or from cutting wages until the economic crisis had passed. The interest in industrial stabilization antedated the Wall Street crash. Stabilization was not merely a short-time expedient; it was a long-range program. Individual industrial and business concerns attempted to regulate production and sales so that they could assure their workers continuous employment on a year-round basis. The stock market collapse infused a sense of urgency into this concern for stabilization.

Proponents of this policy argued that if stabilization were achieved it would mean continuous employment for workers, an assured annual income, and a sense of security which workers had previously lacked. It was obvious why a sense of security was desirable: the workers would be more content in their jobs and more willing and able to spend money. "No one will deny," an economist asserted in 1931, "that during the last year America has been a fear-ridden community. The employed have not dared spend what they have lest they be walking the streets next month." "The basis of this paralyzing fear," he added, "has been the insecurity which characterizes the incomes of the great masses of the population." [14]

At the outset of the depression, however, business leaders, such as Julius Barnes, were sufficiently impressed by individual examples of successful stabilization in industry to contend that it was in the power of industry to eliminate the severe fluctuations of the business cycle. If single industries could stabilize production, the reasoning held, then it was possible for all industries. "During the past decade," Professor Paul H. Douglas of the University of Chicago remarked, "one feature of progressive American thinking upon the problems of management has been the belief that industry could conquer unemployment and stabilize itself." [15]

This belief was more than wishful thinking. Advocates of stabilization could point to some notable successes by specific concerns. Among the more frequently cited were the Procter and Gamble Company, the General Electric Company, Fels-Naphtha, International Harvester, the Dennison Manufacturing Company, and the Standard Oil Company of New Jersey. [16]

Procter and Gamble, the soap manufacturers, operated in

an industry that once had been considered seasonal. Nevertheless, through a series of innovations, the company succeeded in altering its uneven seasonal production and in attaining a high degree of stabilization. Dealers in its products were induced by a policy of price reductions to order well in advance and on an annual basis. Having a definite estimate of its requirements at an early date, the company was able to spread its production evenly over the year. In the slack season, normal production was continued; the company stored the soap itself and then delivered it to the dealers whenever needed. This policy succeeded so well that in November 1930 Procter and Gamble notified Colonel Arthur Woods, chairman of the President's Emergency Committee for Employment, "of the completion of a plan whereby the company virtually guarantees 10,000 workers, drawing wages of approximately $1,000,000 a month, work on a permanent basis." [17]

In the photographic equipment field, where sales were decidedly seasonal, the Kodak Park Works of the Eastman Kodak Company also succeeded in achieving a high degree of stabilization. In the depression year of 1921, the Kodak Park Works, the company's largest manufacturing plant, had laid off 13.5 per cent of its work force. In 1930, lay-offs among productive workers were only 2.5 per cent. The difference in the company's employment record in the two depression years was the result of a detailed study of seasonal sales and an elaborate procedure for stabilizing production. [18]

Kodak's stabilization program involved four major steps: first, a careful, statistical forecast of a year's sales; next, the breakdown of these figures on a monthly sales basis; third, the establishment of "the most convenient and economical production levels throughout a year"; finally, a determination of "the amount of finished stock to be carried at all times of the year." Using this four-step procedure, the Kodak Park Works had been able to transform seasonal production and a high level of labor turnover into stabilized production and employment security.[19]

General Electric's president, Gerard Swope, had long been interested in industrial stabilization. On June 19, 1930, Swope announced the initiation of an unemployment plan designed to cover the company's 75,000 employees. He had first proposed the plan five years earlier, but the workers at that time ("in the heyday of this new economy") were not interested. When unemployment became a serious matter early in the depression, the plan was resubmitted to the workers, reconsidered, and accepted. The plan provided for equal contributions by the employees and the company; it was to go into effect as soon as 60 per cent of the employees of any plant accepted it. Executives were asked to contribute only in times of emergency, when more money was being paid out for relief than was being paid into the fund. This provision was designed to stimulate the interest — and self-interest — of the executives in stabilizing their operations and keeping unemployment down to a minimum.[20]

The policy was most successful in the company's Incandescent Lamp Department. General Electric produced only five styles of incandescent lamps; by eliminating large numbers of styles it had previously produced, the company succeeded also in eliminating seasonal variations in production. After the unemployment plan was submitted to the workers and accepted, Swope publicly announced that the employees of the Incandescent Lamp Department with two years or more of continuous service would be guaranteed fifty weeks of work in 1931.[21]

Not only the larger and better known companies but small concerns as well successfully applied stabilization. The managing director of the Taylor Society, a private research organization interested in promoting scientific management, told an interested congressional committee about one little-known experiment. The company, operating in one of the nation's most unstable industries, cotton textiles, had expanded gradually from a single plant to nine plants scattered throughout the eastern states. The owner-manager, in directing all the plants, developed a technique of scientific management which he applied to all phases of production, selling, and financing. The outcome of this careful planning, Dr. H. S. Persons declared, was that the company "has never discharged an employee for want of work, even in the present depression." [22]

Employers did not always provide the initiative for undertaking programs of stabilization. There were some cases where the inspiration came from the labor unions. In the clothing industry Sidney Hillman, general president of the Amalgamated Clothing Workers of America, was instrumental in this development, as can be seen from the remark of a union associate: "There came from the ranks a man by the name of Hillman who has been able to lead the organization and to see far ahead." [23]

In recalling his work of twenty years, Sidney Hillman emphasized a few landmarks in the long journey toward worker security. There was the 1911 contract with Hart, Schaffner, and Marx in Chicago which first established the policy of an equal division of the available work among all the workers of the factory. Then in 1923, again in Chicago, the clothing industry started its first unemployment insurance fund. By setting aside 4.5 per cent of the total wage bill, provision was made for the worker in times of unemployment. In 1931, a million dollars in unemployment insurance was available for distribution to union members in Chicago. Hillman summed up other practical results stemming from these arrangements with justifiable pride:

> While the industry is now running not more than sixty or sixty-five per cent of its normal capacity, less than five per cent are totally unemployed. Through the unemployment insurance fund and the cooperation of those who are at work, we

are taking care of the people who will have no opportunity to find employment at least for the next six months.

"We have written into our contracts," he declared, "the principle of security for the worker on the job." This was the story of one industry, but Hillman saw a lesson for the nation:

> In the light of this experience it is my judgment that we ought to meet the problems now facing the country by formulating a constructive program, not merely for one industry, or for one plant, but for industry as a whole. The country has a right to expect a constructive program from those in charge of industry, just as during the war, when we were in the midst of a critical emergency, there were created and brought into our life agencies to meet the problems of those times.[24]

This was asking no more of industry than what many others, including a number of businessmen themselves, were insistently urging. They all agreed to the proposition that it was industry's responsibility to provide its workers with security against unemployment. One articulate businessman who agreed was Julius Barnes. "Baffled and bewildered, the worker justly demands opportunity to earn a livelihood, and the industrial order which denies him this opportunity cannot escape indictment on the plea that the giving of it does not lie within its control." Speakers at the 1931 annual meeting of the United States Chamber of Commerce, including the distinguished economist, Wesley C. Mitchell, repeatedly stressed the necessity for industrial stabilization. They soberly warned their audience that, if industry should fail to meet its responsibility, the pressure for federal intervention might become irresistible.[25]

Industry was not insensible to this appeal from both its friends and its critics. Nor were the warnings unheeded. Industry tried out a number of programs and expedients, some new and some old, in an endeavor to satisfy — if not fully, at least partially — the call for industrial stabilization and worker security.

Some plants experimented with a comprehensive training program designed to prepare workers for alternate jobs within the company to which they might be shifted in slack times. There was the "B. & O. Plan," adopted by the Baltimore and Ohio Railroad and imitated by others, which provided for consultation between the workmen and management on how to meet slack times. Others attempted to maintain production in the off seasons by developing sidelines and fillers. Another idea — more of an expedient than a plan — was the separation bonus or dismissal compensation. Companies, unable to provide work for all their employees, gave their discharged workers a lump sum which varied from two weeks' to a year's salary. This was intended to help workers while they hunted for another job. Standard Oil of New Jersey, for example, provided its workers with the benefits of group insurance for six months after they were laid off.[26]

A number of concerns resorted to a system of company loans — a plan pioneered by the International Harvester Company. Regular employees, faced with distress due to prolonged idleness, were given loans which they were to repay in installments from their future earnings. This plan was modified slightly by others, who provided credits in place of loans. Essentials, such as coal, housing, groceries, medical service, and clothing, were made available to the unemployed "on credit either directly by the employer or through arrangements with local stores."[27]

To enumerate, in this fashion, the old and the new plans gives an impression of strength and vitality to the movement for industrial stabilization and worker unemployment protection. It would be misleading to leave that impression. Despite the fervor of its advocates and the successes of some of its practitioners, the experiments were extremely limited in numbers and influence.

The limits of the experiment were brought out repeatedly in Senate hearings held at the close of 1931. James A. Farrell, president of the United States Steel Corporation, in discussing stabilization, acknowledged frankly that "it is very difficult in our business to plan ahead." When asked what United States Steel had done to stabilize production, he replied:

> Of course, production and demand are the two factors of the situation. If our plants were operating at 80 per cent of their capacity, there would be no difficulty about that, but when our production drops to 30 per cent, then we endeavor to allocate the orders to the different plants so there is some work in each place, but it is difficult to create business beyond the demands of buyers. . . .
>
> You see, if all we had to do was to go out, blow a trumpet and say we need more business, we might get the echo, but not the business.[28]

By October 1931 the work force at General Motors had declined by 100,000 from the 1929 total of 260,000 men. Production in the automotive industry was highly seasonal. Alfred P. Sloan, Jr., president of General Motors, answered the question of what had been done to level out the seasonal swing by saying simply that his industry found it extremely difficult to make a very good showing in stablizing production.[29]

In 1931, the Baltimore and Ohio Railroad's earnings were running 33 per cent behind 1929. Approximately 20,000 workers had been laid off during the same period. What had been done to regularize employment? The president of the railroad, Daniel Willard, stressed the disruptive force of the depression on stabilization plans. "We were making considerable advance in that matter up until 1930," he said. "Since that time we have been obliged to make such very great reductions of our working forces that any idea of stabilization has had to be abandoned momentarily." And what had the Baltimore and Ohio been able to do in the way of new construction and repairs? Willard replied briefly and unequivocally:

> We have had to discontinue our purchases. Ordinarily the Baltimore & Ohio puts into its track anywhere from 60,000 to 80,000 tons of new rail for repairs a year. We will not put in over 15,000 this year. We could not do it always, but we can get along for a year or two. We are not painting any buildings. We are not doing a thing that we can help in order that we may preserve, as far as possible, our financial status.[30]

Conditions and prospects in the coal industry were equally dim. Discussing stabilization, Senator Robert M. La Follette, Jr., and George J. Anderson, president of the Consolidated Coal Company, had this exchange:

> THE CHAIRMAN. Has the coal industry made any effort to stabilize its own operations?
>
> MR. ANDERSON. [concluding his reply, said] . . . I return to my weasel answer. Effort upon effort has been made. The coal industry has men of recognized responsibility. Effort after effort has failed due to forces that seem to be almost beyond solution, taking the industry by itself.
>
> THE CHAIRMAN. In other words, you believe the problem is larger than that of any one particular industry?
>
> MR. ANDERSON. Yes, sir; I do.[31]

As the testimony of these business leaders suggested, only a small fraction of the nation's workers were affected by industrial stabilization and unemployment insurance.

By 1930 there were perhaps two hundred enterprises which could be said to have made notable progress in stabilizing production and employment.[32] Since 1930, there had been some new additions, but the over-all effect of the movement was limited. "Despite all the brave talk of stabilization," an economist who had thoroughly studied the subject concluded in 1931, "only a beginning has been made by business in lessening seasonal fluctuations of production and employment and this in the main by industries producing more or less standardized goods." [33]

The record in establishing voluntary unemployment compensation plans was even more disheartening. At the end of 1928 (when the Industrial Relations Counselors, Inc., conducted a nation-wide survey), there were less than 9000 workers covered by plans that had been initiated by employers alone. In percentage terms, company plans covered "one-tenth of one per cent of the total number of wage earners in manufacturing, and less than one-twentieth of one per cent of the total number of industrial workers." There were another 35,000 workers in trade union plans that had been begun by employees alone. In the joint plans of employers and unions, there were an additional 70,000 workers covered — making a total of 114,000 workers with unemployment protection in 1928.

The General Electric plan of 1930 brought in approximately 70,000 additional workers and increased the total to about 195,000. This meant, as Paul Douglas pointed out, that "after a decade of experimentation, less than 1 per cent of the wage earners of the country have found protection against the losses of unemployment." [34]

"One of the most amazing features of our current journey through the wilderness," John T. Flynn remarked, "is, first, the almost universal recognition that we ought to do something about unemployment relief in future crises; and second, that practically nothing *has* been done about it." Flynn's personal estimate was that "the whole episode of individual corporate action has been pitifully limited in point of numbers and pitifully feeble in point of efficiency." The undertaking, he concluded, was too big for business, but business seemed unwilling to allow anyone else to handle the problem.[35]

Edward A. Filene, Boston businessman, was an exception to this generalization. Like other businessmen, his first preference was for industrial responsibility. "I have always held," he admitted, "that the care and provision for industrial workers in sickness, in old age, and in times of idleness should be handled by private industry rather than by the state." But Filene had observed closely the sufferings brought on by depression; nor was he impressed by industry's success in mitigating it. "When we face the tragedy of a national unemployment situation such as we are now passing through," he declared, "we must frankly ask ourselves whether the way out is still to be found through voluntary measures. Because of the insufficiency of relief in the present situation and its inadequacy for any permanent solution of the problem of unemployment, I have come to believe that state insurance is inevitable."

Industry's failure to stabilize production, its inability to prevent unemployment, and the patent inadequacy of its plans to care for its unemployed completed the breakdown of the program that Hoover had persuaded it to accept. The entire program was overwhelmed by the severity of the depression. The industrial-business experiment in voluntary co-operative action, at best a hastily improvised dike, proved to be a slender, vulnerable check. It was all but swept away by the relentless downward plunge of the economy. Business and industrial leadership seemed adrift and helpless.

The inability of industry to care for its own workers meant the failure of voluntary preventive action. The emphasis was now on dealing with the effects of this failure. The immediate and pressing concern became the relief of distress. This threw the burden of caring for the vast majority of the unemployed fully upon private charity, the public welfare agencies, the cities, and the states. These institutions soon faced problems of a magnitude never before known to them.

8

Social Welfare and the Unemployed: Cities and States

> The individual workman, the individual business, the State, are helpless when an economic storm breaks upon the country. Only the coordinated strength of the entire Nation is competent to deal with such powerful economic forces.*
>
> SENATOR ROBERT WAGNER, 1931

> We are making an honor roll of states, cities . . . which can say "We can take care of ourselves." †
>
> LILLIAN M. GILBRETH, 1930

On October 17, 1930, Hoover launched the winter offensive against the unemployment problem with a press statement. "As a nation," he emphatically declared, "we must prevent hunger and cold to those of our people who are in honest difficulties." At the same time, he explicitly rejected suggestions that he call an extra session of Congress to deal with unemployment. Instead, within a few days, he appointed two committees — the Cabinet Committee on Unemployment and the President's Emergency Committee for Employment — to ensure that the unemployed would receive adequate assistance.[1] Hoover, with his Quaker upbringing and with his impressive successes in voluntary relief work — in Belgium, in Europe, Russia, and along the banks of the Mississippi — was convinced that voluntary co-operative action would accomplish the dual purpose of relieving distress and exercising vital national traits. His course in this matter, as elsewhere, was dictated by conviction fortified by experience and success. Unemployment became another text for the teacher and moralizer: congenial roles for Hoover always, strongly evident and persistently held.

The Cabinet Committee was composed of the Secretaries of Commerce, Robert P. Lamont; Agriculture, Arthur M. Hyde; Treasury, Andrew Mellon; Labor, J. J. Davis; Interior, Ray L. Wilbur; War, Patrick J. Hurley; and Eugene Meyer, Governor of the Federal Reserve Board. Lamont was named chairman of this group, whose principal role was to act in an advisory capacity to the voluntary organization.[2]

The President's Emergency Committee for Employment, with Colonel Arthur Woods as its chairman, was quickly organized. As originally established, it consisted of thirty members, prominent individuals drawn from industry, business, and the professions.[3] Many of them, like the chairman himself, served voluntarily and without salary. The committee itself was divided into eight sections so that effective contact could be made with all groups in the nation concerned with unemployment; there were sections to work with federal executive departments, state and local officials, industry, social welfare agencies, public works-construction bodies, statistical organizations, women's groups, and publicity agencies.[4] The federal government paid the committee's expenses by drawing funds from the Department of Commerce. Recalling the principal steps he had taken at this time to prepare the nation for a hard winter, Hoover said:

> I requested the governors of the states to cooperate by forming nonpartisan committees of responsible men and women, in each state, these committees in turn to organize such committees in each municipality and county. This was carried out in each locality where unemployment existed. We thus set up some 3,000 nonpartisan committees of devoted, intelligent men and women. They were given the primary responsibility to see that no one went hungry or cold. In October, 1930, Colonel Woods reported to me that his organization was functioning everywhere.[5]

After a conference with Hoover on October 22, Colonel Woods offered his view of what the President's Emergency

Committee for Employment was supposed to do. "The principal part of our work," Woods explained, "is co-operating with local organizations." "It's a co-ordinating sort of thing, and the best that we can do is to let various places know what others are doing as a guide for their own efforts." The *New York Times* concluded that "this statement by the director of relief, following other indications of the same nature in recent days, was taken as confirmation of the belief that no extraordinary expenditures are planned by the Government." The *Nation*, always less diplomatic in its language, remarked bluntly that "there is the same talk of devising plans, as though unemployment had just come upon us suddenly, the same talk of collecting data, the same talk of cooperation with this, that, and the other group." [6]

The *New York Times* was correct in its conclusion — at least as far as the Executive branch of the government was concerned. Hoover, in his approach to the problems of unemployment and distress, continued to be consistent to his initial program. The role of the federal government was confined to encouraging and assisting the co-operative efforts of those voluntary groups and institutions that customarily cared for the distressed. It was, as he said, their "responsibility to see that no one went hungry and cold." The unemployed would be adequately cared for by the time-honored methods of the American way. No reappraisal of this assumption was apparently necessary at this time — the outset of the second winter of the depression.

Colonel Woods was an old friend and associate of the President. Much of his previous work for the government had been concerned with unemployment; his assumptions and the methods he favored were identical to Hoover's own. It was the Hooverian viewpoint that dominated the Woods Committee.[7] "The President's Emergency Committee," a member wrote, "has definitely adopted the policy of urging that the handling of the unemployment emergency must be done locally. From the relief side, certainly the efforts of the

President's Committee is likely to be only to simulate adequate local organization and resources where it seems likely that local communities would regard such stimulation from Washington as helpful." [8]

This similarity of viewpoints in the Hoover administration between the head and its parts was not fortuitous. Hoover had worked with many men in the long years of his public service. Invariably, they were men who carried away from their association with "the Chief" a strong devotion and a willingness to put aside their own affairs for public service at Hoover's call. And Hoover consistently called those who held remarkably similar philosophies of man, society, and government. Most of them, in fact, when summoned — whether to a cabinet position or as head of a voluntary agency — sounded as if they had just been interrupted reading *American Individualism*. Hoover had the capacity for commanding devoted service; one looks in vain for embittered lieutenants seeking vindication with acid books. Colonel Woods was another of Hoover's faithful following.

"The job of these men," Woods described his committee, "is simply to be of whatever service they can":

> They go to see governors and mayors or committees as they are formed with the idea simply of being in service, of bringing to any individual governor or mayor or chairman of a committee or a committee that is formed to meet this situation any information that they can bring as the result of the experience of other cities so as to help the local committees, mayors, or chairmen in their work.

Although the first principle of the Woods committee was "to get a man a job," it did not itself attempt to place unemployed workers. This was to be done, in accordance with its second principle, by helping to organize "a special committee, a special governor's committee or a special mayor's committee, to meet the situation of unemployment and distress needing relief." [9]

The Woods committee became, in effect, a huge correspondence mill turning out endless letters of encouragement, advice, requests for information, pamphlets, and books. Letters went off to the magazine of social work, *Survey*, asking for copies of its special numbers on unemployment; a request to the director of the Charity Organization Department of the Russell Sage Foundation for copies of Mary Richmond's "Emergency Relief," and "On the Coming Winter"; letters to chairmen of unemployment committees asking a series of questions on local conditions, and ending with: "Will your county be able to handle the situation?" Words of cheer and advice went to trade associations, industrial institutes, and college professors.[10] Then the committee summarized its findings in numerous pamphlets of its own, and urged mayors, governors, and chairmen to incorporate the ideas in their localities.[11] It was, in truth, a gigantic clearing house. But, in addition, it was an organ of exhortation for the American way.

The Woods committee was meant to soothe the nation, not to alarm it; it spoke accordingly of what was being done and not of what was neglected. "The country as a whole," Woods declared, "has responded most heartily to the emergency. Evidence is pouring in that communities are organizing to meet their own problems." He spoke enthusiastically of public works programs, renovations of buildings, "spruce-up campaigns," industrial stabilization and job-spreading — voluntaryism mushrooming everywhere. "From the states themselves to the smallest village and hamlet," he stated, "there has been a recrudescence of that community spirit hitherto reserved for war-time emergencies." [12] All this was splendid — enthusiasm has its place in promoting governmental policies; but if enthusiasm is not to degenerate into "ballyhoo" and become ridiculous, the achievements it celebrates must be fortified by facts. But for the Woods committee, vital facts were indifferently treated or unknown.

Despite its elaborate connections, the President's committee attempted to make no surveys of national unemployment. They knew very little of what was happening in the rural sections of the country. Nor did they attempt to estimate the number of unemployed. When governors asked for the committee's plan, they were told that the committee had none, and the governors received instead a pamphlet on what others were doing. "The aim," Woods repeated to a congressional committee, "has been so to organize the country, so to help the country to organize itself, that it could meet whatever conditions might arise." [13]

Yet, while the President's committee was merely an acknowledged clearing house with sources of information that were extensive but admittedly incomplete, it was placed in the false and embarrassing position of being cited as an authority against people who insisted that widespread distress existed. In November 1930, for example, Woods telephoned each of the governors for information on the unemployment problem and to learn whether or not the states could handle the situation. In many instances Woods started out with a leading question, such as "You do not anticipate any trouble there?" A few of the governors either missed or ignored the hint. Governor John H. Trumbell of Connecticut replied, "I anticipate a hard winter. I do not see much relief in sight. I do not size up the situation as improving at all." "We have," he stated, "a very substantial amount of unemployment in the State." Unemployment, Governor Bibb Graves of Alabama said, "is pretty serious now. They have not arrived at any breadline state, but it is mighty serious. Big steel companies have cut down so much and thrown out so many people, their best people — it is not the ordinary down-and-outer, but the solid substantial working people — they are pretty hard pressed." There were only few replies of this sort, but even more rare was the blunt reply of Governor Fred W. Green of Michigan. "You know," he said, "everybody up here is doing everything they can to relieve employment except the Government." [14]

Most of the governors, however, claimed that the situation was not acute, or if they admitted to an unemployment problem, they insisted that they could handle it. The Governor of Georgia, for example, did not anticipate any trouble at all. "No," he said, "I do not see why we should have, and I do not know of any indication of it anywhere over the State. No, I do not. I do not know of a thing and have not heard of a thing. Of course," he concluded, "there are some people who are out of employment, but I have not heard of anything serious." Replies of this sort permitted Woods to say, when asked by the Governor of Arkansas for the "outlook over the country," that: "Actually I cannot find any place that says the situation is desperate. A number say that there are many people out of employment, but they say it will be taken care of in one way or another. I cannot find one who says the situation will get beyond them." [15]

No one seriously conversant with politics or unemployment considered the governors a reliable source of information on distress. The last man likely to admit that a state was unable to care for its own was its governor. Yet, it was on such information that Hoover repeatedly based his claims that unemployment and distress were being met by the American way. He would have been well advised to look to those who knew the facts: the men and women who ran the nation's private and public welfare agencies. The burden of distress rested with them far more than with the governors. Those who toil in the vineyards can most accurately describe the quality of the grapes.[16]

Philanthropy and privately financed social work both had an important part in the nation's response to unemployment; the danger was in overestimating their accomplishments.[17]

"Almost overnight," the public response to the President's appeal of late 1930 was described, "citizen organizations sprang up for the distribution of money, food, shelter and clothing in the large cities. . . . In New York, Chicago, Boston and Milwaukee . . . prominent laymen entered into co-operation with the charities and municipal governments." [18] The story of New York City well illustrates the determination and resourcefulness with which private charity organizations in the large cities attacked the unemployment problem, as well as the range of activities undertaken.

There were nearly twelve hundred public and private welfare and health agencies scattered throughout New York City. Although many of these organizations ordinarily were not conerned with unemployment relief, the direct and indirect effects stemming from unemployment soon left few of them untouched. As the depression became worse, the overriding unemployment problem soon commanded attention over all the other concerns which normally competed for the attention of charity and welfare groups.[19]

The private organizations, large and small, were active in a variety of ways. The Salvation Army immediately opened six breadlines. Others were established at such places as the "Little Church Around the Corner" and St. Vincent's Hospital. By December 1930, there were in all some fifty-three breadlines, food, and "handout" stations functioning throughout the city. Fourteen private organizations provided lodgings and care for the homeless. The Y.M.C.A., the Y.W.C.A., the settlement houses, the family and relief agencies, and men's and women's clubs were all carrying on some sort of unemployment program.[20]

New York City's newspapers, besides reporting on the charitable activities of others, were actively promoting a number of charity campaigns of their own: campaigns to provide coal, annual holiday campaigns, and "give a job" campaigns. Numerous "associations of churches and ministers, individual churches, lodges, civic and luncheon clubs" organized their own committees to promote private charity. And the Welfare Council, an organization representing several hundred affiliated agencies, attempted to co-ordinate the activities of the major private groups active throughout the city.

By late summer of 1930, leaders of private charity organizations in New York were already becoming apprehensive over their ability to deal with the spiraling number of unemployed. The energetic directors of the two largest, nonsectarian family agencies in Manhattan — Cornelius N. Bliss, president of the Association for Improving the Condition of the Poor (A.I.C.P.), and Walter S. Gifford, executive chairman of the Charity Organization Society — decided that additional funds must somehow be raised to supplement their regular but inadequate budgets. Others quickly and enthusiastically took up their idea; the plan was soon expanded to include the Jewish Social Service Association and Catholic Charities. Together these four organizations formed the principal family-relief agencies in the city.[21]

A group of financial and business executives undertook to raise the extra money for the agencies. At a meeting on October 15, they formed the Emergency Employment Committee, and they chose Seward Prosser, chairman of the board of the Bankers Trust Company, as the chairman of what came to be known as the Prosser committee. The campaign goal, originally set at the conservative figure of $2,000,000, was raised first to $6,000,000 and then to $8,000,000 When the formal campaign ended on December 17, Prosser announced that a total of $8,269,000 had been collected.[22]

The money, dispensed through the Emergency Work Bureau, was used to provide work for unemployed heads of families in the city's parks and at non-profit institutions. Each individual taken on was given three days' employment a week at the rate of $5.00 a day. By December 13, the Emergency Work Bureau had 20,540 unemployed heads of families, both men and women, on its payroll. This meant that the committee was paying out about $400,000 in weekly wages.[23]

In a radio appeal for contributions to the Emergency Work Bureau, Thomas W. Lamont, of J. P. Morgan and Company, estimated on November 26 the number of unemployed in the city at 300,000 — a conservative estimate.[24] It was apparent that the efforts of the family welfare agencies, supplemented by the work relief program of the Prosser committee, reached only a fraction of the unemployed. It represented, as the magazine of social work reported, a drop in the bucket.[25]

Prosser and his co-workers were well aware of the limited effectiveness of the Emergency Employment Committee. In January 1931, he and the members of his committee discussed the situation with Mayor James Walker, and told him frankly that the funds they had raised were insufficient to deal effectively with the city's unemployment needs. They urged that the city appropriate $10,000,000 immediately so that their work relief program might be carried on and extended.

Mayor Walker, who was uncertain whether the city could legally undertake the task, later announced that the city charter did not permit the use of public funds for work relief. No appropriation could be made until the charter was amended. At the time, though, the city was providing funds for the permanent forms of public relief authorized by law: mothers' pensions, aid to veterans, old-age relief, and blind relief.[26]

Since public funds for home relief and work relief were prohibited,[27] Walker concentrated on promoting private charity projects among the city's employees. He created the Mayor's Official Committee, composed of the thirty-seven department commissioners and directed by Welfare Commissioner Frank J. Taylor. The city's 150,000 employees were asked to contribute 1 per cent of their salaries to its unemployment fund, to be distributed through the police department to the city's distressed families in the form of food gifts or checks.[28] In 1930, the Mayor's Official Committee raised $307,609 and assisted 23,417 unemployed. This was increased to approximately one and a half million in both 1931 and 1932.

The public school teachers of New York City, who were not included among those contributing to the Mayor's Official Committee unemployment fund, had their own charity organization — the School Relief Fund. Made up entirely by the teachers' contributions, it was used to provide needy school children with free lunches, clothing, and some cash relief. In 1930, 50,000 children received assistance totaling $53,842. This was increased to $570,635 in 1931 and to $2,092,025 in 1932, aiding some 50,000 to 60,000 children each of these years.

The total amount of relief provided by private and semipublic (Mayor's and teacher's funds) groups in the city totaled $4,569,948 for 1930. In the next year, the amount collected and distributed increased by 347 per cent. In 1932, a peak of nearly $21,000,000 was reached. Since the bulk of these funds went to the Emergency Work Bureau, private charity mainly provided for work relief.[29]

New York's public relief expenditure, which amounted to $9,021,041 in 1930, increased more than three times in 1931. Of this sum, approximately $18,000,000 was used for regular forms of relief and the remainder for work relief — which at the beginning of 1931 had not been allowed by the city charter.[30] In 1932, total relief expenditures jumped to $57,080,-000. The city's total expenditures — private and public — for outdoor relief were $14,668,251 in 1930; $46,274,325 in 1931; and $79,402,963 the next year.[31]

These New York figures were reflected across the nation. Public and private expenditures for relief were rapidly increasing, and the biggest item was now unemployment relief. But the actual need still badly outdistanced the available resources. William Hodson, executive director of the Welfare Council of New York City,[32] pointed out the glaring discrepancy that existed in his testimony before a Senate subcommittee:

> It is estimated by the research bureau of the Welfare Council that in New York City the monthly wage loss by reason of the present unemployment situation is between eighty and ninety millions of dollars. This is probably a minimum estimate. The largest sum that we have ever given in relief in any one month is $4,000,000. In other words, it is perfectly clear that charity can never be substituted for the pay envelope. But the point I want to make is that between the spread of $4,000,000 now paid monthly for relief and the eighty and ninety millions of dollars lost in wages, you have represented a great loss in the standard of living, all the way down to the person who has not enough to live on.[33]

By December 1931, there were some 800,000 persons unemployed in New York City. Not all of them were in immediate need of relief, but it was expected that most of them soon would be. As the depression lengthened, the accumulated savings of the unemployed, the carefully nursed resources, which initially saved them from the humiliation of asking for relief, gradually were exhausted. Eventually, pride became a luxury the unemployed could not longer afford. This slow, wearing process — from an employed status to an unemployed status to a dependent status — became the disheartening necessity of more and more Americans. It was a process known to every social worker in the land, endlessly repeated to them by bewildered, discouraged people. As one social worker summarized it,

> . . . when hard times are prolonged, the great middle class is hit, the white-collar workers, the skilled laborers, the clerks,

the doctors, and the lawyers. They become dependent; and you add to your chronic dependents and your marginal dependents those who never before in their lives have sought charity or assistance in any form.

The thing that happens here is that when the breadwinner is out of a job he usually exhausts his savings if he has any. Then, if he has an insurance policy, he probably borrows to the limit of its cash value. He borrows from his friends and from his relatives until they can stand the burden no longer. He gets credit from the corner grocery store and the butcher shop, and the landlord foregoes collecting the rent until interest and taxes have to be paid and something has to be done. All of those resources are finally exhausted over a period of time, and it becomes necessary for these people, who have never before been in want, to ask for assistance.[34]

By the beginning of the third depression winter, even New York, the largest and wealthiest city in the country, with unmatched resources upon which to draw and an above-average relief organization, had failed miserably in coping with unemployment.[35] And yet what appeared to a New York social worker as relief administered on "a disaster basis" seemed like a "halcyon situation" when it was viewed and evaluated from the perspective of Chicago.

By 1931 Chicago's unemployment problem was more serious than that of New York. According to the April 1930 federal census, there were 167,934 unemployed in Chicago. In October 1931, the Bureau of Statistics and Research of the Illinois State Department of Labor estimated the number to be 624,000. In other words, 40 per cent of the men and women able and willing to work were unable to find it. With a wage loss of approximately $2,000,000 a day, the combined relief expenditures of private and public agencies amounted to a piddling $100,000 per day.[36]

Yet Chicago's private agencies had been active. In November 1930 alone, the non-sectarian United Charities, the largest family relief agency in the city, spent $51,277; Jewish Charities spent $26,500; and Catholic Charities, $30,000. A year later the situation was greatly changed, and the degree of change was reflected in the size of expenditures. United Charities, in November 1931, spent $522,000 — a tenfold increase — Jewish Charities had increased their outlay to $46,000, and Catholic Charities, to $231,000. The needs of the unemployed were simply increasing much more quickly than the resources of the private agencies.

Family relief in Chicago was calculated on the basis of a minimum budget. The food allowance that was provided by the minimum budget — there was no exaggeration in language here — varied from $2.60 a week for a man to $1.50 a week for an infant. But as Chicago was hard pressed for money and needed to stretch the available funds as widely as possible, the minimum budget was lowered by one-fourth! Families on relief received an average allotment of approximately $23.00 a month. But even by operating at these below-minimum standards, Chicago was still spending beyond its means. "We are spending the money faster than we collect it," a Chicago social worker conceded.[37]

Operating in the red, Chicago's private agencies could provide only skimpy assistance; and it was no easy matter to qualify for it. To be unemployed did not ensure assistance; Chicago simply could not help all those who had lost their jobs. The unemployed had first to go through the wringing process described by social workers the country over: the unemployed were given a hearing only after all their personal resources had been liquidated. "We insist," the director of Jewish Charities in Chicago, Samuel Goldsmith, explained, "that the people who come to our private and public agencies . . . shall use up, absolutely use up . . . all their available resources." This policy was a disagreeable necessity forced by a realistic appraisal of the possible; and it was only possible to give to the empty-handed. "The people," Gold-smith said bluntly, "that walk in the shadow of dependency, these hundred thousand families to-day in Cook County and Chicago, [are] the people who have actually been reduced to destitution." [38]

New York and Chicago preferred to deal with their relief problems on a local basis. Neither of them were members of the Community Chest — primarily because each city had a tradition of effective fund-raising by individual agencies. Yet, despite the different manner by which funds were raised, the nation's Community-Chest cities were confronted with the same crisis New York and Chicago endured.

By 1931, the Association of Community Chests and Councils, organized in 1918, included 380 member communities throughout the United States. Of this number, 243 Chests were located in cities with a population of 25,000 or more.[39] Each year these cities conducted a money-raising campaign. Since 65 per cent of the total collected was earmarked for hospitals, visiting nurses, child welfare, crime prevention, and other purposes not directly connected with unemployment, the sum collected did not indicate how much was spent by private charity organizations on unemployment relief.

Two hundred and ninety cities conducted their Chest campaigns in the fall of 1931. Complete returns from two hundred cities brought a total of $67,206,699, while the estimated total for all 380 cities was $100,000,000,[40] which represented a 25 per cent increase over the sum raised in 1928. Yet, while private contributions had increased, relief needs (measured in terms of what was actually spent and not what was actually needed) had increased even faster. And even though a far larger percentage of private funds was set aside for relief purposes, this increase (75 per cent since 1928) was much less than the increase in relief expenditures (400 per cent since 1928). The burden of the relief load was clearly being met from the public funds of city governments.[41]

Investigations into the sources of relief funds showed that private charity contributed a very small part. The most authoritative investigation — that of the Russell Sage Foundation — established the fact that 70 per cent of the money spent on relief came from public appropriations. Given such facts, well known to social workers at the time, it was unrealistic for anyone, even President Hoover, to maintain that private charity alone could handle the nation's relief needs.

On October 18, 1931, Hoover opened a nation-wide drive to assist the private relief agencies in securing the necessary funds to carry on their work. He emphasized the importance of providing security for the unemployed:

> This task is not beyond the ability of these thousands of community organizations to solve. Each local organization from its experience last winter and summer has formulated careful plans and made estimates completely to meet the need of that community. I am confident that the generosity of each community will fully support these estimates. The sum of these budgets will meet the needs of the nation as a whole.[42]

An important role in this endeavor was assigned to the Association of Community Chests and Councils. Earlier, at the request of the President's Emergency Committee for Employment, the Association had agreed to aid the Community Chest drive in cities over 25,000 population. The Association was instructed to discover the relief needs and resources of these cities, evaluate the effectiveness of their relief organizations, stimulate local leadership, and give advice on methods and procedures.[43]

In an exchange with Senator Edward P. Costigan, before a Senate subcommittee considering the unemployment problem, Allen T. Burns, executive director of the Association of Community Chests and Councils, gave a frank evaluation of the results of the national drive.

SENATOR COSTIGAN. You have clearly suggested that certain
goals of community chests were inadequate. Is that statement
a fair one for the country as a whole?

MR. BURNS. Not only their goal but what they raised is inadequate.

SENATOR COSTIGAN. I had in mind the goals in view. Where
exceeded, were those goals adequate for the need?

MR. BURNS. Oh, not at all. They anticipated that 70 per cent
of relief would have to come from public funds. They were
not fooled at all. They had had experience over years, and
they know that as a whole they play a minor part in relief.[44]

"I am stating," Burns said in summarizing his evaluation
of whether the nation's needs would be cared for, "that the
funds we have are altogether inadequate to meet that situation and we are not yet aware that local public funds have
been appropriated in any such amount as to meet the situation." [45] In the face of Hoover's repeated assurances that co-
operative action by voluntary groups could successfully meet
the nation's needs, Burns's testimony was disturbing, to say
the least — disturbing but hardly surprising, if anyone had
paid attention to those experts on the subject: the social
workers.

During the depression, social workers were the voice of the
unemployed. They spoke for the inarticulate. While the nation could see and know the surface aspects of the life of the
unemployed — the bread lines, the soup kitchens, the silent
crowds waiting at the employment agencies — the disintegra-
tion of individual and family life was hidden from their gaze.
Nothing was hidden from the social workers. Their work was
within, beyond the exterior facades erected by pride, where
the full impact of prolonged unemployment was exposed.
They were the voice of the misery, the hunger, the crum-
bling self-respect that confronted them on every side.

One of their most persistent and effective voices was Jacob

Billikopf, executive director of the Federation of Jewish Charities in Philadelphia. At the 1931 annual meeting of the National Conference of Social Work, held at Minneapolis in June, Billikopf asked social workers to consider the question: "What Have We Learned About Unemployment?" His speech, a writer in the *Survey* remarked, touched "the very spinal cord of the economic backbone of the Conference . . . " [46] It was a candid appraisal which cast aside all equivocations.

"With the possible exception of the World War," Billikopf announced gravely, "no phenomenon has arisen in our contemporary life fraught with such consequences as the unemployment problem." Unemployment placed a heavy responsibility upon social workers — a responsibility badly served by those making optimistic statements and soothing reassurances. "I want to warn you, my fellow social workers," he said,

> that we will be guilty of duplicity; we will be betraying the interest of the millions of unemployed who expect us to articulate their needs, if, in our vast enthusiasm to fill our community chests, we should give the impression, directly or even inferentially, that all a community has to do is to raise its chest quota and the unemployed will be provided for.

The times called for clear vision and blunt language from social workers. The nation was faced with a national emergency, and the full resources of the nation were needed to deal with the problem. "This is the way I see the situation," he continued:

> As a result of the policy of drift, and of utter lack of mastery in directing it, our government will be compelled, by the logic of inescapably cruel events ahead of us, to step into the situation and bring relief on a large scale — a scale commensurate with the vast importance and the tragedies of our problem. Private philanthropy is no longer capable of coping

with the situation. It is virtually bankrupt in the face of great disaster. With the bravest of intentions, the community chests, comprising as they do a multiplicity of institutions, are altogether unequal to the task ahead of us. Let us be honest, therefore, and say so — not wait until the disaster assumes larger proportions. Let us be frank and admit that if any American method of meeting unemployment is ever devised, it will be something more fundamental than relief.

In concluding, Billikopf reverted to his earlier admonition. "My friends," he said, "the time has come when you and I, who are so closely in touch with the tragedies of unemployment — the tragedies of despair arising from still other causes — must articulate the needs of those under our care." [47]

Later in the year, at the height of the Community Chest drives, Billikopf, in a letter to the *New York Times*,[48] warned against the mistaken assumption of many newspapers that the funds collected were sufficient to the need. The facts, he pointed out, did not support such an assumption. While the funds collected in 130 cities increased nearly 15 per cent over their 1930 total,[49] relief expenditures in September 1931, compared to September 1930, rose 404 per cent in Philadelphia, 267 per cent in Chicago, 125 per cent in New York, 134 per cent in Cleveland, and 214 per cent in St. Louis. Not only were the optimistic reports of the press mistaken, they were positively dangerous, for they lulled the country into a false sense of security.

The funds were clearly inadequate. In Philadelphia, the Federation of Jewish Charities, during normal times, provided $21.95 weekly as its minimum relief budget for a family of five. Broken down into its component parts, this minimum budget included: food, $9.25; lunches, 60 cents; rent, $5.77; light and cooking, 69 cents; clothing, $2.92; household supplies, 35 cents; car fare, 90 cents; incidentals, 64 cents;

and coal, 85 cents.[50] Now, in December, with 40,000 families being cared for by the emergency unemployment relief committee, this minimum standard could no longer be maintained. "The relief available and distributed by our emergency relief committee," he wrote, "is so far under this standard of adequacy as to be self-evident. It has amounted to $5 per week for a family of five for food only." The other items in the budget, with the exception of milk, were no longer provided.

The wide gap between actual relief expenditures and actual relief needs which these figures poignantly expose existed all over the country, as the testimony of other social workers revealed.[51] Mimimum standards were abandoned, careful case work methods could no longer be applied, and families were aided only when they had reached the point of destitution. Relief was reduced to a disaster basis. And still there was no assurance, even after the economies and corner-cutting, that the funds would hold out. These facts, well known to the experts, thoroughly aired at congressional hearings, and widely advertised by the newspapers and magazines, do not seem to have reached Hoover and his principal advisers.

The successive heads of the national voluntary unemployment committees served the President as his chief advisers on unemployment and relief. These committees, which resulted from presidential prompting, were Hoover's main contribution to the problem. They clearly exemplified his great concern to try co-operative action among voluntary organizations and local government to combat the depression.

The first national committee in this area was the President's Emergency Committee for Employment. The chairman, Colonel Arthur Woods, resigned in April 1931, and was replaced by one of his subordinates, Fred C. Croxton, who served as acting chairman until August 19, 1931, when Hoover appointed as director, Walter S. Gifford, the president of the American Telephone and Telegraph Company and executive chairman of the Charity Organization Society of New York City.[52] Although the committee was then renamed the President's Organization on Unemployment Relief, the basic organization built up by Woods was retained intact. But in order to extend the work to a national basis, Gifford added a new type of organization which worked in close co-operation with the local groups.[53]

Gifford first created an advisory committee, which eventually expanded to some one hundred individuals. From this group, which was publicized as broadly representative of such major interests as industry and labor, Gifford appointed a representative for each state. These state representatives were to act as a contact, gathering and disseminating information, between the national committee and the state organizations.[54]

Five national committees were also established: "a committee to help in the mobilization of relief resources, a committee to help in the administration of relief matters, a committee to advise on employment plans and suggestions, a committee on Federal public works, and a committee on cooperation of national organizations and agencies." [55] Their primary role was to encourage greater local activity and to co-ordinate local efforts. For example, Owen D. Young, chairman of the Committee on Mobilization of Relief Resources, described the function of his committee in this fashion:

> The duties of this Committee are merely to aid local organizations in raising funds for local needs. Our job is not to raise funds ourselves. There is to be no national fund except as it is represented by the aggregate of all local funds everywhere.
>
> There are things which can be done on a national scale to aid local organizations in raising funds which they can-

not do for themselves. For example, many of the great national periodicals have already agreed to contribute pages of advertising. Eight of the best advertising agencies as volunteers are preparing the copy. Both the Columbia Broadcasting System and the National Broadcasting Company are, for the first time in their history, giving the Committee the use of their combined networks. With their cooperation, we have planned a series of four broadcasts. I should say that all of these national activities will occur during the period from October 19th to November 25th, because during that time most of the local campaigns for funds will be under way. Again, the motion picture industry has agreed to contribute reels and releases. The cartoonists to whom we have written have responded universally to the request of our Committee for cooperation. These are among some of the activities which we have been suggesting to nation-wide associations and organizations.[56]

"The central organization in Washington," Gifford explained, "was not to do anything other than encourage the States to do the work; . . . the responsibility was to be left squarely with the States, counties, and communities." [57]

In appointing Gifford, Hoover had chosen another man thoroughly in accord with his assumptions about relief. Local communities, Gifford was convinced, had the primary responsibility of caring for the unemployed. "Where the responsibility can be placed on the local organization," he said, "I think that is the safer and wiser plan and results in better service to the unemployed than any other." Each step taken away from the responsibility of the local community — to the county or to the state level — was a "bad step." Most undesirable of all would be if the federal government made appropriations for unemployment relief. Gifford would not support such a move until the state governments had proved themselves to be "absolutely broke." [58]

Gifford, however, saw little possibility of that eventuality. Describing his work with the committee, he wrote in late November 1931 to Hoover:

> I can report that in particularly all communities requiring organized effort to meet unemployment this winter, such organization is either completed and functioning or is expected to be in the near future. There are several thousand committees, State, County and local, now engaged in this effort reaching to every important point of unemployment.
>
> Governors and members of State committees with their interests and foresight, and local officials and thousands of public spirited members of local committees with their unselfish service and knowledge of local conditions, have united forces to meet the present situation.
>
> As a result, plans are completed in nearly all States and in preparation in the others to the end that all communities with, in some instances, assistance from the County or State, may meet this winter's expected relief burden.

"There is every indication," he concluded, "that each State will take care of its own this winter." [59]

The events of the winter failed to change his mind. "It is only after nearly five months of intensive work on this problem," he informed a Senate subcommittee on January 8, 1932, "that my sober and considered judgment is that at this stage . . . Federal aid would be a disservice to the unemployed . . . and that the situation can be better handled as it is being handled."

Senators Robert M. LaFollette, Jr., and Edward P. Costigan, both members of the Senate Subcommittee, wanted to know the factual basis for this optimistic evaluation. His information, Gifford explained, was based upon telephone conversations with the state representatives of the President's committee; he considered that these reports presented an accurate picture of the relief situation in the states. Did he

think, the senators queried, that the amount of current expenditures for relief met the actual needs of the country? "I
think," he replied, "the money spent is the money needed."
"How many people are out of work and on the verge of want
in the United States?" Senator Costigan asked. Gifford did
not know.

Further questioning revealed that the chairman of the
President's Organization on Unemployment Relief had no
definite figures or definite information on other extremely
vital matters: the number of persons unemployed, the number of families receiving relief, the standards of relief, the
financial condition of the communities and whether they
were able to raise additional money, the relief needs of the
nation's smaller cities without a Community Chest. Gifford
did not know, but he did not think anyone else knew either.
He was right. No one person did have detailed and accurate
answers to these questions. But there was an important difference: some were trying desperately to find out, while Gifford
did not think "the data would be of any particular value." [60]

Up until the end of 1931, the cities and the counties had
carried the major burden of unemployment relief. The states
as a whole had provided little or no financial assistance to the
local private and public welfare groups. The states seemed all
too often mere onlookers to the grim struggle against hunger
and impoverishment. But their days of detachment and com-
placency were rapidly running out. It was apparent, even before the third depression winter of 1931–32, that the nation
was overwhelmed by an economic and social catastrophe. The
basic difficulty was financial: the local sources of income were
rapidly drying out.

This was no sudden revelation; the nation's news media
were pointing out the predicament of the cities as early as
1930.[61] By 1932, their protests had become a clamor. "The
financial troubles of state and local governments," *Business
Week* observed, "have taken on the proportions of a national

problem." [62] Cities, casting about for additional sources of income, found that their normal sources were imperiled. Property taxes, the major source of income, no longer could provide the funds to meet the cities' expenses. This resulted partly from a marked increase in delinquent and unpaid taxes at the same time that expenditures, especially for unemployment, were steadily mounting. Also there was strong resistance to proposals to increase taxes. In Philadelphia, 15,000 demonstrated against a proposed tax increase. Chicagoans invaded the state capital at Springfield to protest. In Rochester, Minnesota, a group of angry farmers clamored about the commission chamber until $75,000 was cut from the budget. Simultaneously, cities that attempted to solve the crisis by borrowing discovered that it was impossible to sell bonds. The municipal bond market had vanished.[63]

City authorities appealed to local bankers in vain. The bankers, many of whom already held unsaleable municipal bonds, advised city officials to balance their budgets — a necessary preliminary before additional borrowing could even be considered. The cities faced an impossible predicament: they needed more money to finance current obligations; to get the money they must curtail their existing services. The result was that cities began to trim their assistance to the unemployed; salary cuts were made; city employees were dismissed; and services which for years had been considered vital were curtailed or abandoned.[64]

In the winter of 1931, Detroit had 223,000 jobless workers; its tax resources were exhausted; and the bankers refused any further loans unless the city demonstrated that it could live within its income. Mayor Frank Murphy described the consequences of meeting this condition:

> We are eliminating part of the 36 services that have grown on the city since 1916, such as our city planning commission, our rapid transit commission; we are just keeping a skeleton

force in the art museum; . . . we are cutting into even the departments for peace and health and safety. The health service is being curtailed, the police and fire departments, the recreation department. We want to leave untouched as much as possible the department of peace and health, but there must be a sharp curtailment of all departments in order to live within the income, and we are going to do that.[65]

When cities such as Detroit were forced to pare essential services, they of course had no resources at hand to deal adequately with the exceptional distress resulting from unemployment. Their work here became a lick, a promise, and sincere regrets. In Philadelphia, for example, where the private agencies ordinarily helped 5000 families, there were 54,532 families receiving some assistance at the begining of 1932. The average allowance per family was $4.25 a week — no provision was made for fuel, clothing, or rent. And this was given only to those who had exhausted every conceivable resource; that is, families absolutely dependent. On June 25, 1932, Philadelphia ran out of funds — private, municipal, and state funds — and its assistance to some 52,000 destitute families was discontinued for three months. And Philadelphia wondered what was happening to these families. A survey of 400 families showed that no one actually starved. "They kept alive," Jacob Billikopf reported, "from day to day, catch-as-catch can, reduced for actual subsistence to something of the status of a stray cat prowling for food, for which a kindly soul occasionally sets out a plate of table scraps or a saucer of milk." "What this does to the innate dignity of the human soul," Billikopf added, "is not hard to guess." [66]

By 1932, Chicago and Cook County were practically bankrupt. Chicago, which had not paid its school teachers in eight months, was preparing to discharge not only some teachers but firemen and policemen as well. "City bonds," a Chicagoan declared, "were not even considered to meet the emergency.

County bonds have been peddled from bank to bank and sold to wholesale grocers like so much second-hand merchandise." [67] Caught between unpaid bills, unpaid salaries, and unsaleable bonds, Chicago attempted in desperation to curtail expenses. "I don't know what else to do," said Mayor Cermak.[68]

The troubles of Detroit, Philadelphia, and Chicago were duplicated with slight variations in cities the country over. And social workers provided first-hand reports on these conditions to Congress and the country: "Practically all community services other than relief have been curtailed" (Cincinnati). "Child-caring agencies have had to limit their intake and . . . some hospitals are threatened with shut down unless additional money is secured" (Cleveland). "We are merely trying to prevent hunger and exposure" (St. Paul). "We are holding taxes down and spreading relief thin" (Scranton). "It will be necessary to discontinue relief in rural sections of the county which include a number of mining communities" (Birmingham).[69]

Cities finally turned to their state governments for financial assistance and succor — as Hoover had schooled them to do — but instead of a sturdy support they found but a slender reed swaying uncertainly before the high economic winds.

New York was the first state to provide substantial funds for unemployment relief. On August 28, 1931, Governor Franklin D. Roosevelt submitted a message to a special session of the legislature requesting that an emergency relief administration be established. Bills were introduced in both houses; they were then combined into one and passed unanimously. On September 23, 1931, Roosevelt signed the bill which created the Temporary Emergency Relief Administration (T.E.R.A.) with a $20,000,000 appropriation for the emergency period, defined as extending from November 1, 1931, to June 1, 1932. Later, at the regular session of the legislature in 1932, another $5,000,000 was added and the emergency period was extended to November 15, 1932.

On October 1, 1931, Roosevelt appointed a three-man administration for T.E.R.A. with Jesse Isidor Straus as chairman; later, on April 23, 1932, Harry L. Hopkins became chairman. The state funds were made available to the local communities for both work and home relief. The work relief program was administered locally by Emergency Work Bureaus, organized in every county, city, and town in the state — the state's share of the expenses being used for wages only, the local governments paying for the materials. For home relief, the state reimbursed the local communities for 40 per cent of their expenditures. This was relief in kind, and was administered by the local public welfare departments.[70]

In the first seven months of its operation T.E.R.A. assisted some 312,000 families. This cost the state $17,484,546; but, in addition, local county and municipal government expenditures for home relief and work relief brought the total to $35,000,000 for unemployment relief. In Illinois, the state legislature provided $18,750,000, on February 6, 1932, to create the Illinois Emergency Relief Commission, which was authorized to grant funds to private relief agencies through the Joint Emergency Relief Fund of Cook County; allocate funds to public relief agencies through its agent, the Cook County Bureau of Public Welfare; and provide for work relief through the Work Relief Committee of Cook County. Very modest appropriations were made in 1931 by Oklahoma, New Hampshire, California, and Ohio. Ohio also passed a law permitting counties, cities, and townships to issue more bonds to finance unemployment relief — assuming that the bonds could be marketed.[71]

In addition, by 1932, Ohio had taken further action by appropriating $25,000,000, New Jersey provided $9,616,033, and Pennsylvania appropriated $10,000,000, to which it added, in August, another $12,000,000. But Pennsylvania's constitution prohibited the state from incurring a debt of over $1,000,000 — it could only increase its taxes. But the state constitution also prohibited a graduated income tax. Governor Pinchot estimated that it would take at least two years to amend the constitution.[72]

Constitutional and tax difficulties of this sort were not at all peculiar to Pennsylvania. States, like cities, depended primarily upon the general property tax for their income; in fact, 50 per cent of state income came from this source. This was supplemented by taxes upon corporations, inheritances, gasoline and sales taxes, and miscellaneous transactions. Only seventeen states had an income tax law in 1931 — increased to twenty by 1932. In most cases, a constitutional amendment —a lengthy process for state legislatures which meet infrequently — was required before new taxes could be imposed. States were also limited constitutionally from giving financial aid to local governments. Senator Costigan stated that "the constitutions of at least 16 States, including Illinois, either expressly prohibit the States from, or specifically limit them in extending credit to or aid or assuming any liability of any county, city, or town." [73]

The practical consequence of tax and constitutional difficulties was that the vast majority of states — even as late as 1932 — were doing nothing to relieve the exhausted cities and counties. Only eight states were providing financial assistance for unemployment relief; and in none of these, not even New York, could it be said that either the cities or the states were "taking care of their own." [74]

"I would like to say," declared Walter West, executive secretary of the American Association of Social Workers, in December 1931, "that I think the social workers of this country would like to be on record here . . . as not at all satisfied with what we call the 'American system' of dealing with the unemployed." When asked by Senator Costigan whether he regarded "the problem as a national one calling for some national assistance," West replied: "It seems to me to be national in origin, national in scope, beyond the reach of any local administrative unit or of the State in its magnitude, and therefore national." A parade of expert witnesses — social workers, economists, public welfare officials — told the same story and reiterated the same conclusion.[75]

In the face of this information, President Hoover clearly had slender ground by 1932 for his optimistic evaluation of the unemployment relief problem. Hoover was frankly in no position to contradict the testimony of those who were closest to the problem. Factually, he did not have a leg to stand on. And yet he did contradict them. As the rising clamor against the President's inactivity showed, his attitude toward the unemployed, his pronouncements, and his relief program constituted a political blunder of the first order.

At the time, no one could prove conclusively that all the states had used up all their resources, nor could it be proved that their ability to issue new bonds or to impose additional taxes was absolutely exhausted. Neither could it be proved that the states were bankrupt. The states as a whole had actually done little for the unemployed — if their efforts were compared with the cities and counties. So that if one accepted Hoover's conditions for extending federal aid to the unemployed, the proper time still had not yet come. But the matter was not judged by the President's standards. The needs of the unemployed overwhelmed traditional institutions. It was futile to insist that the states could handle the problem when they had already demonstrated that they were not handling it. When the modern American is stymied by the perplexities of modern life, when the intricate, economic system breaks down, he does not look to the state houses, he looks to the White House. Telling him to look elsewhere does not alter his expectations. In dealing with the unemployment problem, Hoover did not face this fact. More seriously still, he allowed himself to be put in the position of seeming to quibble with distress. It was an absolutely untenable position.

II

Hoover's Second Program

> The recommendations submitted to Congress were not a series of independent and unrelated proposals, but constituted a unified and integrated program designed to meet the various phases of a progressive economic disease that had been actually diagnosed and which, if it had been permitted to run its course, might have resulted in terrible disaster.* OGDEN L. MILLS, 1932

9

Herbert Hoover:
The Presidency in Peacetime Crisis

Is not this emergency as great as that of war? *
NEW REPUBLIC, 1932

Today we are engaged in a war against depression.† HERBERT HOOVER

When contemporaries attempted to gauge the magnitude of the crisis that confronted American society during the Great Depression, the analogy of war came readily to mind. Nothing in the American experience except war — and great wars such as the Civil War and World War I — seemed comparable to the seriousness, scope, and challenge of the depression. "Not all wars," the editor of *Iron Age* observed in 1931, "are announced by formal declaration. America has been at war for the past 19 months, although many do not know it." And a writer in the *Atlantic* remarked that "huge economic losses and widespread suffering, mental and physical, make the effects of depression direct kin, in the human sense, to those of war." [1]

From the point where the analogy of war was recognized, many made the easy, natural step to the contention that the emergency measures employed to meet a wartime crisis were appropriate for a peacetime crisis as well. Since the crises were comparable, they reasoned, then the national effort that was required to overcome them was also comparable. Professor Richard T. Ely of Northwestern University argued from this assumption when he urged a "Peace Time Army." "We should go to work to relieve distress," he insisted, "with all the vigor and resources of brain and brawn that we employed

in the World War. We have armies to prepare for possible
wars. We should have preparedness for Hard Times." [2] The
editor of the *Nation,* Oswald Garrison Villard, wondered
why the expedients used to meet a wartime crisis were condemned when urged during a peacetime crisis. "When war
came," he reminded an audience at the University of
Virginia,

> it seemed natural and wise for the government to take over
> and operate the railroads, shipping, and coal mines, to super-
> vise our agriculture and many industrial enterprises. Every-
> body acquiesced and nobody questioned. The government
> was urged to take over forests, factories, plants of every kind,
> to build docks, shipyards, railroads, whole villages and towns.
> Nobody declared that this was socialistic or communistic. It
> was just *necessary,* in order to coordinate all the forces of the
> nation, to forge the thunderbolts needed to destroy the
> German military power.[3]

More often the advocates of forceful governmental action
confined the analogy to the federal government's role in expanding credit during World War I, and urged a similar policy to combat depression. Stuart Chase, in advocating an inflation policy, asked pointedly, "What is a people's credit
for?" And then answered his question with another. "When
war is declared," he said with characteristic vividness, "credit
is flung about like a drunken sailor's wages — twenty billions
for the late unpleasantness in France. Why should it not be
used to scotch a more sinister foe?" It was a recurrent, persistent question. "We appropriated money without stint to
meet the demands of war," a Democratic partisan declared.
"In the same spirit we should expend whatever sum is necessary to care for the present severe crisis of peace." [4]

Others who raised the same issue were often inclined to be
pessimistic over the possibility of the war analogy being
translated into policy. "In the past," John M. Keynes noted,

"we have not infrequently had to wait for a war to terminate a major depression. I hope," he added pointedly, "that in the future we shall not adhere to this purist financial attitude, and that we shall be ready to spend on the enterprises of peace what the financial maxims of the past would only allow us to spend on the devastations of war." "Some day," another economist remarked dispiritedly, "we shall realize that if money is available for a blood-and-bullets war, just as much money is available for a food-and-famine war." On that day, he continued, "We shall see that if it is fitting to use collective action on a large scale to kill men abroad, it is fitting to use collective action on an equally large scale to save men at home." But such a realization, he concluded, "will require a change of mental habit." [5]

An attentive eye could have detected that some mental habits were already changing, as the nearest magazine stand could show. "We believe as thoroughly as anyone," the editor of *Business Week* announced, "that government attempts to control prices of any commodity are unsound and futile under ordinary conditions of world trade. They should be resorted to only in a crisis of war-time." "But," he quickly added, "this is such a time and such a crisis." Later, at the time of the furor over a balanced federal budget, he exclaimed with a touch of exasperation: "We are solemnly assured that upsetting the balanced budget by borrowing maketh its sacred cow sister, the Public Credit, sick. Who worried about her health when during the war we borrowed twenty billions for unproductive and explosive purposes?" [6]

The analogy of war seemed particularly pertinent because it represented a concrete and potent parallel to the extremely grave economic crisis. It put the emergency into a proper framework. For to use the analogy of war was to resort to superlatives, and only the superlative appeared adequate to describe the Great Depression. Of even more importance, the analogy of war — especially World War I — invoked the most vivid national experience of contemporary Americans. It recalled the experience of a nation unified by a common cause. It pricked the memory of a massive and successful mobilization of the nation's resources to achieve a common purpose. It suggested that the Great Depression must be fought with all the resources and the determination of a nation at war. But this aspect of the analogy was far easier to state than to utilize.

War and depression do not create identical moods. The issues of wartime, first of all, are far more simple than those of a peacetime crisis. In wartime, there is a definite enemy who must be fought, and a definite objective to which all else is rigorously subordinated: national victory. And the signposts of war — battles that are either won or lost — are more readily comprehensible to the public than those of a peacetime economic crisis. Since the course of war can be more easily followed, the need for personal sacrifice is easier to accept. When the war goes badly, the citizen knows that more will be demanded of him, and the government knows that more will be given.

Moreover, in order to win a war, peacetime scruples in economic, political, constitutional, and social matters are either temporarily set aside or overridden. Neither government nor public opinion will tolerate obstructions to the successful conduct of a war. A diverse society, with its tumult of contradictory opinions, loyalties, and commitments, is transformed by the demands of wartime into an acquiescent society. Under such conditions, the normal obstructions of a complex, heterogeneous, pluralistic society are suspended for the duration.

This transformation is most noticeable at the center. Federal authority, in wartime, has few bounds; in particular, the jurisdiction and exercise of presidential power is greatly enlarged. And all that needs to be done is accomplished with the acquiescence of the public. This willingness to suspend the scruples of peacetime does not happen solely because of military necessity. It is based upon the expectation, fostered by past experience, that the wartime expedients are temporary: that the exercise of the powers, controls, and restrictions of wartime will end with the war. Above all, it is rooted in the belief that the powers employed to conduct a war will not be continued when peace returns.

None of these assurances is applicable in a peacetime crisis. This helps to explain why the challenge of the Great Depression to American society and American institutions was an even more serious and difficult one than that of World War I. Even if President Hoover were willing to combat the depression on the analogy of war, he still faced a more formidable task than had Woodrow Wilson. But was President Hoover willing?

On several occasions Hoover went so far as to use the analogy of war when discussing the economic crisis. In a press statement of February 3, 1932, he said:

> During the great war our people gave their undivided energies to the national purpose. Today we are engaged in a war against depression. If our people will give now the same service and the same confidence to our government and our institutions, the same unity and solidarity of courageous action which they gave during the Great War, we can overcome this situation.

Later in the month, he declared solemnly:

> We are engaged in a fight upon a hundred fronts just as positive, just as definite and requiring just as greatly the moral courage, the organized action, the unity of strength and the sense of devotion in every community as in war.

"Fighting a great depression," he announced in March, "is a war with destructive forces in a hundred battles on a hundred fronts. We must needs fight as in a great war; we must meet these destructive forces by mobilizing our resources and our people against them." [7]

On other occasions as well, the President freely used the language of war — battles, fronts, mobilization, drives — to emphasize the grave nature of the depression crisis. Yet, those who interpreted these pronouncements to mean that Hoover was willing to employ wartime precedents to meet the peacetime crisis were badly mistaken. These statements had to be interpreted within the context of Hoover's philosophy of government and his notion of the presidency as a potent instrument in defense of the American system — and all the ideals which Hoover associated with that system.

As far as Hoover was concerned, these were not ideals for prosperous times alone; they were for the times of national adversity as well. "We are going through a period," he declared in February 1931, "when character and courage are on trial, and where the very faith that is within us is under test." [8] The Great Depression was not a signal to abandon these principles; it was a call to rise in their defense. Those who would sap the vitality of American character by undermining the American system through far-reaching expansions of federal authority and power must be resisted. To allow violations of the American system was to corrupt the very nursery of American ideals. Hoover in his self-conceived role of chief defender of American ideals braced himself to thwart the designs of the innovators.

Whatever might be said of Hoover's philosophy of government and society, it obviously revealed an outlook and temperament that furnished only cold comfort to those who were urging measures based upon the analogy of war. The President's viewpoint was the very antithesis of those who would combat a peacetime crisis with the precedents of wartime. Speaking of the impact that mobilization for World War I had had on American institutions, Hoover emphasized the dangers of that experience:

During the war we necessarily turned to the government to solve every difficult economic problem. The government having absorbed every energy of our people for war, there was no other solution. For the preservation of the state, the Federal Government became a centralized despotism which undertook unprecedented responsibilities, assumed autocratic powers, and took over the business of citizens. To a large degree we regimented our whole people temporarily into a socialistic state. However justified in time of war, if continued in peacetime it would destroy not only our American system but with it our progress and freedom as well.[9]

While Hoover expressed this judgment prior to the stock market crash, it represented an abiding conviction. To those who demanded enlarged federal action to combat the depression, Hoover was prepared to make only slight concessions — concessions hedged with reservations. "I am convinced," he declared emphatically,

> that where Federal action is essential then in most cases it should limit its responsibilities to supplement the states and local communities, and that it should not assume the major role or the entire responsibility, in replacement of local government, which is the very basis of self-government.[10]

To carry out this program, Hoover took the lead in establishing a number of institutions designed to operate on the basis of voluntary co-operative action. The most prominent of these were the National Business Survey Conference, the National Building Survey Conference, the National Credit Corporation, the President's Emergency Committee for Employment, and the President's Organization on Unemployment Relief. These institutions in turn rested upon a host of others, such as the national trade associations, the United States Chamber of Commerce, bank associations, the National Association of Community Chests and Councils, private charity organizations, public welfare agencies, city, county, and state governments.

Measured by what previous depression Presidents had done, this looked like an impressive display of presidential initiative and leadership. But if Hoover's inital program is measured by what all this activity was meant to accomplish, then his policy must be accounted a dismal failure. In no instance did voluntary co-operative action accomplish the purpose that it set out to attain. The President's initial program failed as a whole, and it failed in detail. Why did it fail? And why did Hoover never publicly acknowledge its failure?

Hoover's initial program was set into motion in November 1929 and it continued to be his official program for the next two years. While the original program was enlarged during this period, the additions to it, such as the National Credit Corporation, did not deviate from the spirit or the limitations of the original conception.

From time to time during 1930 and 1931, Hoover declared that he saw definite signs of recovery. In each case the announcement proved premature. Instead of the anticipated upturn, the economy slumped even further. In answer to these downturns — and the jibes of his critics — Hoover advanced an official explanation of the cause of the Great Depression and the reasons for its unexpected prolongation.

"This depression," the President declared in October 1930, "is worldwide. Its causes and effects lie only partly in the United States." The purely American aspect of the depression resulted from the irresponsible, hectic speculation of the "New Era" days which culminated in the stock market crash. This was America's responsibility — the American cause — but, all in all, it was a minor cause. "Had overspeculation in securities been the only force operating." Hoover argued in December, "we should have seen recovery many months ago, as these particular dislocations have generally readjusted themselves." [11]

While the United States was readjusting to the dislocations produced by the Wall Street crash, new and more serious difficulties developed in the world economy. Originating abroad, these difficulties blew over the United States like an ill wind to blight the incipient American recovery. One of the foremost of these "deep-seated causes" was the worldwide surplus in the production of basic raw materials such as wheat, rubber, coffee, sugar, copper, silver, zinc, and cotton. "These major over-expansions," Hoover pointed out, "have taken place largely outside of the United States." They were, he particularized, the product of Brazil, Colombia, Chile, Peru, Mexico, Australia, Cuba, and Java.[12]

Excessive production created glutted markets and a serious price deflation in these commodities. In turn, the collapse of prices precipitated financial crises in many countries and a disruption of world trade. Other major causes enumerated by Hoover included "the political agitation of Asia; revolutions in South America and political unrest in some European states"; Russian dumping of agricultural products in Europe; and the American drought. All these factors, Hoover explained, have "contributed to prolong and deepen the depression." In comparison to the remainder of the world, America's contribution to the depression seemed to pale in significance. "In the larger view," Hoover announced in December 1930, "the major forces of the depression now lie outside of the United States, and our recuperation has been retarded by the unwarranted degree of fear and apprehension created by these outside forces." [13]

Although Hoover argued that disturbances outside the country were prolonging the depression, he also insisted that American recovery need not await world recovery. "We can make a very large degree of recovery independently of what may happen elsewhere." he maintained. "We shall need mainly to depend upon our own strong arm for recovery, as other nations are in greater difficulty than we." An independent American recovery was possible because the American economy was practically self-contained.

The argument for America's economic self-containment was impressive. The United States consumed approximately 90 per cent of all the commodities, including foodstuffs, which it produced. Annual exports, amounting in value to about $5 billion before the depression, accounted for only 10 per cent of America's product. Nor was the nation's foreign trade suddenly obliterated by the depression. American foreign trade during the first years of the depression was valued at about $3.5 billion annually. The $1.5 billion drop in exports, Hoover pointed out, "amounts to only 2 or 3 per cent of our total productivity." [14]

The fact of America's economic self-containment, together with the President's confidence in the success of his initial program, explain the contrast between his own optimism and the prevalent public pessimism concerning prospects for recovery. While Hoover saw signs of recovery, the nation as a whole could only wonder at his optimism. Events proved that the pessimists were the more realistic. Recovery — often predicted and confidently expected by Hoover — failed to materialize. Hoover's explanation for the unexpected continuation of depression, given at the time (and later),[15] provides the key to understanding his subsequent actions and his second program.

According to Hoover, the progress of America's recovery was not derailed by any domestic failings but rather by Europe's financial troubles. Commencing with the difficulties of Vienna's largest bank in April 1931, the financial crisis tottered the national banks of Austria and Yugoslavia, spread to Germany, and culminated in England's abandonment of the gold standard in September. The reverberations of Europe's financial disturbances were soon felt in the United States. There were large-scale withdrawals of foreign gold deposits from the country, and frightened Americans began hoarding gold.[16] Most important of all, the stability of American banks was endangered.

Short-term paper was the connecting link between American banks and the financial crisis of Germany and Central Europe. As heavy investors in European short-term paper — especially German trade bills and bank acceptances [17] — American banks were directly linked to the financial developments of Europe. Since these loans represented American investments, they constituted a part of the assets of American banks. If the German banking system collapsed, defaulting its short-term paper, the assets of American banks holding German paper would suffer a direct loss. This, in turn, would further impair the ability and the willingness of American banks to extend credit at home. The President's recovery program, in which banking and credit were such vital elements, would be seriously hampered.

These European events had an even more important result: they produced a powerful impact upon the thinking of Hoover. What the President had previously seen as the major causes prolonging the depression — world overproduction, the price collapse, political unrest — he now saw as part of a larger pattern of events which tied in with the European financial crisis. And none of them, in Hoover's estimation, was the basic cause of the depression. They were all simply effects that stemmed from one common source: World War I. Now that the root cause was exposed, Hoover quickly adjusted his interpretation of the depression. Speaking in June 1931, with the benefit of his new insight, he said:

A large part of the forces which have swept our shores from abroad are the malign inheritances in Europe of the Great War — its huge taxes, its mounting armament, its political and social instability, its disruption of economic life by the new boundaries. Without the war we should have no such depression.[18]

Americans had indeed been rash in stock speculation, but the persistent tenacity of the depression, like a hangover that would not go away, was not the result of American high life and irresponsibility. It was Europe's folly that had brought about the depression and now was prolonging it. There was nothing basically wong with America except its association with Europe. This being the case, according to Hoover, nothing really needed to be changed in the American system. Since Europe was the seat of the trouble the remedy was obvious: America should isolate herself from the shocks of Europe and permit the self-contained American system an unhampered opportunity to restore prosperity. This interpretation of the cause of the depression and its prolongation served Hoover's philosophy well.

Hoover now proposed a series of acts that constituted a second program. One should not be misled by the terminology, however, since Hoover's second program was more of an extension of certain existing ideas of his initial program than a drastic departure from it. The crisis, for example, was still regarded as essentially financial, and the program devised to overcome it remained a financial one. In this emphasis upon finance, banking, and credit, Hoover made no departure from his initial program. The major difference was in the new program's scope and implementation. Its scope was more narrow, concerned almost exclusively with credit problems. Related difficulties, such as maintaining wages, employment, and construction activity, which had received so much attention in the initial program, were no longer emphasized. Since credit was now more clearly seen as the keystone of the arch, the first and foremost concern must be to fortify its position. Once it was secure, all the other parts of the economic structure would automatically be strengthened. To implement such a vital objective, Hoover was willing to pass beyond voluntaryism into the realm of direct, federal action. In this aspect, then, the second program was broader than the first.

The opening move of Hoover's second program was the moratorium. On June 20, 1931, at the height of the German financial crisis, the President proposed that the creditor nations agree on a one-year postponement "of all payments on intergovernmental debts, reparations and relief debts, both principal and interest . . . not including obligations of governments held by private parties." "The purpose of this action," he explained, "is to give the forthcoming year to the economic recovery of the world and to help free the recuperative forces already in motion in the United States from retarding influences abroad." [19]

Hoover's action in this instance was highly praised by the American press. "The disposition everywhere," the editor of the *Commerical & Financial Chronicle* maintained, "is to look upon the event as marking a turning point in the long period of depression in trade and business." Then, assessing its probable impact, he added, "Confidence that the end of the depression is here will itself contribute in a powerful degree to bring it here." The moratorium, the editor of *Business Week* remarked, "opens the way to that crucial recovery of confidence necessary to persuade private investors to participate in the inevitable expansion of credit which is required to reverse the deflation process and return to productive use the purchasing power frozen by forced liquidation." [20]

The President's proposal succeeded in averting the threatened collapse of the German financial structure and postponed, for at least a year, the consequences that such a collapse would have upon American banks. Hoover hoped to secure a year's respite from European disturbances, a year in which American recovery might proceed unmolested. The moratorium, designed to isolate the United States from the contagion of Europe, represented an American attitude of mind with a long tradition and wide appeal.

On the domestic front, Hoover felt the problem that confronted the nation remained basically the same. The fundamental difficulty was deflation; the first essential for recovery was to stop it. This was to be accomplished by stabilizing and strengthening the banking structure, by inducing the bankers to extend credit more freely, and by encouraging businessmen to borrow. To effect these aims, the President characteristically urged voluntary co-operative action. The bankers, with the strong prodding of the President, established the National Credit Corporation. But, although Hoover succeeded in getting the bankers to create the institution, he could not make them operate it to effect the purpose he envisioned. The venture, as we have seen, was both short-lived and ineffectual.

The remarkable result of this entire episode, however, was not its failure but Hoover's reaction to it. What the sudden collapse of the National Credit Corporation proved was not that bankers could not deal with the problem but that they were unwilling to rise above their self-interest to bail out the weaker banks. The bankers, preoccupied with maintaining liquidity and protecting their own banks, preferred to have the federal government undertake the responsibility. Hoover was fully aware of this fact — and he accepted it.[21] Since the bankers were both unwilling and unable to carry out the program voluntarily, and since the program was considered to be a vital one by the President, the only alternative was to have the federal government step in and do the job. It was either that or let the program go by default. In any case, it was clearly useless to persist in saying that the bankers ought to do the job themselves.

This crisis represents an instructive contrast to Hoover's treatment of other problems, such as relief of the unemployed. In the one case, he faced the facts as he found them and acted; in the other, he persistently denied the facts and refused to act. By taking action in the one instance, he departed from his ideals; by refusing to act in the other, he preserved his ideals. He dealt, in other words, with the banking situation pragmatically, but he handled the unemployment problem idealistically.

On January 22, 1932, Hoover signed the act establishing the Reconstruction Finance Corporation. "Its purpose," he announced, "is to stop deflation in agriculture and industry and thus to increase employment by the restoration of men to their normal jobs." [22] "The essence of the problem," Under-Secretary of the Treasury Ogden L. Mills explained, "is to arrest deflation, to make available the credit needed by American business, industry and commerce, and to encourage its use." [23] To master this problem, Hoover expected a great deal of assistance from the Reconstruction Finance Corporation; but there were others, besides the President, who anticipated that much good would come of the new corporation.

"In the Reconstruction Finance Corporation," *Business Week* stated, "the United States has launched against the depression the most powerful offensive force that governmental and business imagination has, so far, been able to command." Even critics, such as T.R.B. of the *New Republic,* were favorably impressed. "There has been nothing quite like it," he declared, "and even in the face of a crisis, it amazes me that it should be going through Congress with so little modification and amendment." [24]

The Reconstruction Finance Corporation, modeled after the War Finance Corporation of World War I days, was capitalized at $500,000,000 by the federal government, and it was authorized to increase its capital by an additional $1.5 billion by issuing debentures. The corporation was allowed to lend to railroads, banks and other financial institutions, such as insurance companies, mortgage loan companies, building and loan associations, and credit corporations. Planned as both a temporary and self-liquidating institution, the corporation was to be terminated at the end of the emergency and liquidated without causing any permanent increase in the nation's fixed national debt.[25]

As the first measure sponsored by the Hoover Administration frankly based on the analogy of war, The Reconstruction Finance Corporation marked a new phase in the President's anti-depression program. It demonstrated that Hoover was prepared to use the power of the federal government in a direct manner when voluntary co-operative action proved insufficient to handle what he considered a vital function. The Reconstruction Finance Corporation introduced the expansion of federal authority in the fight against the depression and thus represented a new departure in Hoover's attitude and policy.

The moratorium and the act establishing the Reconstruction Finance Corporation were only the first two of a series of measures designed to infuse new life into the nation's credit apparatus. On January 23, 1932, Hoover signed an act which provided an additional $125,000,000 capital for the Federal Land Banks. Its purpose, as well as its hope, was that it would help relieve the farm mortgage situation.[26]

Banks of the Federal Land Bank system, the joint-stock land bank system, and the intermediate land banks were faced with the problem that their primary assets, agricultural mortgages, were frozen fast. This made them reluctant to extend additional credit to their customers and unable to make new loans.[27] A similar situation existed in the home mortgage field. Building and loan associations, co-operative banks, homestead associations, trust companies, and insurance companies, as heavy investors in home mortgages, found that their ability to function as credit institutions was seriously hampered, if not completely thwarted, by frozen assets. One banker expressed the common plight before a Senate subcommittee. "There were so many of those banks that were perfectly solvent," he explained,

but they had taken a large portion of their investment in mortgages. Then the public started to take out its money. The banks paid out all the money they had in the vaults. Then they liquidated their bond accounts. Then they began to call loans. Then they got down to the point where they had nothing really left except a small amount of cash and perfectly good mortgages with the depositors still coming to the bank and saying, "We want some of our money." [28]

While many of these institutions were "perfectly solvent," their inability to find a market for their long-term assets caused them to retrench.

What these institutions needed was a discount bank, supported with federal funds, where they might take their sound but frozen home mortgage assets and obtain loans, using the first mortgage as collateral. They wanted, in short, an institution that would do for them what the Federal Reserve System did for the nation's commercial banks.[29]

The Administration proposed to overcome the credit crisis in the home mortgage field through the Home Loan Bank Bill. First recommended by Hoover on November 13, 1931, it was not enacted until July 1932. This act, authorizing the creation of up to twelve Home Loan banks, was patterned after the Federal Reserve Act and was to provide for the rediscounting of mortgages on small homes. Savings banks, insurance companies, building and loan associations, and homestead associations were eligible for membership in the new system, which was intended to assist them in achieving a more liquid position. Mortgage paper, which was not eligible for discount at the Federal Reserve, could now be discounted at the new banks. With greater liquidity these credit institutions could be more lenient with mortgage holders; could meet their depositors' demands for cash; and, in addition, would make them more able and willing to lend to those eager to become home owners. The ultimate objective of this act was to facilitate and encourage residential construction.[30]

The President's second program, however, was helped more immediately by the Glass-Steagall Bank Credit Bill, a measure which was the companion piece of the Reconstruction Finance Corporation. Described by Hoover as a "national defense measure," and regarded by him as "an essential part of the reconstruction program," the bill was approved by both houses of Congress on February 26, 1932, without even a roll call. "Its adoption," the New York *Journal of Commerce* reported, "was a matter of 10 minutes in the House and but three in the Senate, and the vote was a formality." [31] President Hoover signed the bill the next day.

The Glass-Steagall bill amended the rules governing the operation of the Federal Reserve System in two important respects. It broadened the provisions which defined the types of loan paper eligible for rediscount at the Federal Reserve banks, and it permitted the Reserve System to substitute government securities — previously ineligible — for commercial paper as legal backing for Federal Reserve notes.[32] This second provision had far-reaching consequences. Previously, Federal Reserve notes were backed by reserves consisting of 40 per cent in gold and 60 per cent in commercial paper. That is, for every hundred dollars of federal reserve notes, the government was obliged to hold in reserve forty dollars in gold and sixty dollars in commercial paper of not more than six months' maturity. However, the increasing scarcity of commercial paper created a deficiency in the Reserve System's commercial paper holdings, which was made up by using more gold for reserves. This meant that instead of the Federal Reserve System holding only 40 per cent of the total issue of federal reserve notes in gold, the proportion of gold needed for this purpose rose to 75 per cent.[33] As gold replaced commercial paper in meeting the legal reserve requirement for Federal Reserve notes, the amount of free (or uncommitted) gold diminished. If the United States failed to meet all the demands made upon it for gold, the government would have been forced off the gold standard. The fear of this possibility — and Hoover distinctly feared it — had a direct effect upon domestic financial policy, most notably in the Federal Reserve's open-market operations.

The Federal Reserve Board purchased government securities in the open market whenever it wished to encourage an expansion of credit. In buying government securities, the Federal Reserve increased the member bank's credit at the Reserve bank, thereby permitting the member bank to liquidate its indebtedness to the Reserve bank. The difficulty was that, as a member bank retired its loans from the Reserve bank, it recovered the commerical paper which it had given as collateral to secure the loans.[34] In other words, open-market purchases by the Federal Reserve further depleted its already inadequate stock of commercial paper, and tied up more of its free gold as reserves. In such a situation, the Federal Reserve had no alternative but to suspend its open-market purchases and abandon one of its principal methods of expanding credit.

The Glass-Steagall bill resolved this. In open-market buying, the Federal Reserve purchased and accumulated government securities. The Glass-Steagall bill permitted government securities to be used in lieu of commercial paper as backing for Federal Reserve notes, and so the Federal Reserve could proceed with its open-market operations without further depleting the free gold supply. In fact, since the Federal Reserve held such large amounts of government securities, this provision actually freed a good deal of gold and ended the danger of foreign withdrawals.[35]

With the enactment of the Glass-Steagall bill, the Federal Reserve System immediately commenced a program of large-scale, open-market purchases of government securities. At the end of February, the Federal Reserve banks were buying United States government obligations at the rate of about $25,000,000 a week. In April, the weekly rate was stepped up sharply to about $100,000,000, so that by the end of the month $450,000,000 had been added to the Federal Reserve's holdings. *Business Week,* an enthusiastic supporter of this policy, declared, "It is perhaps the most powerful dose of monetary medicine that has ever been applied to the strengthening of the banking system in a similar period of time." And this was only the beginning. Between February and August, the Federal Reserve banks purchased $1.1 billion of government securities. The system's total holdings in August amounted to $1.85 billion, "a level that was maintained throughout the rest of the year." [36]

The massive February-August open-market operation of 1932 was designed to achieve the same purpose that the far more modest 1929–30 open-market policy had failed to accomplish. It was supposed to strengthen the liquid position of the banks, decrease their indebtedness, and allow them to expand their loans. Not only did both attempts have the same purpose but they faced the same difficulties. The Federal Reserve System, through open-market purchases, could create the conditions conducive to lending; it could not, unfortunately, ensure that the bankers would actually lend or, if the bankers were willing to make loans, the businessmen would actually borrow. The Federal Reserve could do everything short of what absolutely needed to be done if its policy were to succeed. Ultimately, the success of the whole program remained at the mercy of the countless decisions made by the nation's bankers and businessmen — decisions strongly influenced by the climate of confidence that happened to prevail at the moment.

Since the climate of confidence — or, more prosaically, the prospect for profitable investment — was decidedly unfavorable, there had to be something to supplement the conditions created by open-market operations. The government had somehow to persuade the bankers and the businessmen to get on with the business of business: buying and selling, lending and producing.

It was this task of persuasion that Secretary of the Treasury Ogden L. Mills attempted to perform in a series of speeches during the latter part of 1931 and all of 1932.[37] In these speeches, Mills revealed himself as a dedicated and forceful exponent of the Hoover policies.

"The most influential factor in bringing about and prolonging the present depression," he stated in October 1931, "is the fall in prices, both of commodites and securities." Mills emphasized this point repeatedly. "The outstanding fact today," he declared in January 1932,

> is that deflation has proceeded too far. Every additional decline in credit and prices and securities brings with it further bank failures, and bank failures in their turn lead to further contraction in credit and prices. The deflation has now reached a point where it feeds upon itself, and where forces working for economic recovery are nullified by the psychological momentum of the downward movement.

In October 1932, Mills cited some disturbing statistics. Since 1929, wholesale commodity prices had declined by 33 per cent, bond prices by 17 per cent, stock prices by 76 per cent, and rents and wages to a slightly lesser extent. Banking difficulties were aggravated by the extensive hoarding of money, while between October 1929 and June 1932, loans and investments of all banks declined by nearly $15 billion. In the same period, foreign investments in the United States were reduced from $3 billion to $600,000,000.[38] All this spelled grave trouble for the nation's banks.

There was also the more elusive psychological factor of pervasive fear. "The real difficulties," Mills explained, ". . . are those inherent in human nature, in the element of fear which seems to possess the souls of men in the face of an uncertain future and in fixed conceptions and attitudes. From my point of view," he concluded, "there is more to fear from frozen minds than frozen assets." Mills here used fear as just another word for the more familiar phrase, lack of confidence. "Business, as we know it," he pointed out, "cannot be conducted without credit, and credit cannot function without confidence." [39]

The government could act — and was acting — to promote an economic climate favorable to an expansion of credit; yet, it could not itself directly expand credit. "Credit," as Mills emphasized,

> cannot be brought into active use by brute force. The increased employment of credit depends upon an expansion of business activity, that is, the buying and selling of commodities, employment of labor and the acceleration of all the manifold economic activities that form part of the modern economic mechanism. Potential credit is a favorable factor to business recovery, but until the credit actually goes to work it can affect neither business nor prices. It will go to work only when the lender feels secure enough to lend, and the borrower confident enough of the use he can make of the money to borrow. [40]

"What is holding us back," Mills repeated, "is uncertainty and lack of confidence." And the Secretary of the Treasury went to great pains to assure the American people that President Hoover thoroughly understood the nature of the economic crisis, and that his second program (or as Mills termed it, "the reconstruction program") was specifically designed to meet and to overcome the difficulty.

Hoover's recent efforts, according to Mills, aimed to achieve two essential objectives. "First, to underpin the credit structure of the country, and, secondly, to counteract the fearful contraction of credit occasioned by the drain of gold and the hoarding of currency." Since the obstacles blocking the realization of these aims were too formidable "to be dealt with by our normal mechanism," "it is clearly the duty and business of Government to cooperate with business in their removal." Yet, although the government had admittedly undertaken a very large role, it would in no way "impair individual initiative, resourcefulness and responsibility." By stressing the continued responsibility of the business community, Mills strongly echoed Hoover's approach. "Our sole purpose in the development of the reconstruction program," Mills explained,

> has been to set free the recuperative and constructive forces within business itself by removing the pressures which were stifling them — to clear away major obstacles so that the nation's business might have an opportunity to do for itself what the Government cannot hope to do for it, and so that the normal vigor of our economic life might again assert itself.

Then, in an explicit statement of political creed, he added:

> I, for one, reject completely the conception of a national economic life directed from Washington as impracticable in practice, incompatible with American character, and inconsistent with the structure and spirit of our institutions.[41]

Hoover's reconstruction program, while it was a "bold one," merely "supplements rather than supplants existing agencies." It neither transgressed nor endangered the American system. For added assurance, Mills explained that "the program was devised to meet extraordinary conditions, and to avert extraordinary dangers. Once they are over," he promised, "it will automatically come to an end."

All this was simply splendid; the Hoover Administration was going to end the depression again, while, at the same time, preserving the American system inviolate. Yet, a nagging doubt remained: how did Hoover and his Secretary of the Treasury propose to transform the potential credit, which the legislative measures of the second program had fostered, into actual credit? In a word, how could they overcome that paralyzing compound of fear, timidity, and caution — that lack of confidence — on the part of the business community which had frustrated all of Hoover's previous efforts?

To deal with this crucial problem, upon which hinged the success or failure of his reconstruction program, Hoover turned once again to his familiar expedient: voluntary, co-operative action.

The new venture in voluntaryism began in New York City late in May 1932, with the organization of a committee of bankers and businessmen, soon known officially as the Federal Reserve District Banking and Industrial Committee. Owen D. Young was the chairman of the committee, and the area of its responsibility was the Federal Reserve district of New York. Similar committees, all composed of six leading bankers and six leading industrialists and businessmen, were to be set up in the other eleven Federal Reserve districts under the over-all direction of Henry M. Robinson. The objective of these committees, Young explained, was "to discover ways and means of putting excess banking credit to work affirmatively to stimulate employment and business recovery." [42] By encouraging co-operative efforts among bankers and businessmen, the committees were to support the bond market, promote new business undertakings, and assist refunding operations. "The whole idea," *Business Week* concluded, "is an effort to promote recovery by normal capitalistic processes of reviving private captial investment through regular banking channels." [43]

On August 26, 1932, the twelve Federal Reserve District Banking and Industrial Committees met at Washington with government officials for the purpose of establishing a central committee for co-ordination. "The purpose of the conference," Hoover explained in his address, "is to better organize private initiative and to coordinate it with governmental activities so as to further aid in the progress of recovery of business, agriculture and employment." This objective, as anyone familiar with the President's methods would have known, was not to be achieved by vesting the committees with governmental authority, but rather through voluntary action. "It is not proposed," the President said, "that you shall have authority from the Government but that you should join in stimulation of organized private initiative of America." [44]

Later in the proceedings, the President's suggestions were reduced to a six-point program by Secretary of the Treasury Ogden Mills. The six points were then adopted by the conference, and a chairman was appointed to head each of the six subcommittees. Each subcommittee was given the responsibility of implementing nationally one item of the six, which included credit extension, capital expenditures, credit for railroads, repair and improvement of homes, relief of home owners, and spreading of jobs. Prominent businessmen were chosen to carry out each subdivision. [45]

The striking fact about all this activity was that it represented nothing new. The underlying conception and the specific measures marked a reversion by Hoover to the original proposals he had persuaded business leaders to accept in the fall of 1929. It was the National Business Survey Conference resurrected. The only difference was that the original committee had been multiplied by six. All the expectations of the second program, all the legislative efforts to shore up the nation's credit institutions were made to hinge once again on the success of a voluntary program. After three years' journeying in search of a solution to the nation's economic paralysis, Hoover was back where he had started. Conservatism, bereft of new ideas, could only repeat its old and discredited formulas.

But had nothing at all been learned from the experience of depression? What was the lesson of the Hoover years?

If President Hoover had acted during the first three years of depression in the way previous depression Presidents had acted, nothing would have been tried and nothing would have been learned. But instead of imitating the example of patient forbearance, President Hoover had established a precedent of action. Although the President's policy was designed to preserve the virtues of individualism, it was not a policy of "rugged individualism." When Hoover invoked the analogy of war, he had in mind the spirit of unity and cooperation of a people at war, and not the vast expansion of federal authority that many others recalled and urged. In leading America in a war against depression, the President mobilized the nation as a voluntary militia force and not as a conscript army.

Voluntary co-operative action was the idea that permeated Hoover's policy against depression. During three years of acute depression, that idea was consistently applied, the method was thoroughly tested, and both the idea and the method proved grievously wanting. Presidential exhortation did not restore confidence; voluntary action was clearly inadequate; a federal banking program was not enough; and the lesson from all this was clear: the power and authority of the federal government would have to be broadly expanded and vigorously used. For many Americans this necessity was as evident as the fact of failure. This is what had been learned.

Unfortunately this was not the meaning which Hoover brought away from the experience. On November 7, 1932, at the end of his campaign for re-election, the President concluded a short radio address with a reaffirmation of his concept of the presidency. "Four years ago," he recalled,

> I stated that I conceived the Presidency as more than an administrative office; it is a power for leadership bringing coordination of the forces of business and cultural life in every city, town and countryside. The Presidency is more than executive responsibility. It is the symbol of America's high purpose. The President must represent the Nation's

ideals, and he must also represent them to the nations of the world. After four years of experience I still regard that as a supreme obligation.[46]

For one who conceived his position as the defender of the nation's ideals, keeping the faith was more vital than following the logic of the facts. In fact, President Hoover's idealism was proof against the facts of failure.

IO

The President, the Press, and Congress

The main trouble is not that business is in the saddle; the trouble is that nobody is in the saddle.* GEORGE SOULE, 1931

. . . Mr. Hoover thus far has failed as a party leader. He has failed as an economist, although thus far he has had no chance to succeed. He has failed as a business leader because of his fatal economic inheritance. He has failed as a personality because of awkwardness of manner and speech and lack of mass magnetism.† ARTHUR KROCK, 1931

By the rough judgments of politics Mr. Hoover finds himself set down as an irresolute and easily frightened man.‡ WALTER LIPPMANN, 1930

Americans in the 1920's delighted in everything "new." It was their favorite adjective because it very aptly reflected the current, pervading social bustle as well as the optimism they felt about their times and their future prospects. With serene confidence, contemporaries adopted "The New Era" as an appropriate term for their time: its achievements, its spirit, and its bounding expectations. Things new were clearly better than the old, and since more and more innovations were anticipated, continued material progress seemed assured.

As one of the heroes of the New Era, Herbert Hoover was both a product and a spokesman of his own times. When he came to label his 1928 presidential campaign speeches, he chose the simple and eloquently revealing title: "The New Day." And in that new day of America's tomorrow, Hoover vowed that poverty would be wiped from the face of the land. Hoover here simply spoke the sanguine language of his fellow citizens in the 1920's.

Hoover was, moreover, to achieve the high promise of the New Era by introducing a *new* method of executive leadership and public administration. The old type of political leader, adept in the ways of politics and politicians — deals, horse-trading, and personal persuasion (the arts of compromise, in short) — was now to be supplanted by a new style of leadership. In place of messy and unseemly compromising there would be the business efficiency and the scientific method, associated in the public mind with Herbert Hoover — the highly successful mining engineer and public administrator. The expectations of a new viable leadership were no more effectively expressed than by Anne O'Hare McCormick, who, in assessing Hoover's first year as President, recalled its hopeful beginnings.

> We were in a mood for magic. Mr. Hoover was inaugurated, and the whole country was a vast, expectant gallery, its eyes focused on Washington. We had summoned a great engineer to solve our problems for us; now we sat back comfortably and confidently to watch the problems being solved. The modern technical mind was for the first time at the head of a government. Relieved and gratified, we turned over to that mind all the complications and difficulties no other had been able to settle. Almost with the air of giving genius its chance, we waited for the performance to begin.[1]

Public policy was now to be based solidly upon verified facts. As another admirer of the Hoover method wrote: "The right approach to the solution of anything is through the facts. Is it a problem of public opinion? Give the public the facts and trust it for the opinion. Is it a policy to be determined? First of all, find the facts." And the proper agency of fact-gathering, according to Hoover, was an investigating commission staffed with experts. When the self-governing American people were provided with all the essential facts, then they would decide what should be done.[2]

Thus Hoover started his presidency with a high reputation and with respect from newspaper correspondents in Washington. When he was Secretary of Commerce, he had been a valuable source of information and news items, and so had established good relations with the news-hungry reporters.[3] As President, he immediately instituted changes in the presidential press conference which appeared to forecast a marked liberalization of Coolidge's stiff and stilted procedure. As one enthusiastic newsman described the new style proposed by Hoover at his first White House press conference, it was all roses:

> Smiling, cordial, expansive, he informed the 200 assembled correspondents that the worn-out Coolidge ghost, "the White House spokesman," had been abolished in favor of a more liberal system. Under the new rules the reporters would continue to submit written questions in advance, but the President's answers would be divided into three categories, as follows: (1) to be quoted directly in the first person; (2) to be attributed to the White House; and (3) to be used as information given by the correspondents upon their own authority, or as "background." The privilege of quotation was new and very desirable.[4]

The roses, as roses will do, wilted and died. Paul Y. Anderson, Washington correspondent for the St. Louis *Post-Dispatch* and the *Nation*, who confessed himself "one of that confiding multitude who acclaimed the new era of candor and freedom inaugurated by President Hoover in his relations with the press," soon recanted and began to criticize Hoover severely for withholding news from the press. "It is my sad duty to report," Anderson announced not sadly but angrily early in 1930, "that the working of this plan has steadily been narrowed and restricted until now less reliable and printable information comes from the White House than at any time while Coolidge was President." Then, in an itemized summary of Hoover's press relations and the reporters' grievances, he continued:

> Written questions have been so consistently ignored that few reporters any longer trouble to submit them. The direct quotations phase has degenerated into a system of Presidential "hand-outs," palpably propagandist in character and seldom responsive to any inquiry. . . . In addition, the practice of having "fair-haired boys," . . . has been resurrected, whereby the President gives private audiences to correspondents who have demonstrated their willingness and ability to publish stories that he particularly desires published.[5]

By 1931 Hoover's relations with the press, in Anderson's estimation, had "reached a stage of unpleasantness without a parallel during the present century." "They are characterized," he added, "by mutual dislike, unconcealed suspicion, and downright bitterness." This judgement was supported by others, such as the *Nation,* which described Hoover's press conferences as a "bitter joke," while another Washington correspondent concluded that "except for a few favorites who cling to the White House or the Rapidan camp, Mr. Hoover has scarcely a friend or defender among the hundreds of working newspaper men of Washington." [6]

The change in newsmen's attitude toward Hoover's press conferences was accompanied by broadened criticism of his methods of leadership and his ability. Eventually, this derogatory news commentary encompassed the man and all his works in what seemed to be an unrelenting and devastating barrage of hostility. For example, even while praising Hoover's new style and its promise, Anne O'Hare McCormick had some reservations on the efficacy of his methods for achieving results. "President Hoover's procedure so far," she wrote at the close of his first year,

> is that of the administrator rather than the executive, of the technical advisor rather than of the leader. There is hardly

a single instance in which he has come out boldly for his own ideas, rallied the people in support of a cause, or given any indication that he considers such crusading the function of the Chief Magistrate. Rather he has taken the problems he found waiting for him on the Executive desk, gathered all the available data on each subject and passed it on to the regular agency to deal with on the basis of the facts.[7]

This mild doubt *sotto voce* was quickly drowned out by the strident sound of trumpets.

Since Hoover had been highly acclaimed by most of the Washington press at his inauguration, the newsmen were obliged to eat a good bit of crow publicly when they made their about-face. They usually began by acknowledging past error or bad judgment, or simply by making a "me-too" confession that they had been badly taken in by campaign rhetoric. "Hoover's role, as he stepped into the national footlights," the *New Republic* recalled, "was a new and noble one. We all remember it well. He was supposed to be the embodiment of the engineering spirit devoted to human ends. He paid no attention to political stratagems or buncombe; his course was guided by candid study of the facts." "It was one of the chief campaign merits of Mr. Hoover, in the eyes of the intelligent," this editor later added, "that he promised to utilize the best brains available. Faced by a problem, he would appoint a commission and abide by its advice. He understood the language of research." Yes, they had all been thoroughly gulled; Hoover was clearly not the man he had once seemed. "His boosters," Heywood Broun complained, "presented him to us under singularly false colors. Here was a great engineer, the great executive. They said that he knew nothing of practical politics and that his worth lay along the lines of quiet unobtrusive efficiency. By now we know that President Hoover's greatest flair — his only one as far as can be ascertained — is a capacity for publicity." [8]

This type of newsman claimed that he, like everyone else,

had been misled by a gigantic and super-efficient publicity campaign. If Hoover was not a genuine success, then certainly he had had a most successful public relations build-up. "During the whole of Mr. Hoover's public life," the *Nation* declared, "he has shown an incorrigible tendency to substitute words for action, to become a hero by publicity, not by deeds." (Imagine the inarticulate Hoover building a ladder of dazzling words to the nation's political pinnacle.) "Never, perhaps," concluded the *Nation*, "has any other person had a personal publicity machine as powerful and effective as the one that made Herbert Hoover President of the United States." [9] Walter Lippmann used the same argument (or rationalization, or belated insight — as you will). "Mr. Hoover's ascent to the Presidency," he remarked,

> was planned with great care and assisted throughout by a high-powered propaganda of the very latest model. He is, in fact, the first American President whose whole public career has been presented through the machinery of modern publicity. The Hoover legend, the public stereotype of an ideal Hoover, was consciously contrived. By arousing certain expectations, the legend has established a standard by which the public judgment has estimated him. . . . For the ideal picture presents him as the master organizer, the irresistible engineer, the supreme economist.[10]

Newsmen, past masters of the art of publicity, would have it that they had been deluded by their own techniques. It was sad, they conceded, but all too true. "Mr. Hoover's best friends agree," one of the Washington newsmen stated, "that he was badly oversold at the peak of an inflationary period and that the subsequent decline in value has made the contrast between the advertising that went with him and what he has been able to deliver, conspicuous to the point of painfulness." So now they must correct the mistake, reinterpret the man, cut his overblown reputation down to human size. Soon they went from one extreme to the other. In reporting the Hoover image as if it were something listed on the New York Stock Exchange, they caused Hoover's stature to fall even lower than the price of the most wretched common stock. The great engineer had become the newsmen's great fall-guy.[11]

The "real" Hoover, now being as mercilessly exposed as the discredited investment trusts, was really the antithesis of the legend. Everything that previously had been said of Hoover or claimed in his favor was now discounted and the very opposite urged as the more accurate picture of the man. Had it been claimed that Hoover was that rare public servant who was governed by the force and logic of facts? Yes, unfortunately, but it was pure nonsense. "Alas," one writer lamented, "what a blow one year of Hoover efficiency has given to the ideal of training and education in the art of government." Another spoke of "Hoover's contemptuous disregard for facts," while the *Nation,* referring to the Administration's optimistic statements on the number of unemployed, asked: "Is there no limit to the effrontery of the President and his official associates in their effort to deceive the public by denying the most patent and notorious facts?" Nowhere was Hoover more vulnerable to criticism than in his persistent failure to make an accurate accounting on the number of unemployed. During his entire administration, unemployment figures continued to be nothing more than educated guesses.[12]

Once convinced that Hoover neither respected nor was guided by the facts, the newsmen entertained second thoughts concerning his new, scientific method of administration. This was particularly evident in the newsmen's revised opinion on the importance of investigative commissions in determining administration policies. Commissions suffered the same fate as Hoover's reputation; they were thoroughly discredited. It was charged that commissions were used as a device to avoid decisions on important but difficult problems.[13] The *New Republic,* while conceding that Hoover employed commissions extensively, insisted that they were not utilized in the impartial spirit of science; instead, they were made to serve political purposes. "In spite of his pretensions," the *New Republic* said of Hoover,

> he does not really make use of the best that science has to offer. Again and again he distorts statistics; in controversial issues of importance he tries to find support for what he wants to believe instead of trying to discover the truth. Though he pretends that he is going to provide a scientific revision of the tariff through a governmental commission, he begins by ignoring the united protest of the economists against the Smoot-Hawley Bill itself. He avoids decisions which he fears might make him unpopular, and in doing so he sometimes makes an unjustified use of the investigation. . . . Instead of executing the recommendation of a commission, he sometimes substitutes the report for the accomplishment, and when he is overtaken by the consequences of failure to act, he simply inaugurates more research.[14]

"Mr. Hoover." another commentator announced more succinctly, "has been one of the most confirmed drifters ever to occupy the Presidency." [15]

Nor was it any longer correct to assert that Hoover was a forward-looking spokesman of a New Era headed for innovation and progress. Hoover now became a conservative who looked worshipfully to the past. "Strangely enough," commented the editor of the *New Republic* on four of the President's speeches late in 1930, "though he praises our government as representative and democratic, Mr. Hoover seems to regard most of the positive activities it might undertake as the intrusion of an alien sovereignty rather than the cooperative action of a people. The look forward turns out to be really a look backward." And then more sharply in conclusion: "Approaching a winter of physical distress which will, without much question, be one of the worst the United States has ever known, Mr. Hoover has been content to burn incense before the altars of his ancestors." [16]

With the foundation of Hoover's reputation thus thoroughly undermined, the superstructure of his achievements and his prestige soon tumbled down amidst a raucous shout of abuse. He was no scientist in government. Nor was he even competent to deal with economic matters. He was accused of indifference in the face of mass suffering: a hardhearted man falsely disguised in the garb of a humanitarian. Any claim that he possessed leadership qualities was now emphatically discounted; he was neither a leader nor a stateman. "Unless statesmanship consists in the safe laboring of the conventional," Walter Millis stated, "Mr. Hoover could hardly lay claim to being a statesman." Qualities once admired and praised were now the basis for a biting criticism. Hoover's personal traits were described as positive disabilities for one in high political office. "He is thin-skinned and sensitive" (one critic ticked off the list); "he is cautious and a little timorous, as he has betrayed time and again. He has not that lust of battle which would stand him in good stead during the unending warfare between the Capitol and the White House. He has not the equipment to be the successful occupant of an elective office . . ." [17]

Yet, the most damaging — and undoubtedly the most permanent — reinterpretation of Hoover was that he did not possess political talents: he was an inept politician. Paul Y. Anderson, of the *Nation,* for one, was an early and consistent critic of Hoover the politician. Immediately after his inauguration, Hoover dealt as President with Congress for the first time in the special session. Anderson was not impressed. "If the special session of Congress demonstrated one thing for certain," he argued, "it was that Mr. Hoover is totally devoid of skill in getting a legislative program adopted by Congress. He simply has no idea of the proper way to go about it."

"From the beginning," he later added, "Hoover's technique in dealing with Congress has been singularly simple and ineffectual. First he threatens; then he runs." Republican leaders, Anderson reported, had come to suspect "that the President is a poor judge of men, that he is unlearned in the elemental rules of the political game, and that he has no talent for avoiding embarrassing situations and no skill in disentangling himself from them." Hoover simply did not know politics or politicians — and while this was once said in his favor, now it was a serious reproach. "He does not understand the game," Anderson insisted, "and seems totally unable to think his way through a situation in advance. Moreover, he is dreadfully handicapped by the personal hostility of most of his own party leaders." [18] In all of this, Anderson simply said very early what other newsmen were soon repeating. [19]

This legion of detractors, starting from some undeniable facts of Hoover's unpopularity and his political difficulties, succeeded in creating a new stereotype of the man by persistent reiteration and exaggeration. A weak President, who was denied even the consolation of personal popularity, Hoover was disliked in the country at large as well as in the halls of Congress. And the politicians' dislike of Hoover even extended to members of his own party. When Hoover was bitterly and personally attacked in Congress, Republican members failed to come to his defense. And this personal hostility, it was claimed, had important political consequences. Personal popularity and political effectiveness were made to go hand-in-hand. Since Hoover obviously did not have the one, he clearly could not have the other. The result of his failure in political astuteness and finesse was political confusion in Washington. Hoover could not control Congress, and without this essential condition for effective political leadership, he was unable to get important legislation enacted. Unable to dominate Congress, Hoover retaliated by obstruction: blocking the legislative measures proposed by Congress. "Other Presidents have tussled with Congress," the *New Republic* described this tug-of-war, "but it is not the usual thing for a President to be dragging at the end of the rope, with heels dug in against motion. He is usually the active one, the one who has a program, the one who demands promptness and decision, while Congress hangs back, disputes, delays. In this case it is the titular leader who balks while the followers try to make headway." [20] The transformation was now complete: the streamlined, efficient Hoover of yesteryear had become the grumpy, bungling, incompetent man in the White House, who was neither leader nor competent politician.

This evaluation of Hoover the man, the politician, the President was the work of many hands and voices. While writers of the *New Republic* and the *Nation* were certainly conspicuous in their sustained, sweeping criticism of the President and all his works, they constituted merely the solo voices in a chorus of reproach. Similar denunciations and nearly identical denigrations of Hoover's reputation were expressed in *Scribner's,* the *Atlantic, Current History, Harper's, Survey,* the *North American Review,* and others.[21] Hoover was unfortunate in the near-unanimous abuse he received from all directions: a simultaneous, devastating assault.

In the course of time, much of the vindictive bitterness which characterized contemporary news reporting on Hoover has dimmed and been forgotten. The detailed charges and aspersions have faded with the years. But a residue remains; an important residue, as it turns out, since it forms an essential element in the historical evaluation of President Hoover. He remains to this day a favorite illustration of the ineffectual leader, the inept politician, the weak President.

Curiously, Hoover himself has inadvertently contributed some bricks and mortar to support the credibility of this interpretation. In his *Memoirs,* Hoover speaks often and vehemently of his difficulties with Congress. He complains of the serious delay in enacting important measures; the time wasted by Congress that delayed recovery; despite his own inclinations, Congress refused to co-operate; and, as a consequence, much of his program was persistently blocked. In describing his relations with Congress, Hoover uses such phrases as "political sabotage," "sabotage and obstruction tactics," "irresponsible congressional actions," and, finally, depicts himself as "badly battered about." Yet, despite all these difficulties, Hoover claims that ultimately, after serious delays, he won most of the battle. None the less, Hoover unintentionally confirms much of what his critics had charged him with — inability to master the political techniques of leadership in a democratic system.[22]

Before 1937, an incoming President normally had a lull of nine months between his inauguration on March 4 and the first meeting of Congress on the following December. Hoover enjoyed no such period for adjustment to his new office and preparation for legislative matters before he dealt with the national legislature. During the 1928 presidential campaign, Hoover had responded to the demand of agricultural spokesmen, led by Senator William E. Borah of Idaho, for immediate farm relief by announcing that he would, if elected, immediately call congress into special session to consider a farm relief bill and a revision of the tariff.[23]

Three days after his inauguration, Hoover honored his pledge by calling for a special session. On April 15, 1929, the Seventy-first Congress convened to deal with two of the more thorny problems in American politics. Republicans controlled both houses by wide margins. In the Senate, there were 56 Republicans to 39 Democrats and one Farmer Labor representative. The situation in the House was more lopsided: there the Republicans held a majority of 103 at the opening of the special session. Numbers, at least, were on Hoover's side.[24]

On the pressing issue of farm relief, a bill meeting Hoover's specifications was quickly reported to the House by the Committee on Agriculture. Efforts by farm representatives to attach the export debenture plan to the administration bill were defeated. In the Senate, Hoover confronted a more determined opposition. The Committee on Agriculture ignored Hoover's opposition to the export debenture plan, made explicit in a letter he wrote to the chairman of the committee, Senator Charles L. McNary, and reported out a bill with the plan. The bill, as amended, was then accepted overwhelmingly by the Senate. In conference between the two houses, however, the House members supported Hoover and refused to accept the debenture plan. The Senate, opposed by the President and the House, was forced to yield.[25] The Agricultural Marketing Act, approved June 15, 1929, minus the export debenture plan, was practically a carbon copy of what Hoover had promised in his campaign speeches.

The second concern of the special session — tariff revision — was not so expeditiously resolved. The administration's original intention was for a limited revision of tariff rates on agricultural schedules only. This hope was disappointed when both the House Committee on Ways and Means and the Senate Committee on Finance decided upon a general revision. Again, however, Republican discipline in the House prevailed and the tariff bill was passed on May 28, 1929.[26]

The tariff fight continued in the Senate, and it continued through the close of the special session, on November 22, 1929, and into the second session, which began on December 2, 1929. A coalition of western Republicans and regular Democrats, led by Senator George W. Norris of Nebraska, opposed the administration on two major points. They wished to curtail the President's power under the flexible provision,[27] and they were determined to tack on the export debenture plan as an amendment to the tariff bill. In writing the bill, the coalition momentarily succeeded in their aims; but, in conference with the House, these two features were removed. The Hawley-Smoot bill, approved by the President on June 17, 1930, was a high protective tariff; but, since Hoover consistently supported protection before, during, and after his administration, the tariff bill represented a political victory for him over his opponents.[28]

Since Hoover's initial program for dealing with the depression depended primarily upon voluntary effort (and that program coincided in time with the three sessions of the Seventy-first Congress),[29] his requests for new legislation were minimal. Yet, on those matters requiring legislative enactment, it was invariably Hoover's preference rather than those of his opponents which prevailed. His success here was due to the effective partnership he had with the House of Representatives throughout all the sessions of this congress. Hoover did ask for and did receive an income-tax reduction; he requested a $150,000,000 appropriation for public works which the Democrats at first attempted to increase, but finally agreed to a sum slightly below Hoover's figure. And, while the President approved two of Senator Wagner's bills on unemployment (one providing for expanded employment statistics and the second for advanced planning of public works), he stopped the third — a bill creating a system of federally supported employment exchanges — with a pocket veto. Hoover also vetoed Senator Norris's bill on Muscle Shoals, a veto which caused no surprise, since he had made clear his dislike of measures putting the federal government in business. In fact, Hoover suffered only one major defeat; his veto of the measure allowing World War I veterans to borrow up to 50 per cent of their adjusted service certificates was overridden.[30]

During the third session of the Seventy-first Congress, an attempt was made to force Hoover to call an extra session. Senators Norris and Borah, together with Democrats interested in securing legislation for the relief of the unemployed, led this move. The extra session, if it were called, would bring the members of the new Seventy-second Congress to Washington nine months before its scheduled, regular session. Since the 1930 congressional elections had gone strongly against the Republicans, Hoover was not anxious to hurry the acquaintance. Republican strength in the Senate (including insurgent Republicans) was reduced from 56 to 48 — and these now confronted 47 Democrats and one Farmer Labor. In the House, the original count was 218 Republicans, 216 Democrats, and one Farmer Labor representative.[31] Hoover consistently opposed the idea of an extra session for this congress — and there was none.

In the months after the elections in 1930, fourteen vacancies occurred in the House membership. New elections favored the Democrats so that by the opening of the first session of the Seventy-second Congress, on December 7, 1931, the Democrats held 219 seats, the Republicans 214, and the lone Farmer Labor member. At the same time politicians prepared for more politics. President Hoover, the Progressives (Republicans and Democrats), and the Democrats each devised programs for dealing with the depression.

The Progressives, while numerically the most insignificant group, made the greatest show of activity. It was suggested that they break away from both major parties and run their own candidate for President on an independent third party ticket. Professor John Dewey, chairman of the League for Independent Political Action, in December 1931 urged Senator George Norris to stand as the Progressives' candidate for the presidency.[32] Norris declined the invitation, and thereafter he continued to oppose the idea of a third party. "I can see, as the outcome of such a fight," he later wrote,

> that, while the probabilities would be that Hoover would be renominated, yet, if we succeeded in defeating him, we should not be able to name a satisfactory candidate. This, briefly

stated, has been my idea from the beginning. I must say to you, however, that in the progressive Republican group in the Senate, with whom I have had very many conferences, I stand almost alone in this attitude. In fact, I know of but one Senator in this progressive group who agrees with me. The others all believe that a fight ought to be made with a progressive candidate, whether we win or whether we lose. . . .

I have gone over the whole ground with Governor Pinchot, as well as with the progressives in the Senate. I have told the same thing to many other progressives outside of the Senate. . . . It will not be possible, in my judgment, to get this progressive group to enter a movement at this time for an organization that will support some progressive on an independent ticket.[33]

"One of the discouraging things," Norris wrote plaintively to one of his Nebraska constituents, "is that the people expect so much of this little progressive group. They expect so much more than we can possibly accomplish. We are . . . so often expected to perform the impossible. We are sometimes criticized by our friends because we do not accomplish more. What the people do not see . . . is that we are not in control. We are . . . in a very small minority. We are plugging along, fighting an entrenched machine." As an alternative to a third party, Norris, together with Senators Cutting of New Mexico and La Follette of Wisconsin (Republicans), Wheeler of Montana and Senator-elect Costigan of Colorado (Democrats), issued a call, a few days before the adjournment of the Seventy-first Congress, for a Progressive conference to meet in Washington.[34]

"In the midst of depression," announced this little band of Progressives,

the nation is without effective political or economic leadership. The session of Congress now drawing to a close has revealed the imperative need of formulating a constructive legislative program. Months of misery in the industrial centres and on the farms have disclosed lack of any proposals for the solution of one of the greatest economic crises ever confronting the nation.

The disastrous results of failing to meet the responsibilities of this situation will be increasingly evident during the next nine months. The signers of this call for a conference . . . believe that there are certain economic and political problems affecting the welfare of every citizen which must be solved if this Republic is to endure, and realize for all that fullness and richness of life which was the hope that spurred our forefathers to found this government.

"We believe," Norris added, "a legislative program may be evolved and something accomplished of value to the country."

Among the people who assembled at the conference on March 11–12, 1931, were sixteen Representatives and fifteen Senators, economists, university professors, social workers, labor leaders, editors, and businessmen.[35] The Progressives broke down the basic issues requiring immediate attention into five categories, with a committee formed to consider each and devise a legislative program: (1) unemployment and industrial stabilization (La Follette, chairman); (2) tariff revision (Costigan); (3) representative government (Cutting); (4) public electric power (Norris); and (5) agriculture (Borah). Appalled with the futility of past efforts, each speaker urged the need for new and more effective recovery programs, Yet, they ended by generally concentrating on one favorite idea. Economists Leo Wolman and George Soule, for example, called for the beginnings of centralized, economic planning; Father John A. Ryan saw more immediate hope in a $5 billion appropriation for public works; while the President of the American Federation of

Labor, William Green, emphasized the importance of insti-
tuting the five-day work week.[36] While these and other suggestions were urged and debated, none the less, the conference adjourned without adopting a definite program. Instead,
the five committees were charged with the responsibility of
devising concrete proposals for each area during the remainder of the spring and the summer.

While the Progressives debated publicly, Democratic leaders more quietly consulted among themselves about the necessity for a comprehensive program in the next congress.
Some of their efforts behind-the-scenes can be seen through
the correspondence of Senator Thomas J. Walsh. In answer to
a letter from Bernard M. Baruch in which he had urged that
the Democrats should "agree on some definite policy or policies on the great questions that confront us" before the next
congress met, Walsh wrote: "Having in mind the possibility . . . that the Democrats would organize the House without Progressive aid, Cordell Hull and I have been trying to
outline a scheme of legislation for that body so that the party
might be said to have a real constructive program and not
be merely a party of negation." [37] Later, in writing at
greater length to Senator Joseph T. Robinson of Arkansas,
Walsh recounted his labors to formulate a program in more
detail. "I have been giving some thought, as you surmise," he
told Robinson,

> to the matter of a program for the ensuing session, partic-
> ularly as respects action by the House to which the public
> will look for Democratic policies. I am not sure that it would
> be wise to put out anything in the nature of a legislative
> program. More attention will be paid to what is actually
> done than to what is promised or proposed. We ought, ac-
> cordingly, to help as we can in the preparation of bills for
> presentation to the House, duplicates of course . . . in our
> Chamber. I might say in this connection that Mr. Garner's

secretary communicated to me ten days ago a request from
him that I give him some aid in the preparation of a gifts
tax bill. I have consulted in connection with that work with
Cordell Hull and on tariff legislation with him and with
Costigan.[38]

More specifically, Walsh listed eight problems which he
felt that the Democrats should be prepared to cope with legis-
latively. "Something must be done," he suggested first, "to
afford immediate relief to the unemployed." The choice
seemed to be either a public works program or the dole. "If
we shun the dole and advocate public works," Walsh reasoned, "we almost drive the President to join with us." A
closely related problem was to devise plans "to avoid unemployment in the future." Here the Democrats need simply
follow the proposed legislation worked out by Senator
Robert F. Wagner of New York. Democrats also needed to
concoct a tax program that would provide the necessary funds
to balance the budget. Walsh believed that this could be accomplished by increasing the income tax rates and the inheritance tax in the higher brackets, supplemented by gift taxes
and a luxury sales tax.

Although Walsh thought that "it would probably be inad-
visable to attempt a general [tariff] revision," he felt that the
party should repeal the existing flexible provision and reduce
some duties by separate bills on items where general agreement prevailed. Then, continuing the list, he stated: "As the
conviction is general that the debacle of October, 1929,
ushering in the period of depression was the result of gam-
bling on the stock exchange, efforts should be made to eliminate or minimize the evil." He remarked that he was himself
working with Professor William Z. Ripley on proposals requiring that corporations with stock listed on the Exchange
should make more "elaborate reports" to the investing public. On banking: "We must try to make effective the promise

at the President's conference of legislation to rehabilitate the farm loan banks." In addition, there should be made some "drastic provision against the expansion of broker's loans." The seventh item, farm relief, was both important and perplexing. "On this," Walsh wrote, "I confess my inability to propose anything, but we would be well advised, I think, to follow if possible any proposals of the general farm organizations." Finally, the Democrats should declare against "any reduction of the debts owing the government by foreign governments without reliable assurances that the relief afforded will not be utilized to increase armaments or maintain military establishments." [39]

The first session of the Seventy-second Congress, for which all of these efforts and plans were aimed, convened on December 7, 1931. "Often lacking either in leadership or in the will to follow," Professor E. Pendleton Herring observed, "Congress went its muddled way working against great odds and confronted with tasks of great complexity." [40] The Democrats organized the House — the first Democratic majority there since 1919 — and elected as their Speaker, John Nance Garner of Texas. This ended Hoover's alliance with the House against the Senate. Now, perforce, he must lean upon the Senate, where the slim Republican majority (48 Republicans, 47 Democrats, one Farmer Labor) was made extremely uncertain by the presence of "insurgent" or progressive Republican members.

The session considered and acted upon an impressive amount of important legislation, but these measures were neither those of the Progressives nor the Democrats. It was the President's recommendations which were enacted into law. The essential planks of Hoover's second program — the Reconstruction Finance Corporation, creation of a system of Home Loan Discount Banks, the Glass-Steagall bill amending the Federal Reserve's discount and open-market regulations, and an additional appropriation of $125,000,000 for the

Federal Land Bank System — all were adopted. Hoover also approved the Norris-LaGuardia Act limiting the use of the injunction in labor disputes, and two measures which he regarded as inadequate: a tax bill and another for governmental economy and reorganization.

At every opportunity during this session, Hoover had emphasized the absolute necessity of balancing the budget. In a four-month period — between December 1931 and April 1932 — he issued twenty-one messages, statements, and addresses on this subject. Yet, on this vital matter, he remained disappointed. Neither the new tax bill nor the economy measure was sufficient to bring federal finances into balance. Hoover also failed to secure banking legislation to protect depositors and to check speculation.

On other issues Hoover objected to, he succeeded either in blocking the legislation or in having the bills rewritten to meet his requirements before permitting them to pass. In one instance — the House veterans bonus bill — the mere threat of a veto was sufficient to induce the Senate to reject the measure. In all, Hoover used the veto seven times, including such controversial issues as the tariff and unemployment relief bills.[41]

The entire question of using public funds for unemployment relief, by means either of an expanded public works program or through direct federal assistance to the states, produced a protracted struggle between Hoover and Congress. During the session, a number of different relief bills were considered, including those sponsored by Senators La Follette and Costigan, Robinson, Wagner, and the Garner bill in the House. Hoover bitterly opposed the Garner plan, calling it "the most gigantic pork barrel ever proposed to the American Congress," and "an unexampled raid on the public treasury." After much controversy and debate, Wagner's measure was substituted for Garner's in the Senate; and it was this proposal, providing a total of $2.3 billion for relief, which passed both houses on July 9, 1932. Hoover promptly vetoed it. A new bill, meeting Hoover's specific recommendations, was then quickly drafted, passed by Congress on July 13, and signed by the President on July 21, 1932.[42]

The Emergency Relief and Construction Act, an amendment to the Reconstruction Finance Corporation Act, was "to relieve destitution, to broaden the lending powers of the Reconstruction Finance Corporation, and to create employment by providing for and expediting a public-works program." To achieve these ends, the act authorized the R.F.C. to use $300,000,000 of its funds for direct loans to the states "to be used in furnishing relief and work relief to needy and distressed people and in relieving the hardships resulting from unemployment . . ." No more than 15 per cent of the total fund was to be loaned to any one state. Title II permitted the R.F.C. to grant loans to the states in support of financing public projects "which are self-liquidating in character . . ." It could also make loans to private corporations which were formed exclusively to provide low-income housing or were engaged in slum clearance. Title III provided $322,224,000 for emergency construction of certain authorized public works.[43]

This legislation, passed in the very shadow of the forthcoming 1932 presidential election, constituted a marked departure from Hoover's philosophy of government. Together with the creation of the R.F.C. itself, and the attempt at supporting agricultural prices by the stabilization corporations, the policy of federal aid to the unemployed did not jibe with the tenets of the President's American system, nor, for that matter, did the creation of the R.F.C. itself or the attempt to support agricultural price through stabilization corporations. In all these instances, Hoover was pushed beyond what he considered desirable limits by impelling economic and political considerations. None the less, once Hoover had accepted these measures, he typically attempted to limit their operation within narrow bounds. The Emergency Relief and Construction Act, for example, stipulated that before relief funds were granted to the states, the governor must personally ". . . and in each application so made . . . certify the necessity for such funds and that the resources of the State or Territory, including moneys then available and which can be made available by the State or Territory, its political subdivisions, and private contributions, are inadequate to meet its relief needs." Each governor, in short, was required to sign a poverty oath before federal funds would be granted. State governments would find similar difficulties in securing loans for public works projects by the requirement that these projects be self-liquidating, which was defined in the act as including only those projects which "will be made self-supporting and financially solvent and if the construction cost thereof will be returned within a reasonable period by means of tolls, fees, rents, or other charges . . ." [44] The R.F.C. interpreted these safeguards strictly in order to hold down federal expenditures.

Governor Gifford Pinchot of Pennsylvania, in a letter to the R.F.C. dated three days before Hoover signed the relief act, requested a loan of $45,000,000, the full limit permitted to one state. In justification of his request, Pinchot summarized Pennsylvania's plight and its inability to care for its unemployed.

> There are more than 1,150,000 people totally unemployed in Pennsylvania today. . . . It amounts now to more than 30 per cent of the normal working population of the state. . . .
>
> In addition another 30 per cent of our workers are now employed half time or less. Thus only about two-fifths of Pennsylvania's normal working population now holds full-time jobs.
>
> The State is forbidden by its Constitution to incur a debt of over one million dollars — and hence cannot borrow funds

for relief. The levy of a graduated income tax is similarly prohibited. It would take at least two years to amend the Constitution. . . .

The Legislature last winter appropriated ten million dollars for relief. Little or nothing of that ten million dollars is left today. . . .

It is certain that the State, through the Legislature now in special session, cannot provide adequate funds for relief.

The State's political subdivisions are also practically helpless. Most of them have already reached the limit of their legal borrowing power. . . .

The situation in Philadelphia, with 326,000 totally unemployed and 236,000 partially employed is desperate. Private funds are wholly exhausted. Three million dollars, borrowed by the City under special legislation beyond its normal borrowing capacity, have been spent. . . .

In the Pennsylvania coal fields during the last six months unemployment has grown 87 per cent. But in the same period the number of persons on relief has increased 198 per cent, or more than twice as fast. With the exhaustion of almost all sources of aid this story is repeated throughout the State.

Growing unemployment and exhaustion of life savings and of relief money is working havoc with the health of our people. The State Department of Health records a general increase of disease. . . . Twenty-eight per cent of our school children are suffering from malnutrition.

"The $45,000,000," he concluded, ". . . would do no more than keep our destitute citizens on an irreducible minimum of food alone until next April and no longer." [45] The letter closed with the poverty certificate signed by the governor.

This letter, eloquent in its description of Pennsylvania's plight and indicative of not only one state's problems but of a national condition, failed in its object. The $45,000,000 was not forthcoming. Instead, it brought about a protracted controversy between Pinchot and the directors of the R.F.C. over the intent of the law, and whether or not the state had actually exhausted its resources for dealing with the unemployment relief problem. At the close of a conference between a Pennsylvania delegation, led by Pinchot, and the board of directors of the R.F.C., Atlee Pomerene, the chairman, announced, "After a full hearing, we feel persuaded that the legislature of the State of Pennsylvania, and its several political sub-divisions, have not done their full duty with respect to the furnishing of funds for relief purposes." And, he concluded: "We shall defer action with regard to relief for Pennsylvania until we know what the legislature will do for the relief of its own people." [46]

Under this prod, the Pennsylvania legislature appropriated $12,000,000 for relief on August 19, 1932; Pinchot hastily wrote to Pomerene urging immediate reconsideration of his request. Still there were further delays, more hearings were held, additional information was required of Pennsylvania. Finally, on September 8, 1932, Pinchot exploded. "The result of all these maneuvers," he wrote, "is to convince the people of Pennsylvania that the Reconstruction Finance Corporation intends to let us have just as little relief as possible and that little after the longest possible delay. Our people are not in sympathy with splitting hairs while children starve." Then, in conclusion: "I am not asking for a gift but for an advance. I am not asking for this advance as a favor. I am asking for it as the unquestionable right of Pennsylvania under the law of Congress. I am asking for it now, at once, and I ask that too as the right of Pennsylvania." [47] On September 22, 1932, the R.F.C. granted the sovereign state of Pennsylvania its first loan — the sum of $2,500,000. And the struggle continued with undiminished bitterness; but the administration had made its point: federal funds for relief and public works would be doled out with a grudging hand.

The dispute between Pinchot and the R.F.C. illustrates a related but more important dispute between Hoover and Congress. While Congress was busily considering ways of spending money for programs to lift the country out of the depression, Hoover was preoccupied with balancing the budget as an essential prerequisite for economic recovery. There could be no meeting of minds while such a basic difference in outlook existed. "The great problem before the world today," Hoover insisted,

> is a restoration and maintenance of confidence. I need scarcely repeat that the maintenance of confidence in the financial stability of the United States Government is the first contribution to all financial stability within our borders, and in fact in the world as a whole. Upon that confidence rests the credit of the states, the municipalities, all our financial institutions and industry — it is the basis of recovered employment and agriculture.[48]

The difference in viewpoint between the Seventy-second Congress and a disapproving Chief Executive on legislative proposals came down to Hoover's underlying assumption that recovery waited upon the restoration of confidence — which in turn could not come so long as there was the slightest suspicion about the fiscal integrity and soundness of national finances. Great hopes, great days waited upon the realization of a balanced budget. On this point, Hoover held as fast as though he grasped a lifeline.

The burden of expounding the validity of this viewpoint to the American people fell upon the willing shoulders of Hoover's chief lieutenant, Ogden L. Mills. In a long series of speeches and in letters to influential businessmen and bankers, the Secretary of the Treasury explained how the success of Hoover's second program hinged upon balancing the federal budget. Speaking before the Economic Club of New York on December 14, 1931, Mills conjured up the chaos that would be let loose if the national credit were impaired:

> Our currency rests predominately upon the credit of the United States. Impair that credit and every dollar you handle will be tainted with suspicion. The foundation of our com-

mercial credit system, the Federal Reserve Banks, and all
other banks which depend upon them, are inextricably tied
into and dependent upon the credit of the United States
Government. Impair that credit today, and the day after,
thousands of development projects . . . will stop; thousands
of businessmen dependent upon credit renewals will get
refusals from their bankers; thousands of mortgages that
would otherwise be renewed or extended, will be foreclosed.
Merchants who would buy on credit, will cancel orders; factories that would manufacture on part capacity at least will
close down.

It is true that a distressingly large majority of the wage
earners of this country are now out of work. But we must
not forget that a majority still have enough work to make
a living. We have lost much; but we have infinitely more to
lose.[49]

"What is holding us back," Mills informed another audience,
"is uncertainty and lack of confidence." And the cause of this
was clear: "Business fears an unbalanced budget and unsound monetary legislation more than anything else, and it
is this fear and uncertainty rather than any shortage of
money or credit which is today preventing recovery, credit
expansion and price increases." [50]

"If I were a dictator and could write my own ticket," Mills
confided to Owen Young, "the first two goals which I would
reach for would be the balancing of the budget of the United
States Government and the return to the gold standard by
Great Britain." [51] And in a letter to Myron C. Taylor, the
New York lawyer, Mills referred to a speech he had recently
given, and remarked:

It seems to me that the points to be stressed are that fear
and uncertainty play a predominant part in holding back an
economic revival. There is fear and uncertainty as to the
willingness of our Government to put its own house in order;

to balance its budget, and to live within its income. There is fear and uncertainty as to tampering with our monetary system, and there is fear and uncertainty as to conditions abroad and the possibility of further collapse.[52]

The solution, the way of allaying all these fears, was for the government to put its "finances in order and to refrain from any extravagant program of expenditures . . ." This was said in the closing days of the Hoover administration as Mills apprehensively anticipated the coming of the Roosevelt regime.

Hoover's firm conviction of the correctness of this analysis steeled him through the chaotic closing session of the Seventy-second Congress.[53] While Congress gropingly attempted to move the government into new channels of action, the President consistently opposed all measures involving additional expenditures or new expansions of federal authority. Proposals for the domestic allotment plan, expansion of credit and money, establishment of a National Economic Council for centralized planning, huge public works programs, and additional assistance to the nation's unemployed were all raised. None of them was enacted.

Herbert Hoover had his convictions and his own program; there was room for none other. He most certainly was an unpopular President. But despite this disability, Hoover was neither an ineffectual politician nor a weak President. Weak Presidents are ignored or brushed aside; Hoover remained a formidable, effective obstacle to new ideas and innovations until he was blasted away by the presidential election returns.

I I

Conclusion: The Dry Well of Conservatism

> We are confronted by the most extraordinary and baffling paradox. We know that, judged by any economic standards, past or present, the United States is a remarkably rich country, richer than anything dreamed of by any nation in the world. We have vast natural resources, splendid factories, the most complete and up-to-date mechanical equipment, and the finest trained workmen on earth. And yet, there isn't the slightest doubt that . . . we have been and are still going through the most severe depression ever experienced in this country.* OGDEN L. MILLS, 1932

> America in the depression behaves much like a rat in a maze.† GEORGE SOULE, 1933

In the Hoover years, poverty in the midst of plenty became a daily condition of life, a palpable reality. Americans had merely to peer from their private windows at the world outside to see the economic confusion which gripped their land. The national economy — that marvelous machine of abundance — faltered, shook, and then ground to a near halt. But worst of all, the stalled engine defied all the efforts at repair that an energetic, inventive people could devise. Farmer, worker, banker, businessman, the economist, and the public official were all appalled by what they saw. Great resources amid scarcity, a magnificent industrial plant and widespread want, green fields and hunger — here was the paradox. For contemporaries to state the paradox became something of a commonplace, but it ever remained a commonplace uttered in anguish and despair.

Thus the poverty of abundance was the central theme of these years, while America's principal preoccupation was the prolonged exertion to devise means for mastering the predicament. The responsibility centered upon the nation's leadership — public and private — which exercised its control of major institutions to cope with the most serious challenge that the democracy had faced since the First World War.

In fact, the Great Depression posed a challenge to American institutions more difficult than that of war. The techniques of waging war had been tested and refined; the techniques of combating an economic depression in a highly developed industrial economy had not even been begun. The Hoover Administration made the first attempt to use the national government to fashion effective means for controlling the violent fluctuations of the American economy.

Since the autumn of 1929 and during the next four years, the national government had broken away from the fatalism and inactivity of the past, decided that the business cycle was subject to man's control, and inaugurated programs to bring the cycle under that control — an extremely important advance for the nation. No more significant event has occurred in the domestic affairs of the American people during this century. This was the great achievement of President Hoover — an achievement from which nothing can detract, not even failure.

The very fact of novelty itself accounts in good part for the initial directon of the new experiment. President Hoover's program represented a new beginning, and most beginnings tend to be halting, groping, and modest. They tend also to follow closely the pattern of convention. The first program was built close to the people, it relied heavily upon the nation's established institutions, and it drew fully from the leadership of men of recognized power and prestige, all of which was quite natural. Before extreme measures can even be considered, more conventional ones must first be tried. Before coercion will be tolerated, the full potentialities of persuasion must be exhausted. The voluntary militia must first thoroughly demonstrate its incompetence before a professional conscript army can be created. Only when voluntaryism has been tried and found wanting will a free, democratic people be prepared for more extreme measures.

The direction of the new experiment was also dependent upon the personal attitudes of the most powerful and influential man in the nation. President Hoover's predilections were those of an idealist and a conservative. His program was designed to serve the double purpose of overcoming the economic crisis while preserving the American system as he conceived it. His initial program exhausted the possibilities of voluntary co-operative effort. At the end of two years of depression, the ideas and expedients of this approach were used up and discredited. The well of conservatism had been pumped dry.

Hoover did not suddenly abandon his efforts to preserve American ideals and the American system. When his initial program began to merge into the second one, by 1931, he still continued to depend upon voluntaryism. But with the creation of the Reconstruction Finance Corporation in January 1932, federal authority was no longer confined to presidential exhortation. Now federal power was directly committed. And so a new departure began.

The new departure, however, was restricted by old ideas and old assumptions. The R.F.C., for example, was established as a temporary agency; it was authorized to issue debentures and not bonds; and it was to be self-liquidating. Hoover considered it an emergency agency, not a permanent addition to the federal apparatus. This coincided with one of the President's unshakable assumptions: there was nothing fundamentally wrong with the American system. The basic difficulty, he felt, was the psychological one of a persistent but unjustified lack of confidence among many Americans. While Hoover remained exclusively preoccupied with the investing public, others felt that the principal difficulty was with another sector of the public — the consuming public. By 1932, Congress was considering a number of suggestions for relieving the consumers' distress. There were proposals for currency inflation, credit inflation, a large-scale public works program, federal assistance to the unemployed, and a plan to expand the Reconstruction Finance Corporation so that it could lend funds to practically anyone. With the exception of credit inflation, these measures were all opposed by the President.

As Hoover viewed these programs, they all boiled down to the common element of increased federal spending. He opposed them all because they threatened his long-term effort to balance the federal budget. The President firmly believed that a balanced budget was essential for preserving the integrity of the government's financial position. Not only would it protect the government's credit, it would strengthen the bond market, reassure the investing public, and give a powerful boost to confidence. As firmly persuaded as ever that his program would restore the American economy to its normal, prosperous operation, Hoover saw a balanced budget as a vital condition for success.

The President's distaste for enlarging federal authority, together with his analysis of the depression, accounts for his determined opposition to expanding federal activities which he himself had started. In the autumn of 1929, Hoover led this new experiment; by mid-1932, he was the figure hindering the nation in its search for new ways to master the problem which had eluded all his exertions. Herbert Hoover's great achievement was that he led the nation in its struggle against depression; the fact that he forestalled others from continuing and widening the experiment was his great failure.

And, yet, despite the President's intentions, these years anticipated the politics of the future. The American people and the nation's leaders comprehended the failure of Hoover's methods. Hard experience taught them that new methods must now be tried. They understood that the federal government must assume the decisive role in the next ventures. And this public willingness to permit a vast increase of federal power stands in retrospect as one of the most important consequences of the Hoover years. For Hoover, this was an unwanted, an unintended result. He had labored to create a psychological climate of opinion conducive to public confidence; instead, he succeeded in fostering a necessary precondition for the legislative outburst of the New Deal years: the public's conviction that the job of recovery would require the forceful use of federal power. It is primarily in this important sense that Herbert Hoover prepared the way for Franklin Delano Roosevelt and the New Deal.

Notes

ABBREVIATIONS

CLM   Charles L. McNary
FCA   Federal Credit Administration
GWN   George W. Norris
LC   Library of Congress
NA   National Archives
OLM   Ogden L. Mills
PECE   President's Emergency Committee for Employment
POUR   President's Organization on Unemployment Relief
RFC   Reconstruction Finance Corporation
RG   Record Group
TERA   Temporary Emergency Relief Administration
TJW   Thomas J. Walsh

PART ONE

* Thomas N. Carver, "Capitalism Survives," *Current History*, XXXVI (April 1932), 1.

CHAPTER 1

* Herbert Hoover, Address to the President's Conference on Unemployment, September 26, 1921, in *Report of the President's Conference on Unemployment* (Washington, D.C.: Government Printing Office, 1921), p. 28.
† John M. Keynes, "The World's Economic Outlook," *Atlantic*, CXLIX (May 1932), 525.
1. J. M. Kenworthy, "The Way Back to Prosperity," *Current History*, XXXVI (April 1932), 129.
2. "Less Work — More Pay," *Nation*, October 15, 1930, p. 393.
3. Christian Gauss, "Recovery — A Longer View," *Scribner's*, XCII (December 1932), 337.
4. Jasper Jarrow, "Egg-Throwing Champions of Turlock," *Atlantic*, CXLVII (December 1931), 695.

5. Frank J. Warne, "A Plea for Economic Intelligence," *Review of Reviews*, LXXXIV (August 1931), 69.

CHAPTER 2

* Herbert Hoover, *The New Day, Campaign Speeches of Herbert Hoover 1928* (Stanford, California: Stanford University Press, 1928), p. 5.

† Ibid. p. 42.

1. Herbert Hoover has been unusually consistent in his viewpoint. Most of the ideas expressed in the campaign, during his presidency, and later, in his *Memoirs*, are to be found in *American Individualism*. Not only are the ideas expressed time and again, but often they are taken verbatim from this early formulation.

2. *The State Papers and Other Public Writings of Herbert Hoover*, ed. William S. Myers (New York: Doubleday, Doran and Co., Inc., 1934), I, 398.

3. Hoover, *The New Day*, p. 180.

4. Ibid. p. 181.

5. Ibid. p. 41.

6. Hoover, *State Papers*, I, 293.

7. Ibid. I, 198.

8. Ibid, I, 296.

9. Hoover, *The New Day*, pp. 162–3.

10. Ibid. p. 163.

11. Ibid. pp. 164–5.

12. Ibid. p. 213.

13. Ibid. p. 42. While it is important to know Hoover's thinking in this matter, it is also worth recalling that the designation that most adequately covers Hoover's philosophy is enlightened conservatism.

14. Hoover, *The New Day*, pp. 164, 179.

15. Ibid. pp. 182–3.

16. Hoover, *State Papers*, I, 189, 197–8.

17. Ibid. I, 502–3.

18. Ibid. I, 582.

19. Ibid. I, 382.

20. Ibid. I, 34.

21. Hoover, *The New Day*, p. 53.

22. Ibid. pp. 21–3.

23. Ibid. p. 196.

CHAPTER 3

* George Soule, "Which Way Out?" *Forum,* LXXXIII (March 1933), 148.
1. John K. Galbraith, *The Great Crash, 1929* (Boston: Houghton Mifflin Co., 1954), pp. 103–5.
2. William S. Myers and Walter H. Newton, *The Hoover Administration: A Documented Narrative* (New York: Charles Scribner's Sons, 1936), p. 3; Philip Klein, *The Burden of Unemployment* (New York: Russell Sage Foundation, 1923), pp. 5–7.
3. *Report of the President's Conference on Unemployment* (Washington, D.C.: Government Printing Office, 1921), p. 19; Klein, *The Burden of Unemployment,* p. 58ff.; U.S. Congress, Senate, Committee on Appropriations, *Drought Relief and Unemployment — LaFollette Resolution,* Report No. 1264, 71st Cong., 3d Sess., 1931, p. 68.
4. For expressions of this viewpoint, see *Commercial & Financial Chronicle,* May 10, 1930, pp. 3249–50; May 24, 1930, pp. 3600–3607; June 21, 1930, pp. 4289–91.
5. Stuart Chase, "The Case for Inflation," *Harper's,* CLXV (July 1932), 206.
6. Herbert Hoover, *The Memoirs of Herbert Hoover* (New York: Macmillan Co., 1952), III, 30.
7. Ibid. III, 31; *New York Times,* October 26, 1929, p. 1; Hoover, *State Papers,* I, 133; "After the Whirlwind," *Nation,* November 27, 1929, p. 614.
8. Hoover, *State Papers,* I, 133–4.
9. *New York Times,* November 21, 1929, p. 1; *Commercial & Financial Chronicle,* November 23, 1929, pp. 3262–5; November 30, 1929, pp. 3415–19.
10. Hoover, *State Papers,* I, 134.
11. Ibid. I, 136.
12. American Farm Bureau Federation, National Grange, and the Farmers' Educational and Co-operative Union.
13. *Commercial & Financial Chronicle,* November 23, 1929, p. 3264.
14. *New York Times,* December 6, 1929, p. 1.
15. Hoover, *State Papers,* I, 181–3.
16. Garet Garrett, "The First Hoover Year," *Saturday Evening Post,* March 1, 1930, p. 122; *Current History,* XXXI (January 1930), 775; "Mobilizing Business Stability," *Business Week,* December 4, 1929, pp. 30–31. For a succinct statement of this viewpoint, see Julius

Barnes's radio address of January 25, 1930, reprinted in part in *Commercial & Financial Chronicle*, February 1, 1930, pp. 701–2.

17. Money loaned on a day-to-day basis to stock brokers and subject to being called back the next day.

18. Alfred L. Bernheim, "Are Wages Going Down?" *Nation*, November 5, 1930, pp. 489–91.

19. For a vigorous dissent to this view of construction as a major, causal factor in the 1929 market crash, see *Commercial & Financial Chronicle*, January 31, 1931, pp. 721–5.

20. Hoover, *The New Day*, pp. 79–80; William T. Foster and Waddill Catchings, "Mr. Hoover's Road to Prosperity," *Review of Reviews*, LXXXI (January 1930), 50–52.

21. *Commercial & Financial Chronicle*, November 23, 1929, p. 3208; Paul U. Kellogg, "Security Next," *Survey*, December 1, 1931, p. 237.

22. "Whither Prices?" *American Bankers Association Journal*, XXIII (August 1930), 102.

23. Quoted by *Commercial & Financial Chronicle*, November 28, 1931, p. 3502.

24. Soule, *Forum*, LXXXIII (March 1933), 148.

25. "Now Carry It Through," *Business Week*, December 4, 1929, p. 44; Foster and Catchings, *Review of Reviews*, LXXXI (January 1930), 50–52; Alfred L. Bernheim, "Prosperity by Proclamation," *Nation*, December 25, 1929, p. 772; "What Hoover Has Done," *New York Times*, December 1, 1929, Section III, p. 4.

26. The origin of all the proposals of Hoover's initial program can be found in the general recommendations made in the *Report of the President's Conference on Unemployment* (1921). Hoover, as chairman of this conference, told the delegates that, "The remedies for these matters must in the largest degree lie outside of the range of legislation. It is not consonant with the spirit or institutions of the American people that a demand should be made upon the public treasury for the solution of every difficulty. The Administration has felt that a large degree of solution could be expected through the mobilization of the fine cooperative action of our manufactures and employers, of our public bodies and local authorities. . . ." pp. 19–21, 29.

CHAPTER 4

* "Hoover Plays His Part," *New Republic*, December 11, 1929, p. 56.

1. L. M. N., "Not on the Ticker Tape," *New Republic*, July 6, 1932, p. 205.

2. Julius H. Barnes, "Business Grows Up," *Saturday Evening Post*, June 14, 1930, p. 56.

3. Wallace B. Donham, "The Failure of Business Leadership and the Responsibility of the Universities," *Harvard Business Review*, XI (July 1933), 419.

4. Joseph H. Foth, *Trade Associations* (New York: Ronald Press, 1930), pp. 3–4.

5. Ibid. pp. 5–6.

6. Ibid. pp. 4–5.

7. William E. Leuchtenburg, *The Perils of Prosperity* (Chicago: University of Chicago Press, 1958), p. 42.

8. Foth, pp. 36–7, 231–4.

9. Hoover, *Memoirs*, II, 169–73.

10. Ray L. Wilbur and Arthur M. Hyde, *The Hoover Policies* (New York: Charles Scribner's Sons, 1937), p. 47.

11. *Commercial & Financial Chronicle*, January 8, 1930, p. 400; November 23, 1929, p. 3264; "Business Takes Stock of Itself," *Business Week*, December 18, 1929, p. 5. In 1929 there were approximately 1500 national and international trade associations in the United States. This figure is cited by Foth, p. v.

12. Hoover, *State Papers*, I, 183.

13. *New York Times*, November 22, 1929, pp. 1–2.

14. Ibid. April 30, 1930, p. 1. By 1932 some 500 of the trade associations were members of the United States Chamber of Commerce. This figure is given by Julius H. Barnes, "Government and Business," *Harvard Business Review*, X (July 1932), 413. *Commercial & Financial Chronicle*, February 1, 1930, p. 701.

15. Julius H. Barnes, "Facing the Larger Problems of Business Management," *Journal of Business of the University of Chicago*, III (July 1930), 272.

16. *New York Times*, November 24, 1929, p. 2; January 26, 1930, p. 17.

17. Julius H. Barnes, "The New Ebb and Flow of Industry," *Survey*, June 1, 1930, p. 48; Barnes, *Saturday Evening Post*, June 14, 1930, p. 56.

18. Barnes, *Journal of Business of the University of Chicago*, III (July 1930), 276; radio address of January 25, 1930, over the National Broadcasting System, printed in part in *Commercial & Financial Chronicle*, February 1, 1930, pp. 701–2.

19. Barnes, *Journal of Business of the University of Chicago*, III (July 1930), 276; Barnes, "Business in the New Year," *Review of Reviews*, LXXXI (January 1930), 48; *Commercial & Financial Chronicle*, February 1, 1930, p. 701.

20. The members of the Executive Committee were a veritable Who's Who of business leadership; their names and private business positions are listed in *New York Times,* December 13, 1929, p. 1.

21. Barnes, *Journal of Business of the University of Chicago,* III (July 1930), 275; the members of the Advisory Committee, along with the associations they represented, are listed in *New York Times,* December 1, 1929, p. 24.

22. The Reports of the National Business Survey Conference are reprinted in *Commercial & Financial Chronicle,* January 25, 1930, p. 531; March 29, 1930, pp. 2105–6; May 3, 1930, pp. 3065–6; June 7, 1930, pp. 3952–3; July 5, 1930, pp. 19–21; October 4, 1930, pp. 2134–5.

23. Ibid.; *New York Times,* September 9, 1931, p. 21. While Hoover discusses the Washington conferences in his *Memoirs,* he makes no mention whatsoever of the National Business Survey Conference, the organization which developed from these meetings.

24. "President Leads Movement for Stabilization," *Business Week,* November 27, 1929, p. 4; *Commercial & Financial Chronicle,* June 28, 1930, p. 4509; November 30, 1929, p. 3416; January 25, 1930, p. 541.

25. Ibid. November 23, 1929, p. 3262; quoted in ibid.

26. Ibid. November 30, 1929, p. 3418; January 25, 1930, p. 541.

27. "Construction Has Prospects — And Problems," *Business Week,* February 5, 1930, pp. 4–5; *Commercial & Financial Chronicle,* February 1, 1930, p. 701; *Bulletin of the National Business Survey Conference,* February 5, 1930, p. 3.

28. *Commercial & Financial Chronicle,* March 8, 1930, p. 1545; *New York Times,* April 5, 1930, p. 18.

29. Reprinted in *Commercial & Financial Chronicle,* July 5, 1930, p. 5.

30. Ibid. May 3, 1930, p. 3065; June 7, 1930, p. 3952; June 28, 1930, p. 4509; November 8, 1930, p. 2979; December 20, 1930, p. 3976.

31. "The President's Emergency Committee for Employment," *Congressional Digest,* x (January 1931), pp. 3–4; *Commercial & Financial Chronicle,* October 25, 1930, p. 2631. As part of the organization of the new committee, a division on construction was established.

32. Colonel Woods, "The Emergency Committee at Work," *Congressional Digest,* x (January 1931), 5; New York *Journal of Commerce,* November 2, 1930, quoted by *Commercial & Financial Chronicle,* November 8, 1930, p. 2979.

33. *United States Daily,* November 1, 1930, quoted by *Commercial & Financial Chronicle,* November 8, 1930, p. 2979.

34. *New York Times,* December 11, 1930, quoted by *Commercial & Financial Chronicle,* December 20, 1930. p. 3976.

35. The F. W. Dodge Corporation figures are based upon contracts awarded in the 37 eastern states, which, it estimates, cover 91 per cent of total construction in the United States. The figures given here are rounded off in the thousands. "Historical Record of Contracts Awarded 37 Eastern States by Project Type, Valuation, & Floor Area" (New York: n. n., 1939).

36. Joseph B. Hubbard, "The Construction Industry in the Depression: Attempts at Stabilization," *Harvard Business Review*, XI (January 1933), 148–9; "Public Building Leads the Way, But It's Down Instead of Out," *Business Week*, April 13, 1932, p. 27.

37. "Whither Prices?" *American Bankers Association Journal*, XXIII (August 1930), 102; press statements of November 21, 1929, quoted by *Commercial & Financial Chronicle*, November 23, 1929, pp. 3264–5.

38. "This Time They Did Not Cut Wages," *Business Week*, January 1, 1930, p. 23.

39. New York *Journal of Commerce*, February 3, 1930, reprinted in *Commercial & Financial Chronicle*, February 8, 1930, p. 896; *New York Times*, February 1, 1930, reprinted in *Commercial & Financial Chronicle*, February 8, 1930, p. 896.

40. Quoted by *Commercial & Financial Chronicle*, March 15, 1930, p. 1730; May 3, 1930, p. 3064; May 31, 1930, p. 3820.

41. "Employers Try to Keep Wage Truce," *Business Week*, May 21, 1930, p. 6.

42. Ibid.; Howard Florance, "But Wages Have Come Down," *Review of Reviews*, LXXXIV (July 1931), 86–8.

43. "The Building Trades Stand Pat on Wage Despite Unemployment," *Business Week*, June 18, 1930, pp. 9–10.

44. *Commercial & Financial Chronicle*, August 16, 1930, p. 998.

45. Ibid. April 4, 1931, pp. 2466–7.

46. "Wage Truce Hoover Asked Violated By Both Sides," *Business Week*, May 14, 1930, p. 7.

47. "June–July Wage Cuts Exceeded Increases, Changing Long Trend," *Business Week*, August 20, 1930, p. 12.

48. Reprinted in the *Commercial & Financial Chronicle*, October 18, 1930, p. 2477.

49. The effort of business to stabilize employment is discussed in Chapter 7.

50. *Commercial & Financial Chronicle*, February 1, 1930, p. 671; May 23, 1931, pp. 3792–3.

51. Ibid. September 26, 1931, pp. 1990–91; Robert W. Morse, "Reductions in Wages," *Current History*, XXXV (November 1931), 264–5;

address on October 23, 1931, at the American Iron and Steel Institute, quoted by the *Commercial & Financial Chronicle,* October 31, 1931, p. 2834.

52. *Commercial & Financial Chronicle,* September 26, 1931, p. 1991; "Rush of Wage Cutting Follows Big Steel's Lead," *Business Week,* October 7, 1931, p. 6.

53. *Commercial & Financial Chronicle,* September 26, 1931, p. 1963.

54. André Maurois, "How You Have Changed," *Forum,* LXXXV (June 1931), 324.

55. Elmer Davis, "Confidence in Whom?" *Forum,* LXXXIX (January 1933), 31; William T. Foster, "Better than the Bonus," *Forum,* LXXXVIII (August 1932), 88; "The Failure of Big Business," *Nation,* May 25, 1932, p. 586; Donham, *Harvard Business Review,* XI (July 1933), 418.

56. Gerald W. Johnson, "Bryan, Thou Shouldst Be Living," *Harper's,* CLXIII (September 1931), 385–91; G. W. Johnson, "The Average American and the Depression," *Current History,* XXXV (February 1932), 671–5; *New Republic,* November 19, 1930, pp. 4–5; March 4, 1931, pp. 58–9; John T. Flynn, "Mobilizing Deflation," *Forum,* LXXXIII (February 1930), 65–9; *Business Week,* October 29, 1930, p. 40; February 25, 1931, p. 48; *Nation,* April 29, 1931, p. 467.

CHAPTER 5

* Ray B. Westerfield, "Defects in American Banking," *Current History,* XXXIV (April 1931), 17.

1. "Here's What —," *Business Week,* November 5, 1930, p. 40; Edward S. Martin, "With Conventions in Prospect," *Harper's,* CLXV (July 1932), 255.

2. Harold Laski, "The Limitations of the Expert," *Harper's,* CLXII (December 1930), 101; Bertrand Russell, "The Modern Midas," *Harper's,* CLXVI (February 1933), 327–34; Edward S. Martin, "Coming Events, Including the Millennium," *Harper's,* CLXVI *(December 1932),* 125–8.

3. George W. Alger, "Other People's Money," *Atlantic,* CXLVI (December 1930), 736.

4. James T. Adams, "The Responsibility of Bankers," *Forum,* LXXXVI (August 1931), 81; John T. Flynn, "Investment Trusts Gone Wrong, I," *New Republic,* April 2, 1930, p. 181.

5. Garet Garrett, "Wall Street and Washington," *Saturday Evening Post,* December 28, 1929, p. 81; see also, E. C. Harwood and Robert

L. Blair, *Investment Trusts and Funds* (Cambridge, Mass.: American Institute for Economic Research, 1937), pp. 32–3.

6. Garrett, *Saturday Evening Post,* December 28, 1929, p. 81.

7. Adams, *Forum,* LXXXVI (August 1931), 81.

8. William T. Foster, "Better than the Bonus," *Forum,* LXXXVIII (August 1932), 88.

9. "Still To Be Done," *Business Week,* October 14, 1931, p. 48; Francis H. Sisson, "The Strength of Our Banking System," *Review of Reviews,* LXXXVI (December 1932), 30.

10. In 1929, 1177 of the state chartered banks were also members of the Federal Reserve System. The total number of banks, both national and state, in the System was therefore 8707; Sisson, *Review of Reviews,* LXXXVI (December 1932), 30.

11. J. M. Daiger, "Confidence, Credit, and Cash," *Harper's,* CLXVI (February 1933), 283; Merle Thorpe, "Cheerful Facts About 1930," *World's Work,* LX (May 1931), 51.

12. Quoted by *Commercial & Financial Chronicle,* November 23, 1929, p. 3264; Hoover, *State Papers,* I, 145, 182.

13. "Banking in 1930," *Business Week,* January 1, 1930, p. 25; quoted by *Commercial & Financial Chronicle,* October 4, 1930, p. 2128.

14. Daiger, *Harper's,* CLXVI (February 1933), 281.

15. "Banking in 1930," *Business Week,* January 1, 1930, p. 25.

16. *Annual Report of the Federal Reserve Board* (Washington: Government Printing Office, 1934), p. 18; ibid. 1931, p. 4.

17. Ibid. 1932, p. 6; *Commercial & Financial Chronicle,* May 9, 1931, p. 3391.

18. Member bank reserves are kept at the Federal Reserve banks. If the reserve requirement were a straight 10 per cent for all deposits, then for every $100 in deposits there would be required $10 for reserves. At this time, reserve requirements were 3 per cent for time deposits, and 7 to 13 per cent for demand deposits.

19. "Here's What—," *Business Week,* November 5, 1930, p. 40. For a detailed explanation of how this can be accomplished by the banking system, see W. Randolph Burgess, *The Reserve Banks and the Money Market* (New York: Harper & Bros., 1936), p. 7ff.

20. Address delivered in Washington on March 20, 1930, before the American Automobile Association. Reprinted in *Commercial & Financial Chronicle,* March 22, 1930, p. 1955.

21. "General Review of the Year 1930," *Survey of Current Business,* XI (February 1931), 4; *Annual Report of the Federal Reserve Board* (Washington: Government Printing Office, 1931), pp. 1, 7–8.

22. *Commercial & Financial Chronicle,* November 22, 1930, p. 3247; Daiger, *Harper's,* CLXVI (February 1933), 286.

23. *Annual Report of the Federal Reserve Board* (Washington: Government Printing Office, 1931), p. 17.

24. Daiger, *Harper's,* CLXVI (February 1933), 283–4.

25. Ibid. p. 284.

26. *Commercial & Financial Chronicle,* December 6, 1930, p. 3573.

27. Ibid. December 13, 1930, pp. 3745–6; December 20, 1930, pp. 3982–4; *Annual Report of the Federal Reserve Board* (Washington: Government Printing Office, 1931), p. 18.

28. Reprinted in *Commercial & Financial Chronicle,* January 10, 1931, pp. 184–5.

29. *Annual Report of the Federal Reserve Board* (Washington: Government Printing Office, 1932), p. 4; U.S., Congress, Senate, Subcommittee of the Committee on Banking and Currency, *Hearings, on S. 1,* 72nd Cong., 1st Sess., 1931, p. 115; Daiger, *Harper's,* CLXVI (February 1933), 285.

30. Quoted by *Commercial & Financial Chronicle,* March 21, 1931, p. 2074.

31. "Banking Situation Improves by Dint of Long, Hard Work," *Business Week,* September 16, 1931, p. 5.

32. "Next Steps," *Business Week,* October 21, 1931, p. 48; Alfred L. Bernheim, "Are Wages Going Down?" *Nation,* November 5, 1930, p. 489; Leo Wolman, "Objections to Wage-Cutting," *Current History,* XXXV (October 1931), 20–24.

33. *New York Times,* April 2, 1931. Reprinted in *Commercial & Financial Chronicle,* April 4, 1931, pp. 2466–7; *United States Daily,* April 3, 1931. Reprinted in *Commercial & Financial Chronicle,* April 11, 1931, p. 2691; quoted in "The Diminishing Wage," *Nation,* October 7, 1931, p. 351; quoted by *Commercial & Financial Chronicle,* April 25, 1931, p. 3080.

34. Speech of May 19, 1931, before the Brotherhood of Railway Trainmen. Reprinted in *Commercial & Financial Chronicle,* May 23, 1931, pp. 3821–2.

35. "Wisdom of Steel's Wage Cut Yet to Be Proved by Outcome," *Business Week,* May 13, 1931, p. 56; Stuart Chase, "The Case for Inflation," *Harper's,* CLXV (July 1932), 206; Wolman, *Current History,* XXXV (October 1931), 24.

36. William T. Foster and W. Catchings, "Must We Reduce Our Standard of Living?" *Forum,* LXXXV (February 1931), 74–9.

37. "Thunder on the Right," *Business Week,* May 13, 1931, p. 56.

38. Foster, *Forum,* LXXXVIII (August 1932), 89.

39. U.S., Congress, Senate, Subcommittee of the Committee on Manufacturing, *Hearings, on S. 6215, National Economic Council,* 71st Cong., 1st Sess., 1931, pp. 372–3.

40. Ibid. pp. 373–4; *Commercial & Financial Chronicle,* September 12, 1931, pp. 1670–71.

41. *Commercial & Financial Chronicle,* September 12, 1931, p. 1670.

42. *Annual Report of the Federal Reserve Board* (Washington: Government Printing Office, 1932), pp. 18–19.

43. Hoover, *Memoirs,* III, 84.

44. "Emergency Pool to Help Bankers May Serve to Stop Deflation," *Business Week,* October 14, 1931, pp. 5–6.

45. Robert W. Morse, "President Hoover's Plan to Check the Depression," *Current History,* XXXV (November 1931), 263.

46. Hoover, *Memoirs,* III, 86.

47. Hoover opposed the idea of reviving the War Finance Corporation until the very last moment. Proponents of the R.F.C. included private bankers and most importantly, Eugene Meyer, Governor of the Federal Reserve Board. See, Gerald D. Nash, "Herbert Hoover and the Origins of the Reconstruction Finance Corporation," *Mississippi Valley Historical Review,* XLVI (December 1959), 455–68.

48. Hoover, *Memoirs,* III, 86; "Developments in President Hoover's Program to Stabilize Credit," *Congressional Digest,* X (December 1931), 300.

49. At the time, "United States government securities, paper 'arising out of actual commercial transactions' maturing in 90 days, and agricultural paper maturing in 9 months" were eligible by law for rediscount at the Federal Reserve banks. "Proposal to Broaden Reserve Base Debated," *Business Week,* October 21, 1931, pp. 5–6.

50. Morse, *Current History,* XXXV (November 1931), 263–4; "Developments in President Hoover's Program to Stabilize Credit," *Congressional Digest,* X (December 1931), 300.

51. Hoover, *Memoirs,* III, 88–93. Reprinted in the *Federal Reserve Bulletin,* XVII (October 1931), 551–3. Governor Harrison's statement is reprinted in ibid. p. 553.

52. "Developments in President Hoover's Program to Stabilize Credit," *Congressional Digest,* X (December 1931), 300.

53. Paul M. Atkins, "The National Credit Corporation," *Review of Reviews,* LXXXV (January 1932), 68; "Still To Be Done," *Business Week,* October 14, 1931, p. 48.

54. "Bank Relief Pool Organizes, Begins Raising $500-Million Fund," *Business Week,* October 21, 1931, p. 5.

55. See the explanation given by Under-Secretary of the Treasury,

Ogden L. Mills. Reprinted in *Commercial & Financial Chronicle*, October 10, 1931, p. 2366.

56. "Emergency Pool to Help Banks May Serve to Stop Deflation," *Business Week*, October 14, 1931, p. 6; quoted by *Commercial & Financial Chronicle*, October 10, 1931, p. 2303.

57. "Hoover's Golden Torch to Thaw Frozen Assets," *Literary Digest*, October 17, 1931, pp. 5–6; Atkins, *Review of Reviews*, LXXXV (January 1932), 48.

58. Hoover, *Memoirs*, III, 97.

59. *Commercial & Financial Chronicle*, December 26, 1931, p. 4195.

60. U.S., Congress, Senate, Subcommittee of the Committee on Banking and Currency, *Hearings, on S. 1*, 72nd Cong., 1st Sess., 1931, pp. 54–5, 68.

61. Ibid. pp. 67–8.

62. Ibid. p. 176.

63. Rexford G. Tugwell, "Flaws in the Hoover Economic Plan," *Current History*, XXXVI (January 1932), 530. At the end of January 1932, when the Corporation was closing up its operations, it had made, according to the *Wall Street Journal*, "664 loans to 560 banks, the total loans and commitments amounting to $144,000,000." Quoted by *Commercial & Financial Chronicle*, March 5, 1932, p. 1697.

CHAPTER 6

* Hoover, *The New Day*, p. 53.

† Speech of Alexander Legge, Chairman of the Federal Farm Board, before the Chamber of Commerce of the United States, 1930. Reprinted in *The Agricultural Marketing Act* (Washington: Chamber of Commerce of the United States, 1930), p. 13.

1. Hoover, *State Papers*, I, 32.

2. Ibid.

3. The proportion exported varied with different staples; generally, at this time, approximately 25 per cent of the wheat crop was exported; cotton, between 20 and 25 per cent; corn and oats, less than 1 per cent; and livestock, between 7 and 8 per cent. See U.S., Congress, Senate, Committee on Agriculture and Forestry, *Hearings, on S. 123, S. 653, etc., Farm Relief*, 72d Cong., 1st Sess., 1932, pp. 66–7.

4. Testimony of S. H. Thompson, president of the American Farm Bureau Federation, in U.S., Congress, Senate, Committee on Agriculture and Forestry, *Hearings, Farm Relief Legislation*, 71st Cong., 1st Sess., 1929, p. 28.

5. Ibid. pp. 34, 224ff.; U.S., Congress, Senate, Committee on Agriculture and Forestry, *Hearings, on the Agricultural Situation*, 72d Cong., 1st Sess., 1931, pp. 102, 124.

6. For extended discussion and testimony on these plans, see U.S., Congress, Senate, Committee on Agriculture and Forestry, *Hearings, Farm Relief Legislation*, 71st Cong., 1st Sess., 1929, especially Parts II, III, V.

7. George W. Norris to E. W. Rossiter, Decatur, Nebraska, June 19, 1929, in LC, GWN MSS., Box T5B1.

8. Hoover, *The New Day*, pp. 17, 24.

9. Ibid. p. 190, 20–21, 190–95, 103, 22–3, 19, 59.

10. Hoover, *State Papers*, I, 34.

11. Hoover, *The New Day*, p. 19.

12. Ibid. pp. 194–6; Hoover, *State Papers*, I, 34.

13. U.S., *Statutes at Large*, XLVI, Part 1, 11–19.

14. U.S., *Congressional Record*, 71st Cong., Special Sess., 1929, LXXI, Part 1, 125, 129, 369–70; U.S., Congress, Senate, Committee on Agriculture and Forestry, *Hearings, Farm Relief Legislation*, 71st Cong., 1st Sess., 1929, pp. 3–5. The Senate approved the bill, without the export debenture plan, by a vote of 54 to 33, and 8 not voting, U.S., *Congressional Record*, 71st Cong., Special Sess., 1929, LXXI, Part 2, 1269.

15. Ibid. Part 1, 128, 157–8, 296–7, 312ff.

16. Letter from George W. Norris to Senator Peter Norbeck, South Dakota, November 23, 1928; copies sent to Senators Curtis, Borah, McNary, and Brookhart, in LC, GWN MSS., Tray 5, Box 1; Norris to John A. Harvey, Ogden, Kansas, April 1, 1929, in ibid.; Norris to E. Bossemeyer, Jr., May 2, 1929; Norris to Walter Howell, May 2, 1929, in ibid.; Norris to George Peek, May 3, 1929, in ibid.

17. Thomas J. Walsh to Mrs. George F. Stillman, Valier, Montana, September 16, 1930, in LC, TJW MSS., Box 259; Walsh to A. W. Ricker, St. Paul, Minn., January 12, 1931, in ibid.

18. Peter Norbeck to George W. Norris, November 19, 1928, in LC, GWN MSS., Tray 5, Box 1; Norbeck to Charles L. McNary, November 19, 1928, in ibid.; telegram from Charles L. McNary to Herbert Hoover, November 7, 1928, in LC, CLM MSS., Box 5; statement on the Agricultural Marketing Act, 1929, in LC, CLM MSS., Box 23; Walsh to E. R. Kindler, Billings, Montana, December 11, 1930, in LC, TJW MSS., Box 259; Norris to M. W. Osborn, Sidney, Nebraska, June 19, 1929, in LC, GWN MSS., Tray 5, Box 1.

19. Alexander Legge, *The Agricultural Marketing Act*, pp. 13–16.

20. Speech before the American Institute of Co-operation, Baton Rouge, La., July 30, 1929, in Minutes of the Federal Farm Board, NA, FCA, RG 103, I, 47–9, 54.

21. Ibid. p. 53.

22. Statement on the Agricultural Marketing Act, 1929, in LC, CLM MSS., Box 23.

23. Alexander Legge to Charles L. McNary, October 8, 1929, in Minutes of the Federal Farm Board, NA, FCA, RG 103, II, 378.

24. Figures of the Department of Agriculture, cited in Minutes of the Federal Farm Board, NA, FCA, RG 103, I, 52.

25. *First Annual Report of the Federal Farm Board* (Washington: U.S. Government Printing Office, 1930), pp. 7–8; Federal Farm Board, *A Report of the Activities of the Federal Farm Board* (Washington: U.S. Government Printing Office, 1930), pp. 1–2.

26. *First Annual Report of the Federal Farm Board,* 1930, p. 8.

27. Federal Farm Board, "Cooperative Marketing of Farm Products," Bulletin No. 10 (June 1932), p. 26.

28. *Second Annual Report of the Federal Farm Board,* 1931, p. 5.

29. Minutes of the Federal Farm Board, NA, FCA, RG 103, II, 477–8, 510–11.

30. U.S., Congress, Senate, Report of the Committee on Agriculture and Forestry, pursuant to S. Res. 42, *Activities and Operation of the Federal Farm Board,* 74th Cong., 1st Sess., 1935, p. 10.

31. Ibid. pp. 10–11; *First Annual Report of the Federal Farm Board,* 1930, pp. 29–30.

32. U.S., Congress, Senate, Report of the Committee on Agriculture and Forestry, pursuant to S. Res. 42, *Activities and Operation of the Federal Farm Board,* 74th Cong., 1st Sess., 1935, p. 11; *First Annual Report of the Federal Farm Board,* 1930, pp. 32–4.

33. U.S., Congress, Senate, Report of the Committee on Agriculture and Forestry pursuant to S. Res. 42, *Activities and Operations of the Federal Farm Board,* 74th Cong., 1st Sess., 1935, p. 11; U.S., Congress, Senate, Committee on Agriculture and Forestry, *Hearings, on the Agricultural Situation,* 72nd Cong., 1st Sess., 1931, p. 8.

34. *Third Annual Report of the Federal Farm Board* (Washington: U.S. Government Printing Office, 1932), p. 66.

35. U.S., Congress, Senate, Report of the Committee on Agriculture and Forestry, pursuant to S. Res. 42, *Activities and Operation of the Federal Farm Board,* 74th Cong., 1st Sess., 1935, pp. iii–iv.

36. *First Annual Report of the Federal Farm Board,* 1930, pp. 35–6.

37. *Second Annual Report of the Federal Farm Board,* 1931, pp. 37, 63.

38. Alexander Legge to Senator Thomas J. Walsh, February 14, 1931, in LC, TJW MSS., Box 260.

39. U.S., Congress, Senate, Committee on Agriculture and Forestry, *Hearings, on the Agricultural Situation,* 72nd Cong., 1st Sess., 1931, p. 153.

40. Ibid. p. 73.

41. Ibid. pp. 43, 46, 68; U.S., Congress, Senate, Report of the Committee on Agriculture and Forestry, pursuant to S. Res. 42, *Activities and Operation of the Federal Farm Board,* 74th Cong., 1st Sess., 1935, pp. 10–11.

42. Tom Connally to A. Legge, July 25, 1929; Elmer Thomas to Carl Williams, October 18, 1929; O. H. Cross to A. Legge, March 10, 1930; Elmer Thomas to Herbert Hoover, July 21, 1930; H. P. Fulmer to A. Legge, August 15, 1930; Tom Connally to Herbert Hoover, August 21, 1930; Willis G. Sears to Walter Newton, June 20, 1931; L. J. Dickinson to James C. Stone, June 24, 1931; Arthur Capper to J. C. Stone, July 9, 1931; Wright Patman to J. C. Stone, August 13, 1931, in NA, FCA, RG 103, Box 1.

43. U.S., Congress, Senate, Committee on Agriculture and Forestry, *Hearings, on the Agricultural Situation,* 72nd Cong., 1st Sess., 1931, pp. 101–2, 123–4, 153–9.

44. Ibid. pp. 55–7, 57–9, 107, 141–6.

45. Press statement, December 31, 1932, in LC, CLM MSS., Box 23.

46. George W. Norris to H. W. Renquist, July 20, 1932, in LC, GWN MSS., Tray 8, Box 4.

CHAPTER 7

* Stuart Chase, "Prosperity — Believe It or Not," *Nation,* December 25, 1929, p. 774.

1. Paul U. Kellogg, "Security Next," *Survey,* December 1, 1931, p. 238.

2. H. A. Batten, "The Slave Complex," *Atlantic,* CLI (June 1933), p. 733.

3. Henry R. Mussey, "Fighting Unemployment," *Nation,* December 10, 1930, p. 641.

4. Alice Hamilton, "State Pensions or Charity?" *Atlantic,* CXLV (May 1930), 687; "Will New York Lead?" *Nation,* September 10, 1930, p. 262.

5. Stuart Chase, "The Nemesis of American Business," *Harper's,* CLXI (July 1930), 129; Kellogg, *Survey,* December 1, 1931, p. 238; U.S.,

Congress, Senate, Subcommittee of the Committee on Commerce, *Hearings, on S. 3059, S. 3060, and 3061, Unemployment,* 71st Cong., 2d Sess., 1930, p. 39.

6. *Commercial & Financial Chronicle,* November 1, 1930, p. 2803; Hoover, *State Papers,* I, 405.

7. Ibid. I, 431, 497, 504.

8. Ibid. I, 499.

9. "A Better American Way with Unemployment," *New Republic,* December 31, 1930, p. 176; *Nation,* September 23, 1931, p. 294; Sumner H. Slichter, "Doles for Employers," *New Republic,* December 31, 1930, p. 181; "The Week," *New Republic,* January 21, 1931, p. 255; Walter S. Gifford, "Pensions, Charity, and Old Age," *Atlantic,* CXLV (February 1930), 259–65.

10. U.S., Congress, House, Committee on Ways and Means, *Hearings, on H.R. 12353, National Emergency Relief,* 72d Cong., 1st Sess., 1932, pp. 233–5, 265.

11. Edward A. Block, "We Can't Escape the Dole," *Forum,* LXXXVII (March 1932), 130.

12. "Can the Leaders Lead?" *Nation,* April 29, 1931, p. 467; Sumner H. Slichter, "Pharaoh Dreams Again," *Atlantic,* CXLVIII (August 1931), 252; "Business on the Defensive," *Nation,* May 13, 1931, p. 520.

13. Julius H. Barnes, "Business Looks at Unemployment," *Atlantic,* CXLVIII (August 1931), 242.

14. Slichter, *Atlantic,* CXLVIII (August 1931), 251.

15. Paul H. Douglas, "The Partial Stabilization of Workers' Incomes Through Unemployment Insurance," *Annals of the American Academy of Political and Social Science,* CLIV (March 1931), 94.

16. Whitling Williams, "A Challenge to Industry," ibid. p. 3; Jacob Billikopf, "The Social Duty to the Unemployed," ibid. p. 70; Paul H. Douglas, "The Partial Stabilization of Workers' Incomes Through Unemployment Insurance," ibid. p. 95; Frances Perkins, "A Cooperative Program Needed for Industrial Stabilization," ibid. p. 126; U.S., Congress, Senate, Subcommittee of the Committee on Manufactures, *Hearings, on S. 6215, National Economic Council,* 71st Cong., 1st Sess., 1931, p. 140; "This Time They Did Not Cut Wages," *Business Week,* January 1, 1930, p. 23; *Commercial & Financial Chronicle,* November 8, 1930, p. 2979; E. P. Hayes, *Activities of the President's Emergency Committee for Employment* (Concord, New Hampshire, Rumford Press, 1936), pp. 69–73.

17. Perkins, *Annals of the American Academy of Political and Social*

Science, CLIV (March 1931), 127; *Commercial & Financial Chronicle,* November 8, 1930, p. 2979.

18. M. B. Folsom, "Program of Stabilized Production and Employment," *Annals of the American Academy of Political and Social Science,* CLIV (March 1931), 143.

19. Ibid. pp. 143–6; Hayes, *Activities of the President's Emergency Committee for Employment,* pp. 72–4.

20. *Commercial & Financial Chronicle,* November 8, 1930, p. 2979; Gerard Swope, "Management Cooperation with Workers for Economic Welfare," *Annals of the American Academy of Political and Social Science,* CLIV (March 1931), 136; "To Counter Unemployment," *Survey,* July 15, 1930, p. 340.

21. *Commercial & Financial Chronicle,* December 20, 1930, p. 3977.

22. See the testimony of Frances Perkins, at this time industrial commissioner of New York State, in U.S., Congress, Senate, Subcommittee of the Committee on Manufactures, *Hearings, on S. 6215, National Economic Council,* 71st Cong., 1st Sess., 1931, pp. 139–41; 143–6.

23. Murray Weinstein, "Methods Employed in the Clothing Industry," *Annals of the American Academy of Political and Social Science,* CLIV (March 1931), 153.

24. Sidney Hillman, "A Successful Experiment in Unemployment Insurance," ibid. pp. 104–5.

25. Barnes, *Atlantic,* CXLVIII (August 1931), 239; "Business on the Defensive," *Nation,* May 13, 1931, p. 520.

26. "This Time They Did Not Cut Wages," *Business Week,* January 1, 1930, p. 23; Douglas, *Annals of the American Academy of Political and Social Science,* CLIV (March 1931), 94–5.

27. J. Douglas Brown, "The Manufacturers and the Unemployed," *Current History,* XXXIV (July 1931), 519–20.

28. U.S., Congress, Senate, Subcommittee of the Committee on Manufactures, *Hearings, on S. 6215, National Economic Council,* 71st Cong., 1st Sess., 1931, pp. 350, 348.

29. Ibid. p. 376.

30. Ibid. pp. 385–6, 390.

31. Ibid. pp. 385–6.

32. Paul H. Douglas, "Can Management Prevent Unemployment?" *Proceedings of the National Conference of Social Work* (Chicago: University of Chicago Press, 1930), p. 267. There were some two million concerns in business in 1930.

33. Paul H. Douglas, "American Plans of Unemployment Insurance," *Survey,* February 1, 1931, p. 484.

34. Douglas, *Annals of the American Academy of Political and Social Science,* CLIV (March 1931), 101–2. In August 1931, Ethelbert Stewart of the Bureau of Labor Statistics published the findings of another survey. He found 79 unemployment plans in existence. While 226,000 workers were potentially affected, the actual number currently covered was "considerably less." See "Unemployment Benefit Plans Now Operating in the United States," *Congressional Digest,* x (August–September 1931), 200, 223.

35. John T. Flynn, "The Security Wage," *Forum,* LXXXVI (October 1931), 248.

CHAPTER 8

* Senator Robert Wagner, *Congressional Digest,* x (January 1931), 12.

† Letter from Lillian M. Gilbreth, member of the President's Emergency Committee for Employment, to Mrs. C. Clifford Adams, Birmingham, Alabama, November 11, 1930, in NA, RG 73, PECE MSS.

1. Hoover, *State Papers,* I, 402; *Commercial & Financial Chronicle,* November 1, 1930, p. 2803.

2. Hayes, *Activities of the President's Emergency Committee for Employment,* p. 2; "The President's Emergency Committee for Employment," *Congressional Digest,* x (January 1931), 3.

3. The members and their occupations are listed in Hayes, pp. vii–viii.

4. Hayes, *Activities of the President's Emergency Committee for Employment,* p. 5.

5. Hoover, *Memoirs,* III, 53.

6. Quoted by *Commercial & Financial Chronicle,* October 25, 1930, p. 2632; *Nation,* October 29, 1930, p. 457.

7. Hayes, *Activities of the President's Emergency Committee for Employment,* pp. 3, 9.

8. Letter from Porter R. Lee to David C. Adie, Buffalo, New York, November 4, 1930, in NA, RG 73, PECE MSS.

9. U.S., Congress, Senate, Committee on Appropriations, *Report No. 1264, Drought Relief and Unemployment — LaFollette Resolution,* 71st Cong., 3d Sess., 1931, pp. 58–9.

10. Porter R. Lee to Jean W. Jellerson, November 3, 1930; Joanna C. Colcord to Porter R. Lee, November 5, 1930; R. M. Paige to F. D. West, chairman of the Abbeville County Unemployment Committee, South Carolina, February 10, 1931; Arthur Woods to D. A.

Abrams, president, American Concrete Institute, New York City, February 18, 1931; Arthur Woods to Professor Adelbert Amers, Jr., Dartmouth Medical School, January 7, 1931. All in NA, RG 73, PECE MSS.

11. The pamphlets are discussed in Hayes, *Activities of the President's Emergency Committee for Employment*. Hayes, a member of the Woods committee, has written a comprehensive history of its work. There is no comparable account of the organization after August 19, 1931, when it was renamed the President's Organization on Unemployment Relief (or the Gifford committee). The records of both these groups are in the National Archives.

12. Woods, "The Emergency Committee at Work," *Congressional Digest*, x (January 1931), pp. 5, 31.

13. U.S., Congress, Senate, Committee on Appropriations, *Report No. 1264, Drought Relief and Unemployment — LaFollette Resolution*, 71st Cong., 3d Sess., 1931, pp. 59, 60, 63, 67.

14. Typed copies of telephone conversations between Colonel Woods and the governors, November 2 and 6, 1930, in NA, RG 73, PECE MSS.

15. Ibid.

16. Actually, the nation's social workers were a vocal and articulate group. In congressional hearings on unemployment, they documented distress by citing innumerable case studies of families and individuals, and they fortified these personal observations with the best available statistics on their localities. The series of hearings before the subcommittee of the Committee on Manufactures, conducted by Senators Robert M. LaFollette, Jr., of Wisconsin, and Edward P. Costigan, of Colorado, was the most impressive.

17. Social work includes the activities of agencies, such as family and child welfare agencies, that are privately financed. Public welfare is social work conducted with public funds. Social welfare is a broader term including both private social work and public welfare. See *Recent Social Trends in the United States: Report of the President's Research Committee on Social Trends* (New York: McGraw-Hill, 1933), pp. 1168–70.

18. D. E. Wolf, "The United States," *Current History*, xxxiii (December 1930), 436.

19. U.S., Congress, Senate, Subcommittee of the Committee on Manufactures, *Hearings, on S. 174 and S. 262, Unemployment Relief*, 72nd Cong., 1st Sess., December 1931–January 1932, p. 101; *Commercial & Financial Chronicle*, November 15, 1930, p. 3135.

20. "New York Muddles Along," *Survey*, November 13, 1930, pp. 196–7; *Commercial & Financial Chronicle*, November 15, 1930, p. 3135; December 6, 1930, pp. 3641–2.

21. Gertrude Springer, "The Burden of Mass Relief," *Survey*, November 15, 1930, p. 202; Springer, "The Job Line," *Survey*, February 1, 1931, p. 497; *Commercial & Financial Chronicle*, December 6, 1930, p. 3642.

22. Springer, *Survey*, February 1, 1931, p. 497; *Commercial & Financial Chronicle*, October 18, 1930, p. 2445.

23. Ibid.; *Commercial & Financial Chronicle*, December 20, 1930, p. 3976.

24. *Commercial & Financial Chronicle*, November 29, 1930, pp. 3457–8. According to the United States census of April 1930, there were 254,000 unemployed in New York City. Labor leaders maintained that by November there were 300,000 unemployed among organized labor alone. See Springer, *Survey*, November 15, 1930, p. 201.

25. "New York Muddles Along," *Survey*, November 15, 1930, p. 197.

26. U.S., Congress, Senate, Subcommittee of the Committee on Manufactures, *Hearings, on S. 174 and S. 262, Unemployment Relief*, 72nd Cong., 1st Sess., December 1931–January 1932, p. 14, *New Republic*, January 21, 1931, p. 255; March 25, 1931, p. 140.

27. The term relief covered many different types of assistance. Home relief was assistance given to families in their homes (either in kind — food and clothing — or in money), and it was distinguished from work relief and public relief. Initially, public relief did not include assistance of families who were in distress because of unemployment.

28. "New York's First Aid For Heads of Families," *Business Week*, November 5, 1930, p. 7; *Commercial & Financial Chronicle*, November 15, 1930, p. 3135; December 6, 1930, p. 3641; Sumner H. Slichter, "Doles for Employers," *New Republic*, December 15, 1930, p. 182; *Survey*, December 15, 1932, p. 696.

29. "Information for Reconstruction Finance Corporation," T.E.R.A., 1933 (document accompanying loan request from RFC); Frank J. Taylor, commissioner, NYC Department of Public Welfare, to Robert M. LaFollette, Jr., January 20, 1933, in NA, RG 234, RFC MSS.

30. "The New York City budget for 1931 included an appropriation for 'aid to unemployment' of one million dollars charged to current operation and maintenance. This sum was derived from tax levy funds.

"At [the] request of social agencies in the Welfare Council in April 1931, the Board of Estimate authorized a ten million dollar special revenue bond issue [of] short term bonds, for unemployment work relief for which special legislation was necessary. These funds were chargeable to current expenditures for operation and maintenance.

"During 1931 tax notes were issued to the amount of $1,625,000 and used for work relief and charged to permanent improvements — streets and highways.

"In December 1931 the City of New York under the Wicks Law organized its home and work relief bureaus. During that month and the year 1932, the amount expended for unemployment, work and home relief was $33,427,000, of which amount New York City paid $18,238,000 and the State $15,189,000. The City's funds were derived from the sale of serial bonds." "Information for Reconstruction Finance Corporation," 1933, in NA, RG 234, RFC MSS.

31. U.S., Congress, Senate, Subcommittee of the Committee on Manufactures, *Hearings, on S. 174 and S. 262, Unemployment Relief,* 72nd Cong., 1st Sess., December 1931–January 1932, pp. 14–15; ibid. *Hearings, on S. 5125, Unemployment Relief,* 72nd Cong., 2d Sess., 1933, p. 104.

32. The Welfare Council, a private organization, served as the coordinating center for some 900 welfare and health agencies in New York City, nearly all of which were directly concerned with the relief problem.

33. U.S., Congress, Senate, Subcommittee of the Committee on Manufactures, *Hearings, on S. 174 and S. 262, Unemployment Relief,* 72nd Cong., 1st Sess., December 1931–January 1932, p. 15

34. Ibid. pp. 12–13.

35. Ibid. pp. 16–22.

36. Ibid. pp. 19, 28–9.

37. Ibid. pp. 30–31, 39–40; *Hearings, on S. 5125, Unemployment Relief,* 72nd Cong., 2d Sess., 1933, p. 88.

38. U.S., Congress, Senate, Subcommittee of the Committee on Manufactures, *Hearings, on S. 174 and S. 262, Unemployment Relief,* 72nd Cong., 1st Sess., December 1931–January 1932, p. 31.

39. Gertrude Springer, "Funds for Another Bleak Winter," *Survey,* June 15, 1931, p. 302.

40. The majority of the Chest cities held their campaigns in the fall and the early winter, but about ninety of them were held after January. According to figures cited in *Recent Social Trends* (1933), only $83,213,428 was collected in 1931 by 377 Chests, p. 1205.

41. U.S., Congress, Senate, Subcommittee of the Committee on Manu-

factures, *Hearings, on S. 174 and S. 262, Unemployment Relief,* 72nd Cong., 1st Sess., December 1931–January 1932, pp. 124–5, 128.

42. Hoover, *State Papers,* II, 13–14.

43. Springer, *Survey,* June 15, 1931, p. 302.

44. U.S., Congress, Senate, Subcommittee of the Committee on Manufactures, *Hearings, on S. 174 and S. 262, Unemployment Relief,* 72nd Cong., 1st Sess., December 1931–January 1932, p. 127.

45. Ibid. p. 131.

46. Gertrude Springer, "The Challenge of Hard Times," *Survey,* July 15, 1931, p. 380.

47. Jacob Billikopf, "What Have We learned About Unemployment?" *Proceedings of the National Conference of Social Work* (Chicago: University of Chicago Press, 1931), pp. 25, 39, 50.

48. Reprinted in part in U.S., Congress, Senate, Subcommittee of the Committee on Manufactures, *Hearings, on S. 174 and S. 262, Unemployment Relief,* 72nd Cong., 1st Sess., December 1931–January 1932, p. 115. A complete copy of this letter was sent to Walter Gifford by Senator James Couzens, Michigan, who wrote: "It brings up some very important points concerning your particular job in Washington," in NA, RG 73, POUR MSS.

49. The amount allocated for family relief, however, rose by nearly 60 per cent.

50. And 28 cents unaccounted for.

51. See U.S., Congress, Senate, Subcommittee of the Committee on Commerce, *Hearings in 3059, S. 3060, and S. 3061, Unemployment,* 71st Cong., 2d Sess., 1930; U.S., Congress, Senate, Subcommittee of the Committee on Manufactures, *Hearings, on S. 174 and S. 262, Unemployment Relief,* 72nd Cong., 1st Sess., December 1931–January 1932.

52. Commenting on his appointment, Gifford wrote: "It is probably the most difficult one I have ever tackled but here's hoping I succeed in doing something worth while. I am afraid I must rely entirely on my own conscience because no matter what I do I will undoubtedly receive more than a full share of criticisms." Letter from Gifford to Judge Robert McC. Marsh, New York City, September 15, 1931, in NA, RG 73, POUR MSS.

53. Hayes, *Activities of the President's Emergency Committee for Employment,* p. 16; Gertrude Springer, "Where Is the Money Coming From?" *Survey,* October 15, 1931, p. 71; U.S., Congress, Senate, Subcommittee of the Committee on Manufactures, *Hearings, on S. 174 and S. 262, Unemployment Relief,* 72nd Cong., 1st Sess., December 1931–January 1932, p. 309.

54. Gifford submitted a list of names for the advisory committee to Hoover for his consideration. Practically all of the names were those of businessmen, and the greater part of these were bankers. Letters from Gifford to Herbert Hoover, August 26, 1931, and August 27, 1931, in NA, RG 73, POUR MSS.

55. The chairmen of the committees were respectively: Owen D. Young of New York, Fred C. Croxton of Washington, D.C., Harry A. Wheeler of Chicago, James R. Garfield of Cleveland, and Elliott Wadsworth of Boston. U.S., Congress, Senate, Subcommittee of the Committee on Manufactures, *Hearings, on S. 174 and S. 262, Unemployment Relief*, 72nd Cong., 1st Sess., December 1931 January 1932, p. 311.

56. Letter from Owen D. Young to William Randolph Hearst, October 1, 1931, in NA, RG 73, POUR MSS.

57. U.S., Congress, Senate, Subcommittee of the Committee on Manufactures, *Hearings, on S. 174 and S. 262, Unemployment Relief*, 72nd Cong., 1st Sess., December 1931–January 1932, p. 310.

58. Ibid. pp. 316, 321, 332.

59. Walter Gifford to Herbert Hoover, November 28, 1931, in NA, RG 73, POUR MSS.

60. U.S., Congress, Senate, Subcommittee of the Committee on Manufactures, *Hearings, on S. 174 and S. 262, Unemployment Relief*, 72nd Cong., 1st Sess., December 1931–January 1932, pp. 312, 314–15, 319.

61. Bruce Bliven, "No Money, No Work," *New Republic*, November 19, 1930, pp. 12–14.

62. "Local Governments and Taxes Bigger Problem Than Federal," *Business Week*, December 30, 1931, p. 19.

63. Ibid.; *New Republic*, December 16, 1931, pp. 19–20; *Commercial & Financial Chronicle*, January 16, 1932, pp. 362–5; "Cities, Their Credit Poor, Face The Great Dilemma of Depression," *Business Week*, January 20, 1932, p. 14; "The Collapse of Local Government," *New Republic*, January 20, 1932, pp. 254–5; Lothrop Stoddard, "Why Cities Go Broke," *Forum*, LXXXVII (June 1932), 375–9; Henry Hazlitt, "No Taxes to Pay," *Scribner's*, XCIII (January 1933), p. 19.

64. *New Republic*, January 6, 1932, pp. 198–9; Joseph Heffernan, "The Hungry City," *Atlantic*, CXLIX (May 1932), pp. 538–46; *Nation*, June 8, 1932, p. 636; *New Republic*, March 2, 1932, p. 57.

65. U.S., Congress, Senate, Subcommittee of the Committee on Manufactures, *Hearings, on S. 174 and S. 262, Unemployment Relief*, 72nd Cong., 1st Sess., December 1931–January 1932, pp. 283–5.

66. U.S., Congress, House, Subcommittee of the Committee on Labor, *Hearings, on H.R. 206, H.R. 6011, and H.R. 8088, Unemployment*,

72nd Cong., 1st Sess., 1932, p. 95; U.S., Congress, Senate, Subcommittee of the Committee on Manufactures, *Hearings, on S. 5125, Unemployment Relief*, 72nd Cong., 2d Sess., 1933, pp. 8–13. Philadelphia, in the previous two years, had stopped relief on two other occasions: there was no organized relief for six weeks in the summer of 1931, nor was there any, for two weeks in April 1932.

67. U.S., Congress, House, Subcommittee of the Committee on Labor, *Hearings, on H.R. 206, H.R. 6011, and H.R. 8088, Unemployment*, 72nd Cong., 1st Sess., 1932, p. 206.

68. Quoted in the *New Republic*, March 2, 1932, p. 57.

69. U.S., Congress, Senate, Subcommittee of the Committee on Manufactures, *Hearings, on S. 4592, Federal Cooperation in Unemployment Relief*, 72nd Cong., 1st Sess., 1932, pp. 9–13.

70. "Information Concerning State Action for Relief" (two-page report); "Report of the New York Temporary Emergency Relief Administration," October 15, 1932, in NA, RG 234, RFC MSS.

71. Harry Hopkins, "A Summary of the Activities of the Temporary Emergency Relief Administration of New York State from November 1, 1931, to June 1, 1932," in NA, RG 234, RFC MSS. (mimeographed); "First Interim Report of the Illinois Emergency Relief Commission," April 15, 1932; two-page memorandum, n.d., ibid.; Rowland Haynes, *State Legislation for Unemployment Relief*, U.S. Dept. of Commerce, POUR (Washington: U.S. Government Printing Office, 1932), pp. 2–3.

72. James L. Fort, "Memorandum on Relief Provided by the States of New York, New Jersey, Illinois, Ohio, and Pennsylvania," August 5, 1932; letter from Gifford Pinchot to Atlee Pomerene, chairman of RFC, August 19, 1932; Pinchot to the RFC, July 18, 1932, in NA, RG 234, RFC MSS.

73. U.S., Congress, Senate, Subcommittee of the Committee on Manufactures, *Hearings, on S. 174 and S. 262, Unemployment Relief*, 72nd Cong., 1st Sess., December 1931–January 1932, pp. 8, 34; U.S., Congress, House, Subcommittee of the Committee on Labor, *Hearings, on H.R. 206, H.R. 6011, and H.R. 8088, Unemployment*, 72nd Cong., 1st Sess., 1932, pp. 15–16, 120; U.S., Congress, Senate, Subcommittee of the Committee on Manufactures, *Hearings, on S. 5125, Unemployment Relief*, 72nd Cong., 2d Sess., 1933, pp. 31, 220–22, 243–4.

74. U.S., Congress, Senate, Subcommittee of the Committee on Manufactures, *Hearings, on S. 5125, Unemployment Relief*, 72nd Cong., 2d Sess., 1933, pp. 126, 203.

75. U.S., Congress, Senate, Subcommittee of the Committee on Manufactures, *Hearings, on S. 174 and S. 262, Unemployment Relief,* 72nd
Cong., 1st Sess., December 1931–January 1932, pp. 15, 54, 66, 72, 85,
103, 138, 149, 155, 242, 347.

PART TWO
* Ogden L. Mills, speech of September 29, 1932, Detroit, in LC, OLM
MSS., Box 138.

CHAPTER 9
* "The Mob and Its Leaders," *New Republic,* May 18, 1932, p. 5.
† Hoover, *State Papers,* II, 109.

1. Quoted by *Commercial & Financial Chronicle,* April 25, 1931, p.
   3053; George J. Anderson, "Nobody's Business," *Atlantic,* CXLVII
   (May 1931), 637.
2. Richard T. Ely, "Hard Times and a Way Out," *Review of Reviews,*
   LXXXIII (March 1931), 90.
3. Oswald G. Villard, "Government and Business," *Nation,* September 3, 1930, p. 237.
4. Chase, *Harper's,* CLXV (July 1932), 208; Jouett Shouse, "Watchman,
   What of the Night?" *Atlantic,* CXLVIII (February 1931), 255.
5. Keynes, *Atlantic,* CXLIX (May 1932), 525; William T. Foster, "When
   a Horse Balks," *North Atlantic Review,* CCXXXIV (July 1932), 10.
6. "The Wrong Bottle," *Business Week,* July 23, 1930, p. 40; "Brake
   on Recovery," *Business Week,* March 16, 1932, p. 40.
7. Hoover, *State Papers,* II, 109, 112, 137.
8. Ibid. I, 504.
9. Speech at New York City on October 22, 1928, in Hoover, *The New
   Day,* pp. 153–4.
10. Hoover, *State Papers,* I, 429–30.
11. Ibid. I, 376, 428.
12. Ibid.
13. Ibid. I, 428–9.
14. Ibid. I, 376–7, 574–5.
15. Ibid. II, 269–71; Hoover, *Memoirs,* III, 61–84.
16. Hoover, *State Papers,* II, 269; Bernhard Ostrolenk, "Inflation Trends
    in America," *Current History,* XXXVI (March 1932), 773.
17. Hoover estimated that American banks held about $1.7 billion in
    German short-term loan paper. Hoover, *Memoirs,* III, 73.

18. Hoover, *State Papers,* I, 574.

19. Ibid. I, 591–2. The President's proposal was approved by Congress when it reconvened in December 1931, and signed by Hoover on the 23rd. Hoover, *State Papers,* II, 96.

20. *Commercial & Financial Chronicle,* June 27, 1931, p. 4636; "At Last!" *Business Week,* July 1, 1931, p. 40.

21. Hoover, *Memoirs,* III, 97.

22. Hoover, *State Papers,* II, 106.

23. Speech before the American Acceptance Council in New York, in LC, OLM MSS., Box 137.

24. "First Reconstruction Job Is Release of Lending Power," *Business Week,* January 27, 1932, p. 5; T.R.B., "Washington Notes," *New Republic,* January 27, 1932, p. 291.

25. U.S., *Statutes at Large,* XLVII, Part 1, 6; William S. Kies, "Insuring Against Bank Failures," *Review of Reviews,* LXXXV (February 1932), 28; Ostrolenk, *Current History,* XXXVI (March 1932), 775.

26. Hoover, *State Papers,* II, 107; *Commercial & Financial Chronicle,* November 21, 1931, pp. 3358–9; "Congress Sets Powerful Mines To Blow Up the Depression," *Business Week,* July 27, 1932, p. 3.

27. U.S., Congress, House, Subcommittee of the Committee on Banking and Currency, *Hearings, on H.R. 7620, Creation of a System of Federal Home Loan Banks,* 72d Cong., 1st Sess., 1932, p. 40ff.

28. U.S., Congress, Senate, Subcommittee of the Committee on Banking and Currency, *Hearings, on S. 2959, Creation of a System of Federal Home Loan Banks,* 72d Cong., 1st Sess., 1932, p. 220.

29. U.S., Congress, House, Subcommittee of the Committee on Banking and Currency, *Hearings, on H.R. 7620, Creation of a System of Federal Home Loan Banks,* 72d Cong., 1st Sess., 1932, pp. 14, 35.

30. U.S., *Statutes at Large,* XLVII, Part 1, 728; Hoover, *State Papers,* II, 238–40; *New Republic,* November 25, 1931, pp. 31–2; "The Week," *New Republic,* August 17, 1932, p. 2.

31. Hoover, *State Papers,* II, 128–9; New York *Journal of Commerce,* February 26, 1932, quoted by *Commercial & Financial Chronicle,* March 5, 1932, p. 1683.

32. U.S., *Statutes at Large,* XLVII, Part 1, 56–7; "Credit Expansion Is Now Up to Business and the Banks," *Business Week,* February 24, 1932, pp. 5–6.

33. Ernest Angell, "Capitalism Backs Down," *Forum,* LXXXIX (January 1933), 57; Hoover, *State Papers,* II, 302.

34. "Federal Reserve Begins Using Securities to Back Currency," *Business Week,* May 25, 1932, p. 14.

35. Hoover, *State Papers*, II, 128–9; "Credit Expansion Is Now Up to Business and the Banks," *Business Week*, February 24, 1932, pp. 5–6; *Commercial & Financial Chronicle*, March 5, 1932, pp. 1683–4; E. F. Brown, "Congress Adopts Hoover Program," *Current History*, XXXVI (April 1932), 83–4; "Cheap Money Policy of Reserve Heads Off More Drastic Plans," *Business Week*, April 27, 1932, pp. 5–6.

36. "Campaign Against Deflation Has Reached Crucial Stage," *Business Week*, May 11, 1932, p. 7; *Annual Report of the Federal Reserve Board* (Washington: Government Printing Office, 1933), p. 11.

37. Mills was Under-Secretary of the Treasury until February 1932, when he replaced Andrew Mellon as Secretary of the Treasury.

38. Talk of October 7, 1931, for Fox, Paramount and Pathe movietone companies; speech of January 25, 1932, to the American Acceptance Council; speech of October 4, 1932, to the American Bankers' Association, in LC, OLM MSS., Boxes 137–8.

39. "The National Budget and the Public Credit," speech of December 14, 1931, to the Economic Club of New York; speech of April 22, 1932, to the Daughters of the American Revolution, in LC, OLM MSS., Box 137.

40. Speech of February 11, 1933, to the Young Republican Club of Missouri, in LC, OLM MSS., Box 139.

41. Speech of October 4, 1932, to the American Bankers' Association, in LC, OLM MSS., Box 138.

42. Mills, "Statement . . . before the President's Conference of Banking and Industrial Committees," August 26, 1932, ibid.

43. "Confidential History, National Conference of Banking and Industrial Committees," ibid. Box 59 (typewritten); "Congress, Hoover, Young's Group All Seek to Break Credit Dam," *Business Week*, June 1, 1932, pp. 5–6; Hoover, *Memoirs*, III, 167.

44. Hoover, *State Papers*, II, 268.

45. "The Government Ties Business Into the Recovery Program," *Business Week*, September 7, 1932, pp. 5–6. Included among the chairmen chosen were Owen D. Young, A. W. Robertson of Westinghouse, Daniel Willard of the Baltimore and Ohio, Sewell L. Avery of Montgomery-Ward, C. M. Woolley of American Radiator, and Walter C. Teagle of Standard Oil. "Hoover's Business Planning," *New Republic*, September 7, 1932, pp. 85–6.

46. Hoover, *State Papers*, II, 479.

CHAPTER 10

* George Soule, speech before the Conference of Progressives, Washington, D.C., March 11–12, 1931, in *Proceedings of a Conference of Progressives*, p. 23.

† Arthur Krock, "President Hoover's Two Years," *Current History*, xxxiv (July 1931), 494.

‡ Walter Lippmann, "The Peculiar Weakness of Mr. Hoover," *Harper's*, clxi (June 1930), 6.

1. Anne O'Hare McCormick, "A Year of the Hoover Method," *New York Times*, March 2, 1930, v, 1.

2. Garet Garrett, "The First Hoover Year," *Saturday Evening Post*, March 1, 1930, p. 4.

3. Paul Y. Anderson, "Hoover and the Press," *Nation*, October 14, 1931, p. 382; Harris G. Warren, *Herbert Hoover and the Great Depression* (New York: Oxford University Press, 1959), p. 58.

4. Anderson, *Nation*, October 14, 1931, p. 382.

5. Paul Y. Anderson, "A Cross-Section of Washington," *Nation*, April 9, 1930, p. 420.

6. Anderson, *Nation*, October 14, 1931, p. 382; *Nation*, September 9, 1931, p. 243; Elliott Thurston, "Hoover Can Not Be Elected," *Scribner's*, xci (January 1932), 15.

7. McCormick, *New York Times*, March 2, 1930, v, 2.

8. "Humpty Dumpty Hoover," *New Republic*, June 25, 1930, p. 138; "Will Hoover Discredit the Experts?" *New Republic*, August 13, 1930, p. 354; Heywood Broun, "It seems to Heywood Broun," *Nation*, June 25, 1930, p. 723.

9. "Ballyhoover," *Nation*, May 14, 1930, p. 560.

10. Lippmann, *Harper's*, clxi (June 1930), 2.

11. Thurston, *Scribner's*, xci (January 1932), 13. In addition to the disparaging picture of Hoover presented by the nation's newsmen, the Democratic publicity bureau through its publicity director, Charles Michelson, dispatched innumerable critical pieces (articles and speeches) to editors and politicians throughout the country. Frank R. Kent, "Charley Michelson," *Scribner's*, lxxxviii (September 1930), 290–96; see also, Warren, *Herbert Hoover and the Great Depression*, pp. 122–3.

12. Robert Herrick, "Our Super-Babbitt: A Recantation," *Nation*, July 16, 1930, p. 61; Mussey, *Nation*, July 8, 1931, p. 35; "Unemployment: The President's Job," *Nation*, July 9, 1930, p. 30; *Commercial*

& *Financial Chronicle,* January 25, 1930, pp. 540–41; August 3, 1930, p. 1171; *Business Week,* March 19, 1930, p. 48; *New York Times,* March 5, 1930, p. 22; April 5, 1930, p. 18; *Nation,* February 26, 1930, p. 235; April 1, 1931, p. 342; Royal Meeker, "The Dependability and Meaning of Unemployment and Employment Statistics in the United States," *Harvard Business Review,* VIII (July 1930), 385–400.

13. Silas Bent, "Mr. Hoover's Sins of Commissions," *Scribner's,* XC (July 1931), 9.

14. *New Republic,* August 13, 1930, pp. 354–5.

15. Heywood Broun, "It Seems to Heywood Broun," *Nation,* August 13, 1930, p. 171.

16. "Hoover Looks Forward," *New Republic,* October 15, 1930, p. 220.

17. George Soule, "On Blaming Hoover," *New Republic,* October 26, 1932, p. 278; "Hoover's Tragedy," *New Republic,* October 19, 1932, pp. 246–7; Royal W. France, "Why Hard Times?" *Scribner's,* LXXXVIII (December 1930), 65; "Fit to Rule," *Nation,* December 11, 1929, p. 707; "President Hoover's First Year," ibid. p. 234; T.R.B., "Washington Notes," *New Republic,* April 20, 1932, pp. 270–71; Bent, *Scribner's,* XC (July 1931), 9.

18. Paul Y. Anderson, "Hoover's Washington," *Nation,* December 4, 1929, p. 660; "The Hoover Hippodrome," *Nation,* March 12, 1930, p. 293; "Washington Grinds On," *Nation,* May 7, 1930, p. 538; "Hoover the Politician," *Nation,* August 19, 1931, p. 176.

19. Allan Nevins, "President Hoover's Record," *Current History,* XXXVI (June 1932), 387; E. F. Brown, "Congress Plays Its Part," *Current History,* XXXVI (July 1932), 464.

20. T.R.B., "Washington Notes," *New Republic,* May 21, 1930, pp. 16–17; "The United States," *Current History,* XXXII (August 1930), 977–8; "Hoover Uses the Whip," *New Republic,* December 24, 1930, pp. 151–2; Paul Y. Anderson, "Hoover Suffers in the House," *Nation,* March 11, 1931, p. 268; "Wanted — A Government," *New Republic,* March 4, 1931, p. 58.

21. Royal W. France, "Why Hard Times?", *Scribner's,* LXXXVIII (December 1930), 623–6; Elliott Thurston, "Hoover Can Not Be Elected," *Scribner's,* XCI (January 1932), 13–16; Silas Bent, "Mr. Hoover's Sins of Commissions," *Scribner's,* XC (July 1931), 9–14; Walter Millis, "The President," *Atlantic,* CXLIX (March 1932), 265–78; Allan Nevins, "President Hoover's Record," *Current History,* XXXVI (June 1932), 385–94; Arthur Krock, "President Hoover's Two Years," *Current History,* XXXIV (July 1931), 488–94; Walter Lippmann, "The Peculiar Weakness of Mr. Hoover," *Harper's,* CLXI (June 1930), 1–7;

Gertrude Springer, "The Fighting Spirit of Hard Times," *Survey*, June 15, 1932, 260–71; *Business Week*, April 30, 1930, p. 44; William T. Foster, "When a Horse Balks," *North American Review*, ccxxxiv (July 1932), 4–10.

22. Hoover, *Memoirs*, iii, vii, 21, 54, 100–101, 114, 119, 134, 142–8, 159ff. Hoover's intention, in thus recounting his difficulties with Congress, is to demonstrate that, in spite of the political obstruction and intractability of Congress, he was able to get the most substantial portion of his program enacted. He also uses Congress (along with the collapse of Vienna's Kreditanstalt, England's abandonment of the gold standard, and the election of Franklin Delano Roosevelt to the presidency — as well as several other episodes) as one of the causes which prolonged the depression.

23. "President Hoover and the 71st Congress — A Review," *Congressional Digest*, x (April 1931), 117.

24. Arthur W. Macmahon, "First Session of the Seventy-first Congress," *American Political Science Review*, xxiv (February 1930), 38.

25. *Congressional Digest*, x (April 1931), 117–18.

26. Ibid.; Macmahon, *American Political Science Review*, xxiv (February 1930), 51–4.

27. A provision permitting the President, in consultation with the Tariff Commission, to change rates up to 50 per cent.

28. In this case, Hoover's opponents included more than one thousand economists who urged him not to sign the bill. Whether the new tariff was economically wise, however, is a different matter from the political question of victory or defeat. Considered purely in political terms, the tariff provided substantially what Hoover asked.

29. The second session went from December 2, 1929, to July 3, 1930; the third was in session from December 1, 1930, to March 4, 1931.

30. Arthur W. Macmahon, "Second Session of the Seventy-first Congress and Special Session of the Senate," *American Political Science Review*, xxiv (November 1930), 913–46; Macmahon, "Third Session of the Seventy-first Congress," xxv (November 1931), ibid. 932–54; *Congressional Digest*, x (April 1931), 117–20.

31. *Congressional Digest*, x (April 1931), 119; E. Pendleton Herring, "First Session of the Seventy-second Congress," *American Political Science Review*, xxvi (October 1932), 848.

32. "Progressives at Washington," *Manchester Guardian*, March 16. 1931.

33. George W. Norris to Arthur G. Wray, Whittier, California, February 4, 1932, in LC, GWN MSS., Tray 8, Box 4.

34. Norris to J. D. Ream, Broken Bow, Nebraska, March 24, 1931, in ibid.; "Progressives Call Parley on Program," *New York Times,* March 3, 1931.
35. Among those attending were Leo Wolman, George Soule, Charles A. Beard, Father John A. Ryan, William Green, Sidney Hillman, Robert P. Scripps, Rudolph Spreckels. For a complete listing of participants, see *Proceedings of a Conference of Progressives,* 1931 (printed pamphlet).
36. Ibid. pp. 99–102, 123–4, 122, 103.
37. Bernard M. Baruch to TJW, October 10, 1931; TJW to Bernard M. Baruch, October 16, 1931, in LC, TJW MSS., Box 382.
38. TJW to Senator Joseph T. Robinson, Little Rock, Ark., November 7, 1931, in ibid.
39. Ibid.
40. Herring, *American Political Science Review,* XXVI (October 1932), 846.
41. Ibid. pp. 846–74.
42. Ibid. pp. 869–70; Hoover, *State Papers,* II, 196; E. F. Brown, *Current History,* XXXVI (July 1932), 468–9.
43. U.S., *Statutes at Large,* XLVII, Part 1, 709–16.
44. Ibid. pp. 710–12.
45. Gifford Pinchot to the Reconstruction Finance Corporation, July 18, 1932, in NA, RFC, RG 234, Box 88.
46. RFC, August 4, 1932 (mimeographed), in ibid.
47. Pinchot to Pomerene, August 19, 1932, September 8, 1932, in ibid.
48. Hoover, *State Papers,* II, 577.
49. Ogden L. Mills, "The National Budget and the Public Credit," in LC, OLM MSS., Box 137.
50. Ogden L. Mills, speech before the Associated Press, New York City, April 25, 1932, in LC, OLM MSS., Box 138.
51. OLM to Owen Young, December 16, 1932, in LC, OLM MSS., Box 9.
52. OLM to Myron C. Taylor, February 8, 1933, ibid. Box 45.
53. E. Pendleton Herring, "Second Session of the Seventy-second Congress," *American Political Science Review,* XXVII (June 1933), 404.

CHAPTER 11

* Ogden L. Mills, speech before the Associated Press, New York City, April 25, 1932, in LC, OLM MSS., Box 138.
† Soule, *Forum,* LXXXIX (March 1933), 148.

Bibliography

MANUSCRIPT COLLECTIONS

Department of Commerce. Record Group 40, National Archives, Washington, D.C.

Department of the Treasury. Record Group 56, National Archives, Washington, D.C.

Farm Credit Administration. Record Group 103, National Archives, Washington, D.C.

McNary, Charles Linza. Manuscripts Division, Library of Congress, Washington, D.C.

Mills, Ogden L. Manuscripts Division, Library of Congress, Washington, D.C.

Norris, George W. Manuscripts Division, Library of Congress, Washington, D.C.

Reconstruction Finance Corporation. Record Group 234, National Archives, Washington, D.C.

President's Organization on Unemployment Relief. Record Group 73, National Archives, Washington, D.C.

Walsh, Thomas James. Manuscripts Division, Library of Congress, Washington, D.C.

PUBLIC DOCUMENTS

Annual Report of the Federal Farm Board. Washington, D.C.: United States Government Printing Office, 1930, 1931, 1932.

Annual Report of the Federal Reserve Board. Washington, D.C.: United States Government Printing Office, 1929, 1930, 1931, 1932, 1933.

U.S. Board of Governors of the Federal Reserve System. *The Federal Reserve System.* Washington, D.C.: National Publishing Co., 1947.

U.S. Department of Agriculture. *Yearbook of Agriculture.* Washington, D.C.: United States Government Printing Office, 1930.

U.S. Department of Commerce. *State Legislation for Unemployment Relief.* Washington, D.C.: United States Government Printing Office, 1932.

U.S. Federal Farm Board. *A Report of the Activities of the Federal Farm*

Board in Administering the Agricultural Marketing Act. Washington, D.C., 1930.

U.S. House of Representatives, Committee on Banking and Currency. *Hearings on H.R. 5060 and H.R. 5116, Reconstruction Finance Corporation.* 72nd Cong., 1st Sess., December 1931-January 1932.

U.S. House of Representatives, Committee on Labor. *Hearings on H.R. 11055, H.R. 11056, and H.R. 12097, Relief of Distress Due to Unemployment.* 72nd Cong., 1st Sess., 1932.

U.S. House of Representatives, Committee on Ways and Means. *Hearings on H.J. Res. 123, Moratorium on Foreign Debts.* 72nd Cong., 1st Sess., 1931.

U.S. House of Representatives, Committee on Ways and Means. *Hearings on H.R. 12353, National Emergency Relief.* 72nd Cong., 1st Sess., 1932.

U.S. House of Representatives, Subcommittee of the Committee on Banking and Currency. *Hearings on H.R. 7620, Creation of a System of Federal Home Loan Banks.* 72nd Cong., 1st Sess., 1932.

U.S. House of Representatives, Subcommittee of the Committee on Banking and Currency. *Hearings on H.R. 10517, Stabilization of Commodity Prices.* 72nd Cong., 1st Sess., 1932.

U.S. House of Representatives, Subcommittee of the Committee on Labor. *Hearings on H.R. 206, H.R. 6011, and H.R. 8088, Unemployment.* 72nd Cong., 1st Sess., 1932.

U.S. Senate, Committee on Agriculture and Forestry. *Hearings on Farm Relief Legislation.* 71st Cong., 1st Sess., 1929.

U.S. Senate, Committee on Agriculture and Forestry. *Hearings on the Agricultural Situation.* 72nd Cong., 1st Sess., 1931.

U.S. Senate, Committee on Agriculture and Forestry. *Hearings on S. 123, etc., Farm Relief.* 72nd Cong., 1st Sess., 1932.

U.S. Senate, Committee on Banking and Currency. *Hearings on H.R. 11499 and S. 4429, Restoring and Maintaining the Average Purchasing Power of the Dollar.* 72nd Cong., 1st Sess., 1932.

U.S. Senate, Committee on Banking and Currency. *Hearings on S. 4632, S. 4727, etc., Unemployment Relief.* 72nd Cong., 1st Sess., 1932.

U.S. Senate, Committee on Finance. *Hearings pursuant to S. Res. 315, Investigation of Economic Problems.* 72nd Cong., 2d Sess., 1933.

U.S. Senate, *Report of the Committee on Agriculture and Forestry pursuant to S. Res. 42, Activities and Operations of the Federal Farm Board.* 74th Cong., 1st Sess., 1935.

U.S. Senate, *Report No. 1264, Drought Relief and Unemployment — LaFollette Resolution.* 71st Cong., 3d Sess., 1931.

U.S. Senate, Subcommittee of the Committee on Agriculture and Forestry. *Hearings on S. 4167 and S. 4168.* 72nd Cong., 1st Sess., 1932.

U.S. Senate, Subcommittee of the Committee on Banking and Currency. *Hearings on S. 1, Creation of a Reconstruction Finance Corporation.* 72nd Cong., 1st Sess., 1931.

U.S. Senate, Subcommittee of the Committee on Banking and Currency. *Hearings on S. 2959, Creation of a System of Federal Home Loan Banks.* 72nd Cong., 1st Sess., 1932.

U.S. Senate, Subcommittee of the Committee on Banking and Currency. *Hearings on S. 5336, Further Unemployment Relief Through the Reconstruction Finance Corporation.* 72nd Cong., 2d Sess., 1933.

U.S. Senate, Subcommittee of the Committee on Commerce. *Hearings on S. 3059, S. 3060 and S. 3061, Unemployment.* 71st Cong., 2d Sess., 1930.

U.S. Senate, Subcommittee of the Committee on Manufactures. *Hearings on S. 6215, Establishment of National Economic Council.* 72nd Cong., 1st Sess., 1931.

U.S. Senate, Subcommittee of the Committee on Manufactures. *Hearings on S. 4592, Federal Cooperation in Unemployment Relief.* 72nd Cong., 1st Sess., 1932.

U.S. Senate, Subcommittee of the Committee on Manufactures. *Hearings on S. 174 and S. 262, Unemployment Relief.* 72nd Cong., 1st Sess., 1932.

U.S. Senate, Subcommittee of the Committee on Manufactures. *Hearings on S. 5125, Unemployment Relief.* 72nd Cong., 2d Sess., 1933.

U.S. *Statutes at Large of the United States of America.* Washington, D.C.: United States Government Printing Office, 1929–33.

BOOKS AND ARTICLES

Adams, James T. "The Responsibility of Bankers," *Forum,* LXXXVI (August 1931), 81–6.

Amidon, Beulah. "The Civic Front on Unemployment," *Survey,* May 15, 1930, pp. 185–6.

———. "Some Plans for Steady Work," *Survey,* November 15, 1930, pp. 202–4.

Anderson, George E. "Are Bankers Intelligent?" *North American Review,* CCXXXIV (October 1932), 343–6.

Angell, Ernest. "Capitalism Backs Down," *Forum,* LXXXIX (January 1933), 55–61.

Atkins, Paul M. "The National Credit Corporation," *Review of Reviews*, LXXXV (January 1932), 48, 49, 68.

Barnes, Julius H. "Abundance Bogged Down," *World's Work*, LX (February 1931), 34–8.

———. "Business Grows Up," *Saturday Evening Post*, June 14, 1930, pp. 27, 50, 54, 56.

———. "Business in the New Year," *Review of Reviews*, LXXXI (January 1930), 48–9.

———. "Business Looks at Unemployment," *Atlantic*, CXLVIII (August 1931), 238–47.

———. "Facing the Larger Problems of Business Management," *Journal of Business of the University of Chicago*, III (July 1930), 272–8.

———. "The New Ebb and Flow of Industry," *Survey*, June 1, 1930, pp. 232–3.

Beard, Charles A. "The Myth of Rugged American Individualism," *Harper's*, CLXIV (December 1931), 13–22.

Bedford, Caroline. "The Effect of an Unemployment Situation in Family Societies," *Proceedings of the National Conference of Social Work*. Chicago: University of Chicago Press, 1931, pp. 201–10.

Bernheim, Alfred L. "Prosperity by Proclamation," *Nation*, December 25, 1929, pp. 772–4.

Billikopf, Jacob. "The Social Duty to the Unemployed," *Annals of the American Academy of Political and Social Science*, CLIV (March 1931), 65–72.

———. "What Have We Learned about Unemployment?" *Proceedings of the National Conference of Social Work*. Chicago: University of Chicago Press, 1931, pp. 25–50.

Bliven, Bruce. "No Money, No Work," *New Republic*, November 19, 1930, pp. 12–14.

Block, Edward A. "We Can't Escape the Dole," *Forum*, LXXXVII (March 1932), 130–35.

Brown, E. F. "The Campaign of 1932 Opens," *Current History*, XXXVI (September 1932), 716–21.

———. "Congress Adopts Hoover Program," *Current History*, XXXVI (April 1932), 82–90.

———. "Congress Plays Its Part," *Current History*, XXXVI (July 1932), 464–73.

———. "The Unemployment Crisis," *Current History*, XXXVI (July 1932), 411–16.

Burgess, W. R. *The Reserve Banks and the Money Market*. New York: Harper and Bros., 1936.

Burns, Allen T. "Community Chest Results," *Survey*, February 1, 1932, p. 466.

Chase, Stuart. "The Case for Inflation," *Harper's*, CLXV (July 1932), 198–209.

Commercial and Financial Chronicle. 1929–33.

Congressional Digest. 1929–33.

Daiger, J. M. "Confidence, Credit, and Cash," *Harper's*, CLXVI (February 1933), 279–92.

Dodge, F. W., Corporation, New York. "Historical Record of Contracts Awarded 37 Eastern States," n.p.

Dorfman, Joseph. *The Economic Mind in American Civilization*. Vol. V. New York: Viking Press, 1959.

Douglas, Paul H. "American Plans of Unemployment Insurance," *Survey*, February 1, 1931, pp. 484–6.

———. "Can Management Prevent Unemployment?" *Proceedings of the National Conference of Social Work*. Chicago: University of Chicago Press, 1930, pp. 266–72.

———. "The Partial Stabilization of Workers' Incomes through Unemployment Insurance," *Annals of the American Academy of Political and Social Science*, CLIV (March 1931), 94–103.

Duffus, R. L. "Relief by Guess," *New Republic*, October 7, 1931, pp. 196–9.

Edie, Lionel D. "The Federal Reserve and the Price Level," *Annals of the American Academy of Political and Social Science*, CLXXI (January 1934), 104–6.

Ely, Richard T. "Hard Times and a Way Out," *Review of Reviews*, LXXXIII (March 1931), 90–92.

Flynn, John T. "The Birthday of the Slump," *Forum*, LXXXIV (November 1930), 299–304.

———. "Mobilizing Deflation," *Forum*, LXXXIII (February 1930), 65–9.

———. "The Security Wage, *Forum*, LXXXVI (October 1931), 247–51.

Folsom, M. B. "Program of Stabilized Production and Employment," *Annals of the American Academy of Political and Social Science*, CLIV (March 1931), 143–7.

Foster, William T. "Better than the Bonus," *Forum*, LXXXVIII (August 1932), 88–92.

———. "When a Horse Balks," *North American Review*, CCXXXIV (July 1932), 4–10.

Foster, William T., and Catchings, Waddill. "Mr. Hoover's Road to Prosperity," *Review of Reviews*, LXXXI (January 1930), 50–52.

———. "Must We Reduce Our Standard of Living?" *Forum*, LXXXV (February 1931), 74–9.

Galbraith, John K. *The Great Crash, 1929.* Boston: Houghton Mifflin Co., 1954.

Garrett, Garet. "The First Hoover Year," *Saturday Evening Post,* March 1, 1930, pp. 3, 4, 121, 122, 125.

———. "Wall Street and Washington," *Saturday Evening Post,* December 28, 1929, pp. 6, 7, 80–82.

Hall, Helen. "Report of a Survey of the Effects of Unemployment," *Proceedings of the National Conference of Social Work.* Chicago: University of Chicago Press, 1930, pp. 348–57.

Hallgren, Mauritz A. "Hard Times and Hard Facts," *Nation,* March 11, 1931, pp. 266–7.

Hard, William. "Hoover as Individualist," *Nation,* August 26, 1931, pp. 201–3.

Heffernan, Joseph L. "The Hungry City," *Atlantic,* CXLIX (May 1932), 538–46.

Herring, E. Pendleton. "First Session of the Seventy-second Congress," *American Political Science Review,* XXVI (October 1932), 846–78.

———. "Second Session of the Seventy-second Congress," *American Political Science Review,* XXVII (June 1933), 404–22.

Hillman, Sidney. "A Successful Experiment in Unemployment Insurance," *Annals of the American Academy of Political and Social Science,* CLIV (March 1931), 104–7.

———. "Unemployment Reserves," *Atlantic,* CXLVIII (November 1931), 661–9.

Hofstadter, Richard. *The American Political Tradition: And the Men Who Made It.* New York: Alfred A. Knopf, 1948.

Hoover, Herbert. *The New Day, Campaign Speeches of Herbert Hoover 1928.* Stanford: Stanford University Press, 1928.

———. *The Memoirs of Herbert Hoover.* 3 vols. New York: Macmillan Co., 1951, 1952.

Hubbard, Joseph B. "The Construction Industry in the Depression," *Harvard Business Review,* XI (January 1933), 146–55.

Johnson, Walter. *1600 Pennsylvania Avenue: Presidents and the People, 1929–1959.* Boston: Little, Brown and Co., 1960.

Johnson, Wendell F. "How Case Working Agencies Have Met Unemployment," *Proceedings of the National Conference of Social Work.* Chicago: University of Chicago Press, 1931, pp. 189–200.

Kendall, Henry P. "What Can Management Do to Increase Security?" *Annals of the American Academy of Political and Social Science,* CLIV (March 1931), 138–42.

Keynes, John M. "The World's Economic Outlook," *Atlantic,* CXLIX (May 1932), 521–6.

Kies, William S. "Insuring Against Bank Failures," *Review of Reviews*, LXXXV (February 1932), 28–9.

Klein, Philip. *The Burden of Unemployment*. New York: Russell Sage Foundation, 1923.

Krock, Arthur. "President Hoover's Two Years," *Current History*, XXXIV (July 1931), 488–94.

Legg, Alexander. *The Agricultural Marketing Act*. Washington, D.C.: Chamber of Commerce of the United States, 1930.

Macmahon, Arthur M. "First Session of the Seventy-first Congress," *American Political Science Review*, XXIV (February 1930), 38–59.

———. "Second Session of the Seventy-first Congress and Special Session of the Senate," *American Political Science Review*, XXIV (November 1930), 913–46.

———. "Third Session of the Seventy-first Congress," *American Political Science Review*, XXV (November 1931), 932–54.

Maurois, André. "How You Have Changed!" *Forum*, LXXXV (June 1931), 321–6.

Maylick, Clay P. "Toward Unemployment Insurance," *Current History*, XXXVI (May 1932), 178–82.

McCormick, Anne O'Hare. "A Year of the Hoover Method," *New York Times*, March 2, 1930, Section V, pp. 1, 2, 17.

Meeker, Royal. "The Dependability and Meaning of Unemployment and Employment Statistics in the United States," *Harvard Business Review*, VIII (July 1930), 385–400.

Millis, Walter. "The President," *Atlantic*, CXLIX (March 1932), 265–78.

Mitchell, Broadus. *Depression Decade*. New York: Rinehart and Co., Inc., 1947.

Mussey, Henry Raymond. "The President's Economics," *Nation*, July 8, 1931, pp. 34–6.

Myers, William S., and Newton, Walter H. *The Hoover Administration: A Documented Narrative*. New York: Charles Scribner's Sons, 1936.

Nevins, Allan. "President Hoover's Record," *Current History*, XXXVI (June 1932), 385–94.

Ostrolenk, Bernhard. "Inflation Trends in America," *Current History*, XXXVI (March 1932), 773–80.

Perkins, Frances. "A Cooperative Program Needed for Industrial Stabilization," *Annals of the American Academy of Political and Social Science*, CLIV (March 1931), 124–30.

Phillips, C. A., et al. *Banking and the Business Cycle: A Study of the Great Depression in the United States*. New York: Macmillan Co., 1937.

Pinchot, Amos. "We Met Mr. Hoover," *Nation*, January 14, 1931, pp. 43–4.

Proceedings of a Conference of Progressives. Washington, D.C., 1931.

Report of the President's Conference on Unemployment. Washington, D.C.: United States Government Printing Office, 1921.

Report of the President's Research Committee on Social Trends. *Recent Social Trends*. New York: McGraw-Hill Book Company, Inc., 1933.

Schlesinger, Arthur M., Jr. *The Crisis of the Old Order*. Boston: Houghton Mifflin Co., 1957.

Sisson, Francis H. "The Strength of Our Banking System," *Review of Reviews*, LXXXVI (December 1932), 30–32.

Slichter, Sumner H. "Doles for Employers," *New Republic*, December 31, 1930, pp. 181–3.

––––––. "The Immediate Unemployment Problem," *Annals of the American Academy of Political and Social Science*, CLXV (January 1933), 1–12.

––––––. "Pharaoh Dreams Again," *Atlantic*, CXLVIII (August 1931), 248–52.

––––––. "Should the Budget be Balanced?" *New Republic*, April 20, 1932, pp. 262–4.

Soule, George. "On Blaming Hoover," *New Republic*, October 26, 1932, pp. 276–9.

––––––. "Which Way Out?" *Forum*, LXXXIX (March 1933), 148–51.

Springer, Gertrude. "The Burden of Mass Relief," *Survey*, November 15, 1930, pp. 199–202.

––––––. "The Challenge of Hard Times," *Survey*, July 15, 1931, pp. 380–85.

––––––. "The Fighting Spirit in Hard Times," *Survey*, June 15, 1932, pp. 260–71.

––––––. "Funds for Another Bleak Winter," *Survey*, June 15, 1931, p. 302.

––––––. "Getting the Most from Federal Relief," *Survey*, July 15, 1932, pp. 324–5, 335.

––––––. "The Job Line," *Survey*, February 1, 1931, pp. 496–9.

––––––. "Where Is the Money Coming From?" *Survey*, October 15, 1931, pp. 71–3.

Stoddard, Lothrop. "Why Cities Go Broke," *Forum*, LXXXVII (June 1932), 375–9.

Swope, Gerard. "Management Cooperation with Workers for Economic Welfare," *Annals of the American Academy of Political and Social Science*, CLIV (March 1931) 131–7.

The State Papers and Other Public Writings of Herbert Hoover. Edited by William S. Myers. 2 vols. New York: Doubleday, Doran and Co., 1934.

Tolischus, Otto D. "Debts and the Hoover Program," *North American Review,* CCXXXIII (May 1932), 389–98.

Tugwell, Rexford G. "Flaws in the Hoover Economic Plan," *Current History,* XXXVI (January 1932), 525–31.

Van Kleeck, Mary. "Toward a National Employment Service," *Survey,* April 15, 1931, pp. 88–90.

Warren, Harris G. *Herbert Hoover and the Great Depression.* New York: Oxford University Press, 1959.

Wecter, Dixon. *The Age of the Great Depression, 1929–1941.* New York: Macmillan Co., 1948.

Weinstein, Murray. "Methods Employed in the Clothing Industry," *Annals of the American Academy of Political and Social Science,* CLIV (March 1931), 153–4.

Westerfield, Ray B. "Defects in American Banking," *Current History,* XXXIV (April 1931), 17–23.

Whelden, C. H., Jr. "Our Economic Bootstraps," *New Republic,* July 13, 1932, pp. 223–5.

Wilbur, Ray L., and Hyde, Arthur M. *The Hoover Policies.* New York: Charles Scribner's Sons, 1937.

Williams, Whiting. "A Challenge to Industry," *Annals of the American Academy of Political and Social Science,* CLIV (March 1931), 1–6.

Wolf, D. E. "The United States," *Current History,* XXXIII (December 1930), 432–6.

Wolman, Leo. "Objections to Wage-Cutting," *Current History,* XXXV (October 1931), 20–24.

Index

Abundance, 3, 98, 230

Adams, James Truslow, 69

Agricultural Marketing Act, 21–2, 106–7, 122, 214; critics of, 107–9, 110, 120–21

Agriculture, the two-price system, 99; equalization fee, 99–100

Amalgamated Clothing Workers of America, 136

American Association of Social Workers, 171

American Bankers' Association, 71, 92

American Farm Bureau Federation, 99, 122

American Federation of Labor, 80, 127, 218

American Individualism, 10, 146

American Iron and Steel Institute, 63

American Radiator Company, 53

American System, 11, 13, 18, 20, 130, 180, 223, 232

American Telephone and Telegraph Company, 163

Anderson, Benjamin M., Jr., 83–4

Anderson, George J., 140

Anderson, Paul Y., 204–5, 210–11

Association for Improving the Condition of the Poor, 151

Association of Community Chests and Councils, 157–9, 181

Atlantic, 175

Baltimore and Ohio Railroad, 138, 139–40

Bankers, and classical economics, 80–81, 83–5; and confidence, *see* Confidence; and maintaining the price

level, 79–81; and unemployment, 167

Bankers Trust Company, 151

Banking, and confidence, 69; international disturbances to, 185; structure, 70; and trust, 66–9, 86; weakness of, 75

Bank of the United States, 77

Banks, failures, 86; national, 70; state, 70

Barnes, Julius H., 29, 30, 45–9, 50–51, 55, 63, 71, 133, 137

Baruch, Bernard M., 219

Bethlehem Steel Corporation, 64

Billikopf, Jacob, 159–62, 168

Black, John D., 122

Bliss, Cornelius N., 151

Borah, William, 89, 213, 215, 218

Brookhart, Smith, 123

Broun, Heywood, 206

Buchanan, James, 39

Buckner, Mortimer N., 89

Burns, Allen T., 158–9

Business leadership, 6, 28–9, 34, 37, 39–40, 51, 59, 63, 65, 132; and cooperation, 42

Business Week, 35, 45, 54, 58, 59, 60, 61, 62, 66, 71, 78, 80, 90, 92, 166, 177, 187, 189, 194, 198

Cannon, Clarence, 107

Capitalistic system, 7

Catholic Charities, 151; Chicago, 156

Cermak, Anton, 169

Charity Organization Society, 151, 163

Chase National Bank, 82, 83, 87

Chase, Stuart, 25, 81, 127, 176

Chicago, unemployment, 155–7, 168–9
Chicago, University of, 55, 133
Civil War, 39, 40, 125, 175
Collective action, 6; *see also* Co-operation
Commerce, Department of, 44, 54, 144; *see also* Lamont, Robert P.
Commercial & Financial Chronicle, 60, 64, 83, 187
Committee on Mobilization of Relief Resources, 163
Confidence, 33, 35, 48–9, 69, 71, 74, 77, 79, 95–6, 187, 196, 227
Congress, 38, 89, 210–29, 233
Conservatism, 7–8, 13
Consolidated Coal Company, 140
Construction, 30, 33, 51, 54, 57–8
Coolidge, Calvin, 21, 44, 204
Co-operation, 6, 18–19, 22, 40–41; and agriculture, 112–14; and banking, 89–90; and unemployment, 145, 162; *see also* Trade association; Voluntaryism
Co-operatives, 22
Costigan, Edward P., 158–9, 165–6, 171, 217, 218, 222
Credit, and banking, 70, 196; and the stock market, 32
Croxton, Fred C., 162
Cutting, Bronson, 217, 218

Davis, Elmer, 64
Davis, J. J., 144
Delgado Cotton Mills, 59
Dennison Manufacturing Company, 133
Depression, traditional attitude toward, 4, 24–6; impact of, 126; and prosperity, 32–3; *see also* Great Depression
Dewey, John, 216
Doak, William N., 80
Dodge Corporation, 57
Dole, 129–32, 220
Douglas, Paul H., 133, 141

du Pont de Nemours Company, 56
du Pont, Irénée, 56

Eastman Kodak Company, 134–5
Economic Club of New York, 227
Ely, Richard T., 175
Emergency Relief and Construction Act, 223–6
Emergency Work Bureau (N.Y.), 151–2
Equalization fee, 122; *see* McNary-Haugen Bill
Equal opportunity, 12–13, 16, 18, 23, 106
Europe, 12
Export debenture plan, 21, 99–100, 107, 122, 214

Farmers' Educational and Co-operative Union, 120, 122
Farmers National Grain Corporation, 113–14, 115–18
Farrell, James A., 63, 139
Federal Farm Board, 21–2, 106–7, 108, 111–22
Federal Intermediate Credit Banks, 115
Federal Land Banks, 190
Federal Reserve, 27, 70, 72, 91, 191–4; and discount policy, 73; and open market operations, 72–4, 193–4
Federal Reserve District Banking and Industrial Committee, 198–9
Federal Trade Commission, 44
Federation of Jewish Charities (Phila.), 160, 161–2
Fels-Naphtha, 133
Filene, Edward A., 142
First National Bank of Chicago, 94
Flynn, John T., 141
Ford, Henry, 58, 59–60
Ford Motor Company, 58
Fortune, 32
Foster, William T., 35, 81

Garner, John Nance, 89, 221, 222
General Electric Company, 133, 135, 141
General Motors, 64, 139
Gifford, Walter S., 151, 162–6
Glass-Steagall Bank Credit Bill, 191–4
Goldsmith, Samuel, 156–7
Governors, state, 29, 54; and unemployment, 148–9
Grain Stabilization Corporation, 116
Graves, Bibb, 148
Great Crash, 24, 32, 183; and agriculture, 114–15; and banking, 71, 76
Great Depression, 3, 5, 6, 7, 24, 175; and analogy to World War I, 175–81
Green, Fred W., 149
Green, William, 80, 127, 219
Guaranty Trust Company, 87

Harding, Warren, 24, 39, 44
Harrison, George, 88, 89, 93
Hart, Schaffner, and Marx, 136
Harvard University, 55, 122
Hawley-Smoot Bill, 209, 214–15
Herring, E. Pendleton, 221
Hillman, Sidney, 136–7
Hodson, William, 154
Home Loan Bank Bill, 191
Hoover, Herbert Clark, as institutional leader, 8–9; rugged individualism, 9; the American System, 11; philosophy of government, 11–23; equality of opportunity, 12–13; on liberalism, 14–16; bureaucracy, 14; and progressivism, 16; role of the federal government, 16; ideal of self-government, 17–18; on Congress, 19; agricultural problem, 20–23, 101–4; stock market crash, 26–7; National Business Survey Conference, 30; Washington conferences, 27–9; and the business cycle, 33–4;
initial program, 34; voluntary action, see Voluntaryism; maintaining wages, 59–60; creation of National Credit Corporation, 87–8; on agricultural distress, 97–8; unemployment, 128–9, 143; explanation of causes of Great Depression, 182–6; second program, 186ff; the scientific method of government, 203; and the press, 203ff; use of commissions, 208–9; and Congress, 210–29; balanced budget, 222, 223
Hopkins, Harry L., 170
Hull, Cordell, 219
Hurley, Patrick J., 131, 144
Hyde, Arthur M., 106, 144

Individualism, 19, 40–41; and cooperation, 18–19; in farming, 105; and unemployment, 126–7
Individualistic creed, 6; inappropriateness of, 6; see Individualism
Industrial leaders, see Business leadership
Interior, Department of, 55
International Harvester, 133, 138
Institutions, 7, 36–7, 128, 132; functioning of, 8
Investment trust, origin of, 67; growth, 68
Iron Age, 175
Irving Trust Company of New York, 49–50

Jewish Charities (Chicago), 156
Jewish Social Service Association, 151
Jones and Laughlin Steel Corporation, 64

Keynes, John M., 176–7
Kodak Park Works, see Eastman Kodak Company

Labor, 29; see American Federation of Labor; and Green, William

LaFollette, Robert M., Jr., 82, 140, 165, 217, 218, 222
Lamont, Robert P., 52, 53, 55, 144
Lamont, Thomas W., 152
Leadership, defined, 39–40; see Business leadership
Legge, Alexander, 109–12, 119
Lincoln, Abraham, 14
Lippmann, Walter, 35, 207
Louisville Trust Company, 75

Maurois, André, 64
Mayor's Official Committee (N.Y.), 152–3
McCormick, Anne O'Hare, 203, 205–6
McNary, Charles L., 108–9, 111, 117–18, 121, 124
McNary-Haugen Bill, 21, 108
Mellon, Andrew, 25, 87, 144
Meyer, Eugene, 93, 144
Millis, Walter, 210
Mills, Ogden L., 93, 189, 195–9, 227–9
Minnesota, University of, 55
Mitchell, Wesley C., 137
Moratorium, 187
Morgan and Company, 87, 152
Murphy, Frank, 167
Muscle Shoals, 215

Nation, 5, 7, 26, 65, 127, 145, 175, 205, 207, 208
National Bank of Kentucky, 75
National Beet Growers Association, 114
National Building Survey Conference, 53–4, 181
National Business Survey Conference, 30–32, 35, 44–5, 47–51, 53, 55, 59, 80, 89, 181, 199; demise, 51; origin, 30; see Barnes, Julius H.
National City, 87
National Credit Corporation, 91, 188; formation, 87–9, 181–2; incorporation, 90

National Electric Light Association, 52
National Fruit and Vegetable Exchange, 114
National Grange, 99, 122
National Industrial Conference Board, 62
Navy Department, 55
New Deal, 234
New Era, 24, 182, 202
New individualism, 19, 120
New Republic, 7, 189, 206, 209, 212
New York City, 150–55; Emergency Employment Committee, 151; Welfare Council, 151
New York Herald Tribune, 52
New York Journal of Commerce, 59, 80, 192
New York Stock Exchange, 24
New York Times, 27, 36, 59, 79, 92, 145
New York Trust Company, 89
Norbeck, Peter, 108–9, 121
Norris, George W., 100, 107–8, 109, 124, 214, 215, 216–17, 218
Norris-LaGuardia Act, 222

O'Neal, Edward A., 122

Peek, George N., 108
Perkins, Frances, 127
Persons, H. S., 136
Pierson, Lewis E., 49
Pinchot, Gifford, 171, 217, 224–6
Pomerene, Atlee, 226
Poverty, 3, 12, 202, 230; as a new problem, 5; extinction of, 20
President's Committee on Economic Changes, 51–2
President's Emergency Committee for Employment, 52, 143, 158, 162, 181; organization of, 144; see Woods, Colonel Arthur
President's Organization on Unemployment Relief, 163, 166, 181

Procter and Gamble Company, 133–4
Progressives, 216–19
Prosser, Seward, 151
Public utilities, 52–3

Railroads, 52
Reconstruction Finance Corporation,
    93, 189–91, 192, 222, 225–6, 232–3
Republic, 14
Richmond, Mary, 147
Ripley, Willam Z., 220
Riverside and Dan River Cotton
    Mills, 59
Robinson, Henry M., 198
Robinson, Joseph T., 219, 222
Roosevelt, Franklin Delano, 169–70,
    234
Rugged individualism, 10, 23, 200
Russell Sage Foundation, 147, 158
Ryan, John A., 218

St. Louis Post-Dispatch, 204
St. Vincent's Hospital (N.Y.), 150
Salvation Army, 150
School Relief Fund (N.Y.), 153
Schwab, Charles M., 64
Securities exchange, 37
Sherman Anti-Trust Law, 43
Simpson, John, 120, 122
Sloan, Alfred P., Jr., 199
Sloan, Matthew, 52
Smith, Adam, 25, 80
Social Work, 149, 159; National Con-
    ference of, 160
Soule, George, 35, 218
Speare, Charles F., 77, 78
Spillman, W. J., 122
Stabilization corporations, 111, 115;
    see also Agricultural Marketing
    Act
Stabilization, industrial, 132–41
Standard Oil Company of New Jer-
    sey, 133, 138
Stewart, Ethelbert, 79

Stock market crash, see Great Crash
Stone, James C., 120
Straus, Jesse Isidor, 170
Supreme Court, decisions of, 43–4
Survey, 125, 127, 147, 160
Swope, Gerard, 135

Taber, Louis J., 122
Taylor, Frank J., 152
Taylor, Myron C., 228
Taylor Society, 135
Temporary Emergency Relief Admin-
    istration, 169–70
Trade association, 30, 42; origin and
    development, 42–4
Traylor, Melvin A., 94
Treasury, Department of the, 55
Trumbell, John II., 148
Tugwell, Rexford G., 95
Turck, Fenton B., Jr., 53

Unemployment, 125ff, 222–3; and
    cities, 167–9; and states, 169–72; see
    also Social Work
Unemployment, Cabinet Committee
    on, 55, 143–4
Unemployment Conference of 1921,
    24–5, 55
United Charities (Chicago), 156
United States Bureau of Labor Sta-
    tistics, 61–2, 79
United States Chamber of Commerce,
    29, 44–5, 81, 109, 137, 181; see also
    Barnes, Julius H.
United States Daily, 79
United States Rubber Company, 64
United States Steel Corporation, 63–4,
    139

Van Buren, Martin, 24
Villard, Oswald Garrison, 176
Voluntaryism, 18, 44, 65; and banks,
    188, 198–200; and unemployment,
    129–30, 147

Wages, maintaining, 59–64
Wagner, Robert F., 215, 220, 222
Walker, James, 152
Walsh, Thomas J., 108, 109, 119, 219–21
War Department, 55
War Finance Corporation, 189
West Branch, Iowa, 21, 104
West, Walter, 171–2
Wheeler, Burton K., 217
Wiggin, Albert H., 82–3
Wilbur, Ray L., 144
Willard, Daniel, 139–40

Wilson, M. L., 122
Wilson, Woodrow, 24, 39, 179
Wolman, Leo, 81, 218
Woods, Colonel Arthur, 55–6, 134, 144–9; assumptions and viewpoint, 145–6; resignation, 162
World War I, 43, 175, 176, 177, 185

Y.M.C.A., 150
Young, Owen D., 163, 198, 228
Young, Roy A., 73
Youngstown Sheet and Tube, 64